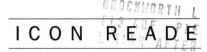

Charles Dickens

Great Expectations

EDITED BY NICOLAS TREDELL

Consultant editor: Nicolas Tredell

Original series editor: Richard Beynon

ICON BOOKS

This edition published in 2000 by Icon Books Ltd.,
Grange Road, Duxford, Cambridge CB2 4QF
e-mail: info@iconbooks.co.uk
www.iconbooks.co.uk

Previously published in the Icon Critical Guides series in 1998
(original series editor Richard Beynon)

Distributed in the UK, Europe, Canada, South Africa and Asia by the
Penguin Group: Penguin Books Ltd., 27 Wrights Lane, London W8 5TZ

This edition published in Australia in 2000 by Allen & Unwin Pty. Ltd.,
PO Box 8500, 9 Atchison Street, St. Leonards, NSW 2065

Consultant editor: Nicolas Tredell
Managing editor: Duncan Heath
Series devised by: Christopher Cox
Cover design: Simon Flynn
Typesetting: Wayzgoose

ISBN 1 84046 140 3

Printed and bound in Great Britain by
Cox & Wyman Ltd., Reading

CONTENTS

A NOTE ON REFERENCES AND QUOTATIONS

Cross-references to the extracts printed in this Guide, and references to the 1993 Clarendon Dickens edition of *Great Expectations*, are given in brackets in the text of the Guide. All quotations from the novel have been amended to accord with the Clarendon Dickens, which is now the authoritative text. Other references are given in the endnotes. As the Clarendon edition retains, in one volume, the original volume divisions and chapter numbers of the novel, references are given in the Guide in the following form: volume number; chapter number; page number. For example, 2:20 p.313 means volume 2, chapter 20, p.313. As many modern editions, for instance the Penguin English Library edition, number the chapters consecutively without reference to the original volume numbers, a list of chapter equivalents is given in Appendix B at the back of this Guide.

In any quotation, a row of three dots indicates an editorial ellipsis within a sentence or paragraph, and a row of six dots (that is, two ellipses) indicates an editorial omission of a paragraph break, or of one or more paragraphs.

INTRODUCTION

GREAT EXPECTATIONS is now regarded as one of Dickens's greatest
novels. It has attracted critics of a vast range of persuasions, including Christians, Marxists, Freudians, liberal humanists, symbolists,
structuralists, post-structuralists, deconstructionists, and feminists. It has
survived the decline in Dickens's reputation in the later nineteenth
century, the dismissal of F.R. Leavis in the mid-twentieth century, and the
demolition of the canon of Dead White European Males in the post-modern
era. Its title, themes and characters are part of contemporary culture, points
of reference when people want to talk about large hopes and disappointments.[1] This Guide will examine the fascinating fortunes of *Great Expectations*
and present a selection of the most insightful critical texts it has provoked.
This introduction sets *Great Expectations* in the context of Dickens's life
and work, and outlines the critical history that the Guide explores.

Dickens started to write *Great Expectations* in response to a crisis in the
affairs of his magazine *All the Year Round*. On 18 August 1860, the magazine
had started to publish a serial called *A Day's Ride: A Life's Romance* by the
Irish novelist Charles Lever, and it soon became clear that this was failing
to hold readers. Sales of the magazine started to fall, and decisive action
was needed. As Dickens observed in a letter to his friend and biographer-
to-be John Forster, '[t]he property of *All the Year Round* is far too
valuable, in every way, to be much endangered'. On Tuesday 2 October
1860, Dickens called 'a council of war' at the magazine's office and drew
up his battle plan. 'It was perfectly clear to me that the one thing to be
done was, for me to strike in.'[2] He began a serial that would be the same
length as *A Tale of Two Cities* (1859), and that would be called *Great
Expectations*.

The first instalment appeared in *All the Year Round* on 1 December
1860. Dickens explained to Forster that the book would 'be written in
the first person throughout' and that 'the hero' would be 'a boy-child'
like David Copperfield. He told him that, to safeguard against any
'unconscious repetitions' in the new story, he had just re-read *David
Copperfield* (1849–50) and had been greatly affected by it. He assured
Forster that *Great Expectations* would not lack humour, calling the opening
an 'exceedingly droll' one in which he had 'put a child and a good-

natured foolish man, in relations that seem to me very funny'. As well as this reference to Pip and Joe Gargery, Dickens also referred to Magwitch in terms of his function in the plot: '[o]f course I have got in the pivot on which the story will turn too – and which indeed, as you remember, was the grotesque tragi-comic conception that first encouraged me'.[3]

The commercial success of Dickens's new novel exceeded expectations. It saved the fortunes of *All the Year Round*, boosting the circulation to about 100,000 copies weekly. The three-volume edition of 1,000 copies that Chapman and Hall published in July 1861 sold out quickly and was followed by a second impression of 750 copies in August, a third of similar size in late August, a fourth of 500 in September and a fifth impression, once again of 750 copies, in October. The circulating libraries seem to have purchased a large number of copies, which was a further sign of the novel's popularity as they had often shied away from Dickens's earlier work. In the USA, *Great Expectations* was serialised in *Harper's Weekly* and then published by Harper and Brothers in two volumes, and the novel came out in Germany in Tauchnitz's Series of English Writers. In 1862, a one-volume English edition appeared and in 1863 there was a cheap edition of 5,000 copies, although by this time demand was falling.[4]

The commercial success of *Great Expectations* was not quite matched by the critical response. Dickens's position at the time of the novel's appearance was complex. World-famous and wealthy, with twelve substantial novels already to his credit, he aroused both admiration and aversion to a heightened degree. There were growing doubts about the quality of his more recent fiction, both from those who had enjoyed his earlier work but detected a decline in the later novels, and from those who were starting to believe that the novel was a serious art form with standards that Dickens did not satisfy. This pressure on his literary reputation was compounded by pressures in both his public and private life, which his fame made it difficult to keep apart. In 1858, after twenty-two years of marriage, he had finally separated from his wife Catherine, the mother of his ten children, in an atmosphere of recrimination and scandal. He had made matters worse on 12 June 1858 by publishing, on the front page of his magazine *Household Words*, a statement headed 'Personal' in which he attempted to quell 'all the lately whispered rumours' about 'his domestic trouble' – a move only likely to exacerbate such 'rumours'.[5] Further scandal threatened because of his troubled relationship with a young actress, Ellen Ternan. He had also begun a gruelling series of public readings. The restlessness that had always possessed him seemed to wind up to fever pitch. Driving himself too hard, involved in public readings and a host of other activities, he went on to complete one more massive novel, *Our Mutual Friend* (1864–65) and to start a new one, *The Mystery of Edwin Drood* (1870), before collapsing after a full day's work at his desk. He died on the evening of the next day, 9 June 1870. He was fifty-eight.

The first chapter of this Guide examines the early reviews of *Great Expectations*. These demonstrate both the diversity of opinion as to the achievement of the novel, and the way in which the first reviewers focused on topics that were to be taken up and developed by later critics, such as the question of Pip's 'snobbery', Dickens's techniques of characterisation, his representation of women, and the role of Orlick. Chapter two traces the fluctuating curve of the reputation of Dickens in general, and of *Great Expectations* in particular, from its decline after his death, epitomised by G. H. Lewes's critique, through its temporary rise at the turn of the century as a result of the advocacy of Andrew Lang, Swinburne, Gissing and Chesterton, to its real revival in the later 1930s and the 1940s through the work of Bernard Shaw, T. A. Jackson, George Orwell, Edmund Wilson and Humphry House. The example of F. R. Leavis in this chapter will demonstrate, however, the powerful resistance that still remained in the late 1940s, at least in the UK, to accepting Dickens as a serious major author.

This resistance continued to some extent through the 1950s. It was perhaps the inhibiting influence of Leavis, above all, which resulted in a relative neglect of Dickens by British critics in the 1950s, even at a time when academic literary criticism was expanding. The major critical work on Dickens in that decade was done outside England. Chapter three of this Guide considers a range of important accounts of *Great Expectations* produced in the 1950s: Jack Lindsay's powerful critical biography, which draws on Marx and Freud; Dorothy Van Ghent's rich exploration of crime and guilt in the novel; G. Robert Stange's elegant analysis of *Great Expectations* as the 'classic legend' of the nineteenth century; and J. Hillis Miller's formidable reading of the novel, which draws on phenomenology and existentialism. The 1960s and 1970s were a period of consolidation in *Great Expectations* criticism, in which the pioneering work of the 1950s was taken up, developed and sometimes challenged in both the USA and the UK, and which also saw some new departures. Chapter four of this Guide explores Julian Moynahan's analysis of the role of Orlick as Pip's *alter ego*; Barbara Hardy's appetising account of the role of food in *Great Expectations*; Robert Garis's original and penetrating vision of the novel as a performance in what he calls 'the Dickens theatre' that dramatises the argument of Freud's *Civilization and its Discontents* (1930); Q. D. Leavis's suggestive exploration of the roles of guilt and shame in Pip's life; Peter Wolfe's innovative exploration of Dickens's 'double plot' of the novel; and Harry Stone's fascinating pursuit of the magical symbolism of hands in the novel.

Great changes came over literary criticism in the UK and the USA in the 1980s, and these were immediately and powerfully evident in *Great Expectations* studies. Indeed, the 1980s produced a bumper crop of interpretations, each of them bringing new perspectives to bear in provocative and illuminating ways. The best of these are gathered in chapter five of this Guide. The chapter starts with Peter Brooks's compelling analysis of the plot of *Great Expectations* in relation to Freud's *Beyond the Pleasure Principle* (1920); moves on to consider Steven Connor's insightful application of Lacanian theory to Dickens's novel, and Jeremy Tambling's perceptive deployment of Foucault to unlock its concern with crime and imprisonment; and concludes with the questions raised by Kate Flint and Carolyn Brown about its representation of women. The final chapter of this Guide examines three major readings of *Great Expectations* in the 1990s, each of which opens important new directions for critical investigation: Edward W. Said's provocative exploration of the post-colonial dimension, William A. Cohen's teasing pursuit of the auto-erotic and homoerotic suggestiveness of Dickens's text, and Caroline Waters's lucid and rigorous analysis of the representations of women and the family in *Great Expectations*.

Great Expectations has fascinated readers and critics for 137 years. This Guide should deepen that fascination; it offers a voyage of discovery through its mysteries conducted by its most perceptive and provocative critics. Its aim is to promote a more intelligent and informed understanding of the novel and to stimulate further discussion and interpretation; it is hoped that the Guide will pay homage to Dickens's achievement by offering, on the level of criticism, the excitements, enigmas, discoveries, revelations and challenges that *Great Expectations* so richly provides on the level of art.

CHAPTER ONE

Early Expectations: Reviews 1861–62

WHILE *GREAT Expectations* was coming out in serial form in 1861, a caricature of Dickens appeared in London shop windows that delighted the novelist himself. It portrayed him with a huge head and a small body, turning from his writing desk to search for inspiration, his right hand holding a quill pen, the forefinger of his left hand pressed to his temple 'to knock an idea out'.[1] The caption below read: 'From Whom We Have Great Expectations'.[2] It was a caption that played on the double meaning that the title had at the time of the novel's appearance: for 'great expectations' indicated not only the theme of the novel but also the expectations of Dickens's readers. There was a sense, however, that such expectations might not be fulfilled. For if Dickens, in 1861, was England's most famous author, his position was, nonetheless, not wholly secure. His work had come under criticism from two main angles, which corresponded, to some extent, to a growing split in the Victorian reading public. On the one hand, there was the view that his recent novels showed a falling-off from the good humour and inventiveness of his earlier fiction, especially *The Pickwick Papers* (1836–37); on the other hand, there was the view that much or all of his work lacked the qualities that were increasingly required by those whom the writer G. H. Lewes would later call 'cultivated and critical readers':[3] probability, psychological depth and unity. These doubts about Dickens were echoed and amplified in the review responses, which ranged from those whose expectations had been more than fulfilled to those who felt very disappointed.

One of the first reviews appeared in the *Athenaeum* on 13 July 1861. Like almost all the reviews of *Great Expectations* listed in George J. Worth's *Bibliography* (1986), it was unsigned; but Worth attributes it to H. F. Chorley.[4] Chorley offers high praise of *Great Expectations* but also anticipates and aims to disarm some possible criticisms. He classifies the novel primarily as a 'romance', but also commends its realism in several respects. Comparing its descriptions of nature with those of the English

Gothic novelist Ann Radcliffe, author of *The Mysteries of Udolpho* (1794) and with the North American novelist James Fenimore Cooper, author of *The Last of the Mohicans* (1826), Chorley points out that Dickens achieves romance, not by evoking remote locations, but by infusing 'familiar and tame' and apparently very unromantic scenery with picturesque and romantic qualities, rendering such landscapes poetical in the way that Dutch painters do. Chorley also commends the psychological accuracy and penetration of the novel – its 'deep and tender knowledge of the secrets of a yearning human heart' – and contends that real-life counterparts to Miss Havisham and Satis House, and to Wemmick's Walworth Castle, might well exist in mid-Victorian England.

To an extent, Chorley presents *Great Expectations* as a revision of Romanticism for the age of realism. Pip is seen as a kind of Romantic hero in cramped circumstances. It is interesting to note, however, that Chorley feels that Pip may not be of interest to many readers and has to affirm that Pip's struggles and dreams exemplify experiences that many have had. His feeling contrasts with the views of some of the critics met later in this Guide, who regard Pip as representative of his age and even as a kind of Everyman (see, for example, Shaw, Jackson, House, Van Ghent, Stange). Chorley's remarks suggest that not all Victorian readers would immediately recognise Pip as a representative or universal figure.

Like the reviews of Edwin S. Whipple and E. S. Dallas discussed later in this chapter (pp. 20–24, 24–27), Chorley's review mentions the fact of the serial publication of *Great Expectations*, and hints at contemporary concerns about how this way of bringing out 'serious' fiction might affect the form of novels – some of these concerns are more fully explored by E. S. Dallas. Chorley stresses the strength of the plot of Dickens's latest novel, pointing out how it both satisfied the demand for suspense when the novel came out as a serial and contributed to a coherent whole when the novel was read in volume form. He emphasises, in particular, the way in which the plot winds around Magwitch, and he homes in on the power of the night scene of Magwitch's return. In these ways, he picks out aspects of *Great Expectations* that much future criticism will take up and explore. Chorley also anticipates future criticism in two other important respects: he is concerned to defend Dickens against charges of being 'maudlin or sentimental' in his portrayal of Magwitch's last days; and he highlights the ambiguity of the ending, the absence of a clear affirmation that Pip marries Estella. In serial form, and in the 1861 edition that Chorley would presumably have used for his review, the final clause of *Great Expectations* reads: 'I saw the shadow of no parting from her' (3:20, p. 480); from 1862, this was amended to the version that appears in most modern editions (though not in the Clarendon Dickens): 'I saw no shadow of another parting from her'. Edgar J. Rosenberg, in an essay of 1981 on the novel's endings, cites the view of Walter Dexter, in *The Dickensian* in 1938, that Dickens made this change to avoid ambiguity, but also points out that Angus Calder, in his 1965 Penguin edition of the novel, finds the second version no less ambiguous.[5] The debate continues: Chorley's response in 1861 demonstrates that the ending of *Great Expectations* could be seen as ambiguous, as posing a problem, even before John Forster's revelation in 1874 that Dickens had originally written another ending. Moreover, by plumping for the view that Pip did *not* marry Estella, Chorley also shows that the preference for an 'unhappy' ending is not the prerogative of modern critics.

The extract below begins at the start of Chorley's review, with its bold claims for the achievement of *Great Expectations*; then moves on to key extracts from later paragraphs that discuss issues of Romanticism, realism, plot and characterisation:

■ Whether the library of English fiction contains a romance comparable with *Great Expectations* is a matter which admits of doubt – because with the breathless interest of a tale of mystery and adventure, with descriptions in which familiar and tame scenery is wrought up so as to exceed in picturesqueness the Apennine landscapes of a[n] [Ann] Radcliffe, or the deep-sea storms of Fenimore Cooper, are combined such variety of humour, such deep and tender knowledge of the secrets of a yearning human heart, as belong to a novel of the highest order. Grant the two leading inventions of the tale as romantic, but not impossible; grant a certain exaggeration, so artfully distributed over the whole work as to amount to nothing more than a high tone of colour, and *Great Expectations* can be charged with only one fault; – that of being too short. It stands the test of collection, too, as few tales published in its fragmentary fashion can. Every week almost, as it came out, we were artfully stopped at some juncture which made Suspense count the days till the next number appeared, – again to be baulked, and anew to count. – Yet, on reading through the romance as a whole, there is no feeling of shock or spasm, still less any impression of 'dropped stitches' but a sense that we have to do with a work of Art arranged from the first moment of conception with power, progress, and a minuteness consistent with the widest apparent freedom . . . this is the creation of a great artist in his prime. . . .

It is not lost time, neither a case of 'painting the lily', to insist on certain details and characteristics of a tale already in thousands of hands. – No scenery could be imagined less romantic than the marshes in which the romance begins and ends; the soaking flat country, with its pollards, – with its 'broads,' in the furthest of which lie moored the convict-hulks, the old churchyard on the verge of this district, the sluices, and the limekiln. – But out of such common materials a Cuyp, or a Ruysdael, or a Hobb[e]ma makes a poetical landscape; and so with his pen does Mr. Dickens [*Editor's Note*: Aelbert Cuyp (1620–91), Salomon van Ruysdael (about 1600/3–70) and Meindert Hobbema (1638–1709) were all seventeenth-century Dutch landscape painters]. The scene holds the reader from the first; the boy, born to be tormented by his 'great expectations', is as much a dreamer, in right of his natural surroundings, as if he had been born at the feet of the Jungfrau, or bred in that Paradise of heaven, earth and sea, 'the Golden Shell' of Palermo. – That Nature has influences apart from her sublimities, and that they speak to all who have ears to hear, is told with the decision of a key-note clearly touched, in the very first lines of this strong story. The return to the key, from time to time, is masterly, in the fullest sense of the word, because never monotonous.

The hero of the tale – a dreaming, ambitious boy, with a grain of genius in him, and flung out by Fate into a narrow and cramping existence, which in no respect contents his yearnings, – may interest few people; and yet he is true to a life with which many have struggled, and to dreams which have put right, or put wrong, many a better man than himself. His shrewish guardian sister, with her perpetual apron (a household ephod [Jewish priestly vestment] of self-defence and assertion), and her sycophants, may be, we trust, more shrewish than are the sisters of many child-dreamers; but how admirably is her bitterness and vulgarity (fed by parasites) balanced by the sweet, truthful nature of Joe, with his dull wits and his meandering speech, and his huge hands like two forge hammers, and his tender, loving heart . . . . . .

Most admirable is the manner in which the plot of the tale winds round the wretched hunted jail-bird. Those who from the first understood the delusion of the boy's great expectations, – who felt or saw that they had nothing to do with the ghastly recluse in the deserted house, and her brooding revengeful sense of the wicked wrong which had laid her woman's life waste – were, therefore, all the more terribly held in thrall by the knowledge that the convict would return some day, and the air-castle be blown into fragments as by a whirlwind. – It is much to say, that the suspense so strongly excited is followed by a catastrophe as fearfully and forcibly outdoing expectation as if it had not been foreseen. There is nothing in English fiction, not even 'the print of the man's foot in the sand' in [Daniel Defoe's] *Robinson Crusoe* (1719),[6] fuller of engrossing and legitimate terror, than the night scene of the convict's return, dogged from its first moment by Death. – From this point to its close, the interest of the romance increases with a resistless and steady power never before attained by Mr. Dickens. Nor has he ever used his own language with such poignant muscular force as here . . . Adventure follows adventure – each one more riveting than the last – each one, too, adding some softening and redeeming light to the character of the poor hunted '"warmint"' (1:19, p.19), without making the close of his sad story maudlin or sentimental . . .

There are those who will say that Miss Havisham's strange mad life is overdrawn; but such have not been conversant with the freaks and eccentricities which a haughty spirit in agony can assume: nor the manner in which a resolution once taken becomes a law never to be broken. We have no doubt, that, even now, in remote places of England, rich old mansions might be found as strangely peopled as the deserted brewery – with its spectre in white. Satis House, with its dank and weed-grown garden and the mouldering bridal feast, is as real, to us, as the lonely church on the marshes, – or the wonderful estate in Walworth, with its works of art and ingenuity[7] – the original of which, by the way, we have heard claimed for half-a-dozen different localities.

One word more. In no late fiction has Mr. Dickens been so happy in his group of what may be called accessory characters. Mr. Jaggers, with his handkerchief, Mr. Wopsle, with his dramatic instincts, – the greedy, sycophantish seedsman [Pumblechook], – that wonderful thorn in everyone's side, Trabb's boy – are all capital. We fancy that at the outset he may have meant to make more of Mr. and Mrs. Matthew Pocket, – but they are not missed – Herbert is as fresh and genial an *Horatio* as a hero could desire; and most particularly are we grateful for the uncertainty in which the tale closes, as we interpret it. We do not believe that Pip *did* marry Estella, though there are two opinions on the subject.

. . . *Great Expectations*, we are satisfied, will add to Mr. Dickens's reputation, and is the imaginative book of the year.[8] □

A review of the same date as Chorley's, in *The Literary Gazette*, did not quite share this enthusiastic response. The reviewer, who has not been identified,[9] could not wholly endorse the opinion that *Great Expectations* surpassed all Dickens's previous works – an opinion which, the review claimed, had often been expressed while the novel was appearing in serial form. Nonetheless, the review affirms that *Great Expectations* is 'in many respects, one of the most original, imaginative, and romantic stories that he has ever written, and in point of sustained effort and charm of style, it is unequalled'. It compares Dickens's new novel favourably with its predecessor, *A Tale of Two Cities*, maintaining that the later work is pervaded by 'a hearty, manly, national tone . . . which, without debarring it from cosmopolitan admiration, will make it especially welcome in many an English home'.[10] It is interesting to relate this judgement to the interpretations of *Great Expectations* in terms of colonialism and homo-eroticism that have begun to emerge at the end of the twentieth century – for instance, the readings of Edward W. Said and William A. Cohen, which are discussed in the final chapter of this Guide (see pp. 144–49 and pp. 149–59).

Like Chorley, the *Literary Gazette* reviewer aims to anticipate and rebut possible criticisms, in this case of improbability in the plot and exaggeration in the characterisation. The review contends that Dickens, as a great writer of fiction, is a 'poet', and that it is the duty of a poet to produce characters 'typical of a class' by combining 'the humours and peculiarities of many men' in order to create characters who are 'ideal, but not unnatural'. The review particularly praises Joe Gargery as an 'almost perfect character', very rare in real life, but nonetheless 'perfectly probable and natural' and 'destined to be one of the most popular characters in English fiction'.[11] Miss Havisham and Magwitch are seen as '[t]he two most abnormal and mysterious characters' in the novel; the reviewer has some difficulty in bringing Miss Havisham within the bounds of probability, finding her 'melancholy madness . . . horribly weird and wild' and noting 'something that borders upon exaggeration' in the way that she 'trains' Estella to be the taunter of Pip. Nonetheless, the review argues, the extent of Miss Havisham's sufferings is sufficient explanation for her bizarre behaviour, while Magwitch's 'whole conduct and career are made natural and probable by the wonderful power with which they are described'.[12] Pip's narrative is commended for its 'truthfulness and reality', especially in its accounts of childhood feelings.[13] *The Literary Gazette* registers the lack of 'the pungent satire with which [Dickens] has sometimes assailed political abuses or social injustice' – a point that would also be echoed by an essayist in *The Eclectic Review*, as shall be seen later in this chapter (p. 28) and which would be taken up in a particularly interesting way 104 years later by Robert Garis in *The Dickens Theatre* (1965 – see p. 106 of this Guide). The review goes on to suggest, however, that the novel is 'all the more artistic' because it does not have 'one special serious purpose' and to assert that it still permits 'indirect and incidental moral teaching . . . of the highest and truest kind'.[14] It is interesting that the review initially seems to regret the *absence* of specific social and political concerns, thus implying a very different criterion from those critics, both in Dickens's own time and in the twentieth century, who regret the *presence* of such concerns in a work of fiction; but it then moves to the position that the absence of such concerns enhances the artistry of a work of fiction – which is, to some extent, the ostensible position of critics who do object to the presence of social and political concerns.

The review of *Great Expectations* in *The Examiner* of 20 July 1861 was possibly written by Dickens's friend and biographer-to-be, John Forster, or by Henry Morley.[15] It starts by attacking those who would prefer Dickens's earlier work, charging them with limited taste and lack of maturity. It explicitly invokes the criterion of unity in a way that partly anticipates the aesthetics of Henry James, when it affirms: '[e]verything in art, good or bad, should have, and usually has, a central thought to which its parts bear some harmonious relation'.[16] Aspects of the novel that contribute to its unity are commended: 'the construction of a plot that . . . knit[s] every fragment of its detail into one round and perfect whole';[17] the way in which the characters 'fit into the plot as a stone into an arch'; the necessity of every piece of dialogue; and 'the sense of a perfect continuity and harmony [in] the whole work'. The criterion of probability is also implied, when the reviewer argues Estella is revealed to be Magwitch's daughter 'by a network of incidents in no point violating probability' – an opinion that was not shared by 'J. A.' in the *Ladies Companion and Monthly Magazine* (see p. 32) or by Margaret Oliphant in *Blackwood's Edinburgh Magazine* (see p. 34).

The *Examiner* review also praises *Great Expectations* for its suggestiveness and subtlety – '[t]he delicacies of Joe's character are often suggested rather than told' and '[t]here is a subtle indication . . . of the servile and broken wife that such a woman as Mrs. Joe would have made, if subjected to violence from her husband'. As in the affirmation of the importance of 'a central thought' in art, the criteria of suggestiveness and subtlety anticipate those of Henry James. There is a foreshadowing, in this review, of the criteria that will come to dominate criticism of the novel later in the nineteenth century and which will persist well into the twentieth century – criteria to which Dickens, and *Great Expectations*, can be made to conform only with some effort on the part of critics. The review is also interesting in relation to critical debates about Pip's motives for his rejection of Magwitch's patronage, in that it attributes the rejection partly to shame but also to reason, calling the convict 'a humiliating patron from whom great expectations cannot *rationally* be allowed to flow' [*Editor's italics*].[18]

The *Spectator* review of *Great Expectations* appeared on the same date as that of the review in *The Examiner*, 20 July 1861. Possibly by Meredith Townsend,[19] it spotlights what it sees as a key weakness of Dickens's characterisation. At its best, his technique of characterisation involves 'that large assemblage of minute, coherent habits which go to make up such a figure as Mrs. Gamp [in *Martin Chuzzlewit* (1843–44)] or Mr. Weller [in *The Pickwick Papers*]'; but this can give way to the use of 'mere external label[s]' that fail to give the essence of his characters and which do not constitute 'a high style of art'. This occurs especially when he is dealing with 'the more educated ranks' in society whose characters are less obviously marked in their speech and behaviour than are those of the lower orders. In a way that is both amusing and almost proto-structuralist, the *Spectator* reviewer provides the following table of the mere 'labels' that Dickens employs in *Great Expectations*:

■ PERSON	TRAIT
Mrs. J. Gargery	Harps perpetually on having brought her brother up "'by hand.'"
Mr. J. Gargery	Pulls his whiskers when embarrassed; and shows kindness by helping to gravy.
Mrs. Camilla	Ends sentences with "'The ide-a!'"
Mr. Jaggers	Bites the side of his forefinger at people by way of menace.
Mr. Wemmick	Posts biscuit down his mouth, which is always called "'the post-office.'"
Mr. Wemmick, senior	Is stone deaf, and always answers his son, "'All right, John, all right.'"
Mr. Matthew Pocket	Lifts himself up by his hair when in despair.
Mrs. Matthew Pocket	Drops her handkerchief incessantly, and laughs when it is returned to her by Flopson.
Miss Havisham	Lives by candlelight, wears only one shoe, and the bridal dress in which she had suffered her disappointment, and takes exercise round the table where the bridecake is getting mouldy.
Mr. Pumblechook	Says "'May I? May I?'" by way of soliciting to shake hands with a prosperous acquaintance.[20] □

The *Spectator* reviewer stresses, however, that 'this false art' does not comprise the whole of the novel, and praises Dickens's portrayal of a child's mind since 'no childish mind can well be outlined with that artificial sharpness which is Mr. Dickens's greatest danger, and the point of view of a child, that of observant imbecility, exactly suits the style of Mr. Dickens's fun'.[21] The portrayals of village life are also commended for their humour and accuracy, and the characterisation of Joe and Wemmick is praised insofar as it goes beyond the 'mere external label[s]' identified in the table above. But these aspects apart, 'there is very little in this book which any true admirer of Mr. Dickens would wish to preserve from destruction'. The '"Miss Havisham and Estella" element is nearly as shrill as the melodrama in *Dombey and Son* (1846–48), and far more extravagant'. Moreover, in contrast to the praise of the plot in the *Examiner* (p. 17) or the *Atlantic Monthly* (pp. 20, 21–22), the *Spectator* review contends that Dickens's 'genius is not suited to a unity of plot' and that '[h]e needs the freedom to ramble when he will and where he will'; otherwise he 'gets too much interested in his own plot, and forgets the characters in his interest in the story'. The review concludes by counselling Dickens to 'take a vow of total abstinence from the "Estella" element in all future tales, and limit himself religiously to vulgar life', adding that 'we do not use the word [vulgar] in the depreciating sense'.[22] The *Spectator* review is an interesting mixture of penetrating analysis and an unashamed class consciousness.

A third review, which appeared on 20 July 1861, by an unidentified writer in *The Saturday Review*,[23] was qualified in its praise, calling the novel 'a story with excellent things in it rather than an excellent story'. Like the *Spectator* review, though without the reference to class, it targeted 'one great fault' that was evident throughout Dickens's work and with which *Great Expectations* was 'strongly marked': the fault 'of exaggerating one particular set of facts, a comic side in a character, or a comic turn of expression, until all reality fades away, and the person who is the centre of the extravagance becomes a mere peg or clothes-horse on which the rags of comedy hang loosely and flutter backwards and forwards'.[24] Where *The Spectator* uses the metaphor of the 'label' to denote this technique, the *Saturday Review* writer employs that of the 'ticket', saying that 'Miss Skiffins . . . like most of Mr. Dickens's minor characters, has one peculiarity to ticket her'.[25] Miss Havisham is seen as 'one of Mr. Dickens's regular pieces of melodramatic exaggeration', and Mrs. Pocket is judged to be 'even less like a possible woman than Pumblechook is like a possible man', a portrayal in which 'we get away from the follies of flesh and blood to the oddities of puppets and to the kind of fun that lights up the pages of *Charivari*'.[26] These are interesting comments in the light of feminist critiques in the 1980s and 1990s of Dickens's representations of women, for example that of Catherine Waters discussed in the final chapter of this Guide (see pp.159–66).

Like H.F. Chorley (pp.12, 13), Edwin P. Whipple (p.21) and E.S. Dallas (pp.24, 25–26), the *Saturday Review* writer mentions the fact of serial publication; but while Chorley, Whipple and Dallas all affirm that Dickens has escaped its dangers, this reviewer suggests that the pressures of publishing in such a way partly account for the faults of the novel; they force the pace of Estella's 'moral restoration', compel the wholesale alteration of characters so that the 'amiable dreamy' Herbert, 'incapable of business', suddenly 'comes out all at once as a shrewd, successful Levant merchant', and cause villains – the example given is Orlick – to be 'sketched in and smeared out again'.[27] Like *The Spectator*, however, *The Saturday Review* praises Wemmick, and indeed does so more enthusiastically, calling him 'the great comic creation' of the novel.[28] It also praises the portrayal of Pip as 'a much more thorough study of character than David Copperfield ever was' and finds that, although *Great Expectations* shares the faults of Dickens's previous novels, it does 'surpass them in one point. There are passages and conceptions in it which indicate a more profound study of the general nature of human character than Mr. Dickens usually betrays'.[29]

A review in the *Atlantic Monthly* in September 1861, whose author has been identified as Edwin P. Whipple,[30] takes a much more positive view of *Great Expectations* than the *Spectator* or the *Saturday Review* writers; but he puts forward his case with an awareness of certain critical criteria against which the novel is to be measured. One of these criteria is probability, and Whipple tackles this by setting it in the context of a more general analysis of Dickens's work, identifying in that work 'two diverging tendencies' – a power of accurate observation of people and things, and an inclination to 'pathetic or humorous idealization'. Whipple finds that *Great Expectations* displays Dickens's power of accurate observation but that it is successfully combined with his inventive, creative capacity to produce a work that does not conform to the criterion of probability. He says of the 'series of events' in the novel that 'it is difficult to conceive of [it] as actually "happening"', but maintains nonetheless that *Great Expectations* offers an especially keen insight into real life and the world. It is an argument similar to that which George Gissing would later make in his turn-of-the-century defence of Dickens, discussed in the next chapter of this Guide (see pp. 41–43).

The criterion that a sense of artistic necessity should inform the unfolding of the events in a novel is also evident in Whipple's review of *Great Expectations*. Thus he commends the 'leading events' of the plot as 'artistically necessary', offering us 'the movement of a logic of passion and character' rather than being 'a mere succession of humorous and pathetic scenes'. A further criterion is that of unity: the characters are 'better fitted to each other and to the story in which they appear than is usual with Dickens' and '[t]hey all combine to produce [a] unity of impression'. Whipple also implies a criterion of linguistic transparency – that is, the idea that the language of a novel should not obtrude on the reader's attention but should provide as clear a view as possible of what it depicts. He commends those narrative and descriptive passages in *Great Expectations* in which, he feels, 'we are hardly conscious of the words, in our clear apprehension of the objects and incidents they convey'. As shall be seen in chapter four of this Guide, this is a view that would be challenged, 104 years later, by Robert Garis when he argues that Dickens, in *Great Expectations* as in his other work, draws attention to himself as linguistic performer (see pp. 104–108).

Whipple's remarks on both Pip and Magwitch are also worth noting. His description of Pip as 'the subject and the victim' of *Great Expectations* anticipates those readings of the 1980s and 1990s that emphasise Pip's subjection and 'decentring' in the narrative of which he is the ostensible subject and master. Two notable examples of such readings, by Steven Connor and Jeremy Tambling, are discussed in chapter five of this Guide (pp. 130–36, 136–41). Whipple's observation that the 'powerful' character of Magwitch 'furnishes pregnant and original hints to all philosophical investigators into the phenomenon of crime' suggests the way in which crime, at this point in mid-Victorian England, was becoming an object of 'philosophical investigation' and relates to Michel Foucault's investigation in *Discipline and Punish* (1976) of the links between power and knowledge in the nineteenth century. As shall be seen in chapter five of this Guide, Tambling's essay applies Foucault's work to *Great Expectations*.

An extract from Whipple's review follows. As with Chorley's review at the start of this chapter, it begins with Whipple's first paragraph, in which, like Chorley, he discusses the experience of reading *Great Expectations* in serial form. He then goes on to comment on the plot of the story, on the two 'diverging tendencies' of Dickens's mind, on the unity of impression the novel produces, on Pip and Magwitch, and on the relative transparency of Dickens's style, before rounding off with a ringing endorsement of 'a masterpiece':

■ The very title of this book indicates the confidence of conscious genius. In a new aspirant for public favour, such a title might have been a good device to attract attention; but the most famous novelist of the day, watched by jealous rivals and critics, could hardly have selected it, had he not inwardly felt the capacity to meet all the expectations he raised. We have read it, as we have read all Mr. Dickens's previous works, as it appeared in instalments, and can testify to the felicity with which expectation was excited and prolonged, and to the series of surprises which accompanied the unfolding of the plot of the story. In no other of his romances has the author succeeded so perfectly in at once stimulating and baffling the curiosity of his readers. He stirred the dullest minds to guess the secret of his mystery; but, so far as we have learned, the guesses of his most intelligent readers have been almost as wide of the mark as those of the least apprehensive. It has been all the more provoking to the former class, that each surprise was the result of art, and not of trick; for a rapid review of previous chapters has shown that the materials of a strictly logical development of the story were freely given. Even after the first, second, third, and even fourth of these surprises gave their pleasing electric shocks to intelligent curiosity, the *dénouement* was still hidden, though confidentially foretold. The plot of the romance is therefore universally admitted to be the best that Dickens has ever invented. Its leading events are, as we read the story consecutively, artistically necessary, yet, at the same time, the processes are artistically concealed. We follow the movement of a logic of passion and character, the real premise of which we detect only when we are startled by the conclusions.

The plot of *Great Expectations* is also noticeable as indicating, better than any of his previous stories, the individuality of Dickens's genius. Everybody must have discerned in the action of his mind two diverging tendencies, which, in this novel, are harmonized. He possesses a singularly wide, clear, and minute power of accurate observation, both of things and of persons; but his observation, keen and true to actualities as it independently is, is not a dominant faculty, and is opposed or controlled by the strong tendency of his disposition to pathetic or humorous idealization. Perhaps in *The Old Curiosity Shop* (1840–41) these qualities are best seen in their struggle and divergence, and the result is a magnificent juxtaposition of romantic tenderness, melodramatic improbabilities, and broad farce. The humorous characterization is joyously exaggerated into caricature, – the serious characterization into romantic unreality. Richard Swiveller and Little Nell refuse to combine. There is abundant evidence of genius both in the humorous and the pathetic parts, but the artistic impression is one of anarchy rather than unity.

In *Great Expectations*, on the contrary, Dickens seems to have attained the mastery of powers which formerly more or less mastered him. He has fairly discovered that he cannot, like Thackeray, narrate a story as if he were a mere looker-on, a mere 'knowing' observer of what he describes and represents; and he has therefore taken observation simply as the basis of his plot and his characterization . . . In *Great Expectations* there is shown a power of external observation finer and deeper even than Thackeray's; and yet, owing to the presence of other qualities, the general impression is not one of objective reality. The author palpably uses his observations as materials for his creative faculties to work upon; he does not record, but invents; and he produces something which is natural only under conditions prescribed by his own mind. He shapes, disposes, penetrates, colours, and contrives everything, and the whole action is a series of events which could have occurred only in his own brain, and which it is difficult to conceive of as actually 'happening'. And yet in none of his other works does he evince a shrewder insight into real life, and a clearer perception and knowledge of what is called 'the world'. The book is, indeed, an artistic creation, and not a mere succession of humorous and pathetic scenes, and demonstrates that Dickens is now in the prime, and not in the decline of his great powers.

The characters of the novel also show how deeply it has been meditated . . . they are better fitted to each other and to the story in which they appear than is usual with Dickens. They all combine to produce that unity of impression which the work leaves on the mind. Individually they will rank among the most original of the author's creations. Magwitch and Joe Gargery, Jaggers and Wemmick, Pip and Herbert, Wopsle, Pumblechook, and 'the Aged', Miss Havisham,

Estella, and Biddy, are personages which the most assiduous readers of Dickens must pronounce positive additions to the characters his rich and various genius had already created.

Pip, the hero, from whose mind the whole representation takes its form and colour, is admirably delineated throughout. Weak, dreamy, amiable, apprehensive, aspiring, inefficient, the subject and the victim of 'Great Expectations', his individuality is, as it were, diffused through the whole narrative. Joe is a noble character, with a heart too great for his powers of expression to utter in words, but whose patience, fortitude, tenderness, and beneficence shine lucidly through his confused and mangled English. Magwitch, the '"warmint"' (1:3, p.19) who '"grow'd up took up"', whose memory extended only to that period of his childhood when he was '"a thieving turnips for his living"' down in Essex (3:3, p.344), but in whom a life of crime had only intensified the feeling of gratitude for the one kind action of which he was the object, is hardly equalled in grotesque grandeur by anything which Dickens has previously done. The character is not only powerful in itself, but it furnishes pregnant and original hints to all philosophical investigators into the phenomenon of crime. In this wonderful creation Dickens follows the maxim of the great master of characterization [Shakespeare] and seeks 'the soul of goodness in things evil'. [*Editor's Note*: In Shakespeare's *Henry V* (probably 1599), Act 4, Scene 1, lines 4–5, King Henry says: 'There is some soul of goodness in things evil,/Would men observingly distil it out – '.[31]]

The style of the romance is rigorously close to things. The author is so engrossed with the objects before his mind, is so thoroughly in earnest, that he has fewer of those humorous caprices of expression in which formerly he was wont to wanton. Some of the old hilarity and play of fancy is gone, but we hardly miss it in our admiration of the effects produced by his almost stern devotion to the main idea of his work. There are passages of description and narrative in which we are hardly conscious of the words, in our clear apprehension of the objects and incidents they convey. The quotable epithets and phrases are less numerous than in *Dombey and Son* and *David Copperfield*; but the scenes and events impressed on the imagination are perhaps greater in number and more vivid in representation. The poetical element of the writer's genius, his modification of the forms, hues, and sounds of Nature by viewing them through the medium of an imagined mind, is especially prominent throughout the descriptions with which the work abounds. Nature is not only described, but individualized and humanized.

Altogether we take great joy in recording our conviction that *Great Expectations* is a masterpiece . . . a work which proves that we may expect from Dickens a series of romances far exceeding in power and

artistic skill the productions which have already given him such a preeminence among the novelists of the age.[32] ☐

Whipple's enthusiasm was not matched by *The Times*'s review of *Great Expectations* on 17 October 1861. The writer, who has been identified as a critic quite well known in his own day, E. S. Dallas,[33] begins by invoking those readers who had felt disappointed at what they saw as Dickens's move away from 'the old *Pickwick* style . . . with its contempt of art, its loose story, its jumbled characters, and all its jesting that made us laugh so lustily'.[34] Such readers, he suggested, will find something of that style in his latest novel. Dallas does not, however, claim that the novel marks an all-out return to the old style, and he is careful to keep his distance from those who want it. While claiming that the 'flowing humour' of *Great Expectations* 'disarms' and 'defies' criticism, he also indicates his awareness that criticisms could be made, and indeed he makes some of them, for example when he suggests that *Great Expectations* consists of '[a] wild story, odd characters, absurd situations, whimsical descriptions'.

Like Chorley and Whipple, Dallas mentions the fact of serial publication; he provides, however, a more extended discussion of the uncertainties and anxieties aroused by what was seen, he suggests, as a dangerous experiment – the use of a method previously 'connected with publications of the lowest class' to bring out 'important', 'good' novels. Dallas claims that Dickens has led the way in this experiment and created a situation in which most 'good' novels are now published in serial form. He also makes a specific comparison between *Great Expectations* and a previous novel published in serial form in Dickens's magazine, *Household Words*: Wilkie Collins's *The Woman in White* (1859–60). Dallas makes the comparison to Dickens's advantage; Margaret Oliphant makes the comparison to Dickens's detriment, as shall be seen later in this chapter (p. 34). Dallas then goes on to compare *Great Expectations* with an earlier Dickens novel – not the most obvious one, *David Copperfield*, but *Oliver Twist* (1837–39). In his comparison, Dallas indicates – perhaps not in an altogether conscious way – the ambiguity of the figure of the benefactor, implying a parallel in *Oliver Twist* between the thieves and the benevolent Mr. Brownlow, in that both have 'intentions' for Oliver, and pointing out how, in *Great Expectations*, the representative of crime and the benefactor are combined in the figure of Magwitch: Magwitch is Pip's Mr. Brownlow. In the twentieth century, the comparison between Magwitch and Mr. Brownlow was also to be made (though without explicit reference to Dallas's review) by J. Hillis Miller in *Charles Dickens: The World of His Novels* (1958), where he calls Magwitch 'a nightmare permutation of Mr. Brownlow [in *Oliver Twist*] and Mr. Jarndyce [in *Bleak House* (1852–53)]'.[35] It is also interesting to note Dallas's observation that Pip, once he discovers that his benefactor is a convict, 'behaves rather like a snob'. This looks forward to a sometimes heated twentieth-century debate about whether *Great Expectations* is, in Humphry House's famous phrase, 'a snob's progress' (see p. 66). The perception of Pip as a snob is expressed more forcefully in another contemporary review of Dickens's novel in the *Dublin University Magazine*, which is discussd later in this chapter (see pp. 30–31).

Dallas starts his review by observing the comeback of the old Dickens in *Great Expectations*:

■ Mr. Dickens has good-naturedly granted to his hosts of readers the desire of their hearts. They have been complaining that in his later works he has adopted a new style, to the neglect of that old manner which first won our admiration . . . [but] Mr. Dickens has in the present work given us more of his earlier fancies than we have had for years. *Great Expectations* is not, indeed, his best work, but it is to be ranked among his happiest. There is that flowing humour in it which disarms criticism, and which is all the more enjoyable because it defies criticism. Faults there are in abundance, but who is going to find fault when the very essence of the fun is to commit faults? . . . In foregoing [*sic*], to some extent, the correct and highly proper style of his more recent productions, and in falling back upon the jovial extravagancies of his younger days, is it to be supposed that so masterly a writer is not quite aware of what he has done, and has not deliberately chosen his path? A wild story, odd characters, absurd situations, whimsical descriptions – it is easy to make a long catalogue of such crimes. To do so, however, were merely to give the body without the soul, – to hang, draw, and quarter the body, and to present its dead fragments as specimens of the living man . . .

The method of publishing an important work of fiction in monthly instalments was considered a hazardous experiment, which could not fail to set its mark upon the novel as a whole. Mr. Dickens led the way in making the experiment, and his enterprise was crowned with such success that most of the good novels now find their way to the public in the form of a monthly dole . . . . . . The periodical which he conducts is addressed to a much higher class of readers than any which the penny journals would reach, and he has spread before them novel after novel specially adapted to their tastes. The first of these fictions which achieved a decided success was that of Mr. Wilkie Collins – *The Woman in White*. It was read with avidity by hosts of weekly readers, and the momentum which it acquired when published in fragments carried it through several large editions when published as a whole. The novel was most successful, but if we are from it to form a judgement of the sort of story which succeeds in a weekly issue our estimate will not be very high. Everything is sacrificed to the plot – character, dialogue, passion, description; and the plot, when we come to examine it, is not merely improbable – it is impossible . . . After Mr. Wilkie Collins's tale, the next great hit was this story of Mr. Dickens . . . It is quite equal to *The Woman in White* in the management of the plot, but, perhaps, this is not saying much when we have to add that the story, though not impossible like Mr. Wilkie Collins's, is very improbable. If Mr. Dickens, however, chose to keep the common herd of readers together by the marvels of an improbable story, he attracted the better class of readers by his fancy, his fun, and his sentiment. Altogether, his success was so great as to warrant the conclusion, which four goodly editions already justify, that the weekly form of publication is not incompatible with a very high order of fiction . . .

[T]he resemblance between [*Oliver Twist* and *Great Expectations*] is . . . one of subject very much and of treatment. The hero of the present tale, Pip, is a sort of Oliver. He is lowborn, fatherless and motherless, and he rises out of the cheerless degradation of his childhood into quite another sphere. The thieves got a hold of Oliver, tried to make him a pickpocket, and were succeeded in their friendly intentions by Mr. Brownlow, who thought that he could manage better for the lad. Pip's life is not less mixed up with the ways of convicts. He befriends a convict in his need, and henceforth his destiny is involved in that of the prisoner. The convict in the new story takes the place of Mr. Brownlow in the old, and supplies Master Pip with every luxury. In either tale, through some unaccountable caprice of fortune, the puny son of poverty suddenly finds himself the child of affluence. If we are asked which of the tales we like best, the reply must be that the earlier one is the more fresh in style, and rich in detail, but that the later one is the more free in handling, and the more powerful in effect. It is so, even though we have to acknowledge in the work some of Mr. Dickens's worst mannerisms. For example, it is a mere mannerism that in all his tales there should be introduced some one – generally a woman – who has been confined indoors for years, and who, either from compulsion or from settled purposes, should live in dirt and gloom, never breathing the fresh air and enjoying the sunshine. A lady who has a whim of this sort is here, as in most of Mr. Dickens's tales, the blind of the story. Making every allowance, however, for repetitions, the tale is really worthy of its reputation, and is well worth reading . . .

Of the story we have indicated nearly enough . . . This fellow, Pip, at the time of the convict's return, was enjoying himself very much, forgetful of his early poverty-stricken friends, and thinking chiefly of present needs. He is horrified to find that his benefactor is a convict, and behaves rather like a snob . . . In the course of this story several characters are introduced which will take rank with some of Mr.

Dickens's best, such as Joe the blacksmith, Pumblechook the corn-dealer, and Wemmick the lawyer's clerk . . .

When Mr. Dickens gets into the third [volume] he is driven along by the exigencies of the story, and he can no longer afford to play with his subject. The interest is still sustained, but it is of a different kind . . . The public insist upon seeing in Mr. Dickens chiefly the humorist; and, however great he may be in other directions, they count all as nothing beside his rare faculty of humour. To those who may not be satisfied with a work of this author's unless humour superabounds most we can heartily commend *Great Expectations*.[36] □

As well as this review in *The Times*, October 1861 also saw the appearance of an essay on Dickens in *The Eclectic Review*, whose writer has not been identified.[37] Although this essay is called 'Charles Dickens's *Great Expectations*', it is mostly a general account of Dickens's fiction that praises him as 'the epic poet of city life'[38] whose 'bulky volumes . . . are like nothing so much as the streets of London, with all the shifting and crowding, and jostling passengers, moving to and fro'.[39] The essay does, however, offer some significant scattered comments on Dickens's latest novel. Its observation that '[a] new work . . . by Charles Dickens is an event always regarded with interest by general readers'[40] is notable in that it invokes the idea of the 'general reader' rather than G.H. Lewes's 'cultivated and critical reader'. The writer is aware, however, that Dickens's recent work has not been well received by either general or cultivated and critical readers; the essay alludes to the severe treatment meted out to *Little Dorrit* (1855–57), which 'was felt to be a failure',[41] and to *A Tale of Two Cities*, which 'pleased nobody'.[42] Commending *Great Expectations* for being 'more free from objectionable material than most of our author's writings' since there are 'no sneers at the Sabbath and Sabbath observances' from a writer who 'knows as much of the ways and manners of religious people as a Hottentot', the essay goes on to express 'the delight with which we have read *Great Expectations*',[43] but also to register a sadness in the novel:

■ It is, even more than is usually the case, shaded by the peculiar pensiveness of effect, which remains when the hearty excitements of the episodes of mirth with which our author indulges his readers have passed away. Many stories flow together into the one, and every story is sad – Miss Havisham's, Provis's, Estella's, Pip's, and Joe's. Amidst much that charms to laughter, there runs the perpetual feeling of a thoughtful mind to whom life[,] and man, and society, present perpetual thoughts of sorrow and of mystery.[44] □

Like *The Literary Gazette, The Eclectic Review* observes that Dickens 'has not in this, as in most of his later works, set himself to the task of specially rectifying social sins and abuses'; but, in contrast to *The Literary Gazette*, it makes no comment about the effect of this upon the quality of the novel, only commending 'the deserved ridicule and admirable humour with which he brings into contempt the solemn farce of funerals, and the woeful ways of undertakers'![45] Dickens's capacity for 'ludicrous combination and exaggeration',[46] for 'see[ing] in the most out-of-the-way objects grotesque, and queer, and comical analogies'[47] is seen both as a 'wonderful spirit'[48] and as 'the vice of his writings', but in *Great Expectations*, 'there is less of this than in perhaps any [of his] other work – less to interfere with the march and unity of the whole story'.[49] This 'grotesqueness' remains evident in some aspects of the portrayal of Wopsle and Pumblechook, however, and can become 'weird and ghastly',[50] as in our first introduction to Miss Havisham. But Wemmick and 'the Aged' are ranked 'among the most distinct and individual of his creations' of men and women with 'eccentricities . . . whom he has animated with real human hearts'.[51]

The review of *Great Expectations* in the December 1861 issue of the *Dublin University Magazine*, attributed to L.J. Trotter,[52] starts by speaking of the disappointment that Dickens's later work had aroused, the sense of 'the growing weakness of a once mighty talent', which had led to 'very small expectations' of his new novel. The review acknowledges, however, that '[e]xpecting little, we gained on the whole a rather agreeable surprise'.[53] While the novel cannot be ranked 'with any of those which lifted him into his present leadership in the realm of letters'[54] – the reviewer appears to have in mind novels such as *The Pickwick Papers* and *Martin Chuzzlewit*[55] – it is better than *Bleak House* and *Little Dorrit*. The story is 'absurd in outline and fantastic in details', and the characters are 'strange to our experience of any other world than that of farce or popular fiction',[56] but there is skill and humour in the novel. In contrast, however, to *The Spectator*'s praise for Dickens's portrayal of a child's mind, the *Dublin University Magazine* says, with regard to the novel's first two paragraphs, that 'none but their actual author would have been held excusable for putting into a child's brain fancies at once so laughably original and so ingeniously absurd' – a point that anticipates Robert Garis's argument that behind Pip, we are always aware of Dickens performing his act (see pp. 104–106). The *Dublin University Magazine* does, however, share *The Spectator*'s aversion to Dickens's reiteration of features such as Wemmick's post-office mouth and Jaggers's finger-biting, and it objects as well to Dickens's 'old weakness for the funniest-sounding and least-possible words that ever were hashed out of our English alphabet', as in names like Pirrip, Gargery and Wemmick. In his use of such tricks, Dickens is like 'some popular comedian [who] might raise an additional laugh by making faces now and then aside at his audience'. The review makes several references to Dickens's capacity for broad farce, a 'department in which he has gained the doubtful honour of a foremost place',[57] and finds that, in *Great Expectations*, 'the natural is largely overlaid by the farcical'. It echoes the objections of the *Eclectic Review*'s essayist to Dickens's extravagant analogies, calling them a 'merciless pumping-up of grotesque or ridiculous fancies', and making an interesting comparison with 'the similar weakness of an otherwise different writer' – the North American writer Nathaniel Hawthorne, in his *Transformation* (1861; the English title of *The Marble Faun*).[58] In 1970, as shall be seen in chapter four of this Guide, Q. D. Leavis would make a comparison between *Great Expectations* and Hawthorne's *The Scarlet Letter* (1850), though in terms favourable to both novels (see p. 109).

The *Dublin University Magazine* does praise the structure of *Great Expectations*, though in a somewhat roundabout way; the writer suggests that Dickens 'aimed at engrafting on his own faulty methods the yet faultier subtleties of Mr. Wilkie Collins', putting Collins in the category of those novelists who believe that 'the art of story-telling lies in the weaving of sheer riddles, the putting together of puzzles that claim attention from their intricacy alone'. Though no credit is given to any conscious artistry on Dickens's part, the result of this 'flounder[ing]' into Collins's 'rut'[59] has had 'results in their own way remarkably successful'.[60] *Great Expectations* is '[m]ore compact than usual in its structure' and Dickens's plot, 'like his characters however improbable, has a kind of artistic unity and clear purpose, enhanced in this case by the absence of much fine-drawn sentiment and the scarcity of surplus details'.[61]

Surveying the characters, the *Dublin University Magazine* applauds Joe as 'the simple, manly, faithful-hearted blacksmith [who] approves himself as one of nature's truest noblemen' and praises Biddy's 'quiet thoughtfulness for the folk at the forge, and . . . loving endurance of Pip's overbearing priggishness'.[62] Among Pip's London friends, Herbert Pocket is judged 'perhaps the most natural', but Wemmick 'is certainly the most entertaining'. The reviewer also commends the portrayal of Jaggers as 'one of those powerfully unpleasant beings whose real worth . . . shines out clearest after dark', and finds in Magwitch a bold and affecting, if not natural, character. Apart from these figures, and Pip himself, the rest of the characters are held to 'belong either to farce or melodrama, or a mixture of both'. The 'whole conception' of Miss Havisham's character is 'morally and physically absurd' and Estella 'bears small resemblance to any possible daughter of Eve'. Orlick is 'a ruffian without paint',[63] although the scene in which Orlick takes Pip prisoner in the sluice-house (3:14), is judged to 'gain in melodramatic horror' what it 'lose[s] . . . in likelihood' and to possess 'the double merit of being strikingly conceived and powerfully painted'[64] – a more positive judgement than that of

'J.A.' in the *Ladies Companion and Monthly Magazine*, or Margaret Oliphant's in *Blackwood's* (see pp.32, 34). As for Bentley Drummle, he 'has little more reality than his own surname'. The review concedes, however, that Pumblechook and Wopsle are '[m]ore cleverly, if not more soberly drawn'.[65]

The *Dublin University Magazine*'s forceful, amusing and provocative account of Pip himself is worth quoting in full. Pip is seen as a character who forfeits our interest once he leaves the village, and this is partly attributed to what this writer, like the *Spectator* reviewer, sees as Dickens's difficulty in portraying the higher ranks of society. As was seen earlier in this chapter (p.26), E.S. Dallas, in *The Times*, saw Pip as behaving 'rather like a snob' when he discovers that his benefactor is a convict; the writer in the *Dublin University Magazine* asserts much more strongly that Pip is a 'feeble' and 'weak-minded' snob once he falls under the influence of Satis House, and especially during the time that he lives in Barnard's Inn with Herbert. Interestingly, this review suggests that Pip's snobbery may be due to his love for Estella. In the light of recent analyses of the representation of women in *Great Expectations* – there is a notable example by Catherine Waters, in the last chapter of this Guide (see pp.159–66) – the following extract demonstrates the way in which Estella is seen as imaginary – 'mere moonshine' – and as emasculating, 'melt[ing] away [Pip's] manlier qualities'. Here, then, is the *Dublin University Magazine*'s view of the hero, and heroine, of *Great Expectations*:

■ About Pip himself, the apparent hero of his own story, we hardly know what to say. As long as he remains at the forge, trying to teach Joe his letters, or seeking to enlarge his own stock first under Mr. Wopsle's great aunt, and then under that stage-stricken hero himself, he still maintains in our eyes somewhat of the interest first evoked by his meeting with the terrible convict in the dreary church-yard by the marsh. Under Joe's roof, even during the years of his apprenticeship, he seems to win for himself a little of the love so largely due from us to his companion. But time and fortune, combined with the weakness that mars all Mr. Dickens's attempts at painting the social life of the more polished classes, go far to efface our first impressions, and make us wonder whether the original Pip might not have died in early boyhood, leaving some worthless substitute to trade thenceforward on his good name. Anyhow Pip's acquaintance with Estella seems gradually to turn him into as feeble a snob as ever was palmed off on the novel reader for a hero. Under the blighting influence of Satis House, his character grows as shadowy as the greatness of his own expectations proves at last to be. The growth of his mad love for a girl of mere moonshine, melts away his manlier qualities, and renders him weakly ungrateful alike to his first and his latest benefactor. Between his

departure for London in the character of a new made gentleman and
the reappearance of Abel Magwitch, the story of his life is a broad
waste of sluggish unreality, relieved once or twice by a bit of green
oasis in the form of a visit from Joe Gargery, or of an evening spent at
Walworth in the company of Pip's quaint friend, Wemmick. After a
time, indeed, the march of events brings him once more nearer to our
human sympathies; but even then we are anxious far less about himself than about the rough-mannered, kind-hearted outcast, whose
invincible longing to look upon the gentleman of his own making,
tempts him to dare the risk of discovery, and consequent death, by
coming back to the land from which his judges' doom had banished
him for ever. If Mr. Dickens had tried his best to portray the idle
young man of Barnard's Inn as a mere weak-minded snob in fine
clothing, he could not have succeeded better than he has perhaps
unwittingly done. It may be that a love so foolish as that of Pip for
Estella would weaken the fibres of never so brave a heart, and that a
youth just new to the enjoyment of wealth and personal freedom
would for the moment fling away all remembrance of his former
friends. But Pip's tiresome maundering about his sweetheart, his consciously prolonged avoidance of poor Joe, and his morbid loathing of
the kind but coarse-mannered wretch to whom his rise in the world is
wholly due, seem to our thinking as little needed for working out the
first conception of Pip's character, as they are likely to increase our
interest in a hero whose claim thereon was never of the clearest.
Repentance comes, indeed, to him at the last, but by that time our
attention is fixed on far more notable objects; and in the whirl of incidents that wind up the story, we hardly care to know whether the
nominal hero is to end his days in a debtor's prison, to pine abroad a
poor lonely bachelor, or to marry in good time the lady who has mean-
while given herself away to a worthless rival.[66] □

The comparison between Dickens and Wilkie Collins, which the *Dublin
University Magazine* makes when it discusses the structure of *Great
Expectations*, provides the starting-point of the review of the novel by
'J.A.'[67] in the *Ladies Companion and Monthly Magazine*. In contrast to the
Dublin University Magazine, 'J.A.' does not identify Collins as belonging in
the ranks of the intricate puzzle-makers, but sees him primarily as 'the
English chief' of 'the Romantic school'. Claiming that Collins's influence
upon Dickens has been 'very much greater' than Dickens's upon Collins,
it finds that the stronger influence has largely been to Dickens's good.
Like Edwin P. Whipple, 'J.A.' discerns two opposed tendencies in
Dickens – a professed 'extreme naturalism'[68] and a 'native romanticism'.[69]
But where Whipple commended Dickens's power of accurate observa-
tion, 'J.A.' argues that his 'extreme naturalism' leads to falsity and

singles out the technique, also deprecated by *The Spectator*, *The Saturday Review*, and the *Dublin University Magazine*, of '[s]eizing upon some external point or trait in a man [or woman]' like 'Wemmick's post-office', 'Jaggers's finger-biting, hand-washing, boot-creaking', 'Joe's whisker-feeling' and 'Mrs. Gargery's apron'.[70] 'J.A.' feels, however, that the faults of an 'extreme naturalism' are less in evidence in *Great Expectations* than in Dickens's earlier novels, that one could, in his works, 'trace, step by step, the over-mastering of false naturalism by native romanticism'[71] and that *Great Expectations* was 'the legitimate offspring of Dickens's true genius'.[72] In the emergence of Dickens's true romanticism, the influence of Wilkie Collins had largely been beneficial, though the 'romance of *Great Expectations* is a little too much like *The Woman in White*'.[73]

'J.A.' contends that readers who 'know Mr. Dickens's ideal world, and can translate the ghosts thereof into the real flesh and blood of this world'[74] will find Jaggers 'a notable creation' and will discover in Joe 'some glimpses of a human soul' that might well 'blind their eyes with tears'.[75] But the review had little time for the other characters. In terms of plot, it criticises the 'queer coincidences with regard to Estella, her papa and mamma' as 'most impossible absurdities', though it concedes that the 'skill of the story-teller' prevents such revelations from seeming 'very ludicrous' as one reads the novel. In terms of structure, it judges that the scene in which Orlick holds Pip prisoner in the sluice-house – a scene praised by the *Dublin University Magazine* – would be 'excellent' as a short story but is 'thoroughly out of place' in the novel. Its most interesting structural comment bears on the scenes of Pip's London life; like the *Dublin University Magazine* writer, 'J.A.' feels that these are unsuccessful, but it accounts for them, not in terms of Dickens's incapacity to portray fashionable society, but in terms of a failure to provide a sufficiently strong contrast between Pip's London life and the life at the forge: the failure is thus located primarily on the level of structure, in the absence of one term of a binary opposition between luxury and frugality:

■ [In the London scenes, we] might have expected a contrast of luxury and extravagance . . . to the old blacksmith life – a preparation by exquisite sensitiveness of honour and position, and so forth, that should make the discovery of the convict-origin of his wealth fall with the greater force. We find nothing of the kind. Pip does not enter high life; he gets but moderately into debt; his nerves do not become exquisitely sensitive. He of course cuts Joe, the blacksmith (what else could he do? particularly when instigated thereto by Estella); and he comes to look upon those youthful dealings with the convict as the black spot in his life – the one action thereof which makes him unfit for the companionship of Estella.[76] □

This comment is also interesting in that, in contrast to some of the reviews we have considered, it offers no condemnation of Pip as a snob or as anything else, regarding his disavowal of Joe as inevitable, especially in view of his love of Estella. In seeing no reason for condemnation, it anticipates an issue focused by Julian Moynahan a hundred years later, in an essay discussed in chapter four of this Guide: the possible disproportion between Pip's sense of guilt and his actual deeds (see pp. 95–100).

In 1862, three more accounts of *Great Expectations* appeared. The *British Quarterly Review*, in January of that year, published an essay covering all Dickens's novels to date (and the *Christmas Books* (1843–48)). The unidentified writer[77] generally approves of *Great Expectations*, claiming that it 'may fairly rank among Dickens's most powerful works', although wishing that the story had been 'less sombre in character and some of the incidents less unnatural'. The essay praises the portrayal of Pip (though wishing he had been given 'a better name') as 'most naturally drawn' and finds 'nothing melodramatic' about Magwitch. It shrewdly highlights the contradiction that arises from the fact that, in 'making his boy "a gentleman"', Magwitch has 'placed an insurmountable bar between them'.[78] Joe is seen as 'admirable' and as the ideal husband for Biddy, 'simple, upright, kind-hearted as he'. On the other hand, Wemmick is judged 'scarcely natural'. Miss Havisham is even less natural, and both she and Estella are 'most unpleasing' characters who should have been omitted or 'softened'. The *British Quarterly Review* writer is especially hostile to Estella, calling her 'cold and cruel through mere waywardness' and doubting 'if the mere discipline of a brutal husband for some five or six years could have availed to tame [her] sufficiently to make her a suitable wife for Pip'.[79] These comments are revealing, particularly in the light of modern feminist readings of *Great Expectations*, for the stereotypes of femininity they employ and for their apparent legitimisation of violence towards women as a means of 'discipline'.[80]

A second review of 1862 is a short notice in *The Rambler*, which mainly discusses Dickens in general terms. Its authors, who have been identified as John Moore Capes and the famous historian Lord Acton,[81] compare Dickens unfavourably to Thackeray – who has that capacity to create general types that characterises '[a] novelist of a more creative genius' – and criticise his attitude to religion, ranking him with those who 'ma[k]e humanity their God' and charging that 'he knows nothing of sin when it is not crime'.[82] As it happens, the guilt-laden text of *Great Expectations* might be cited as a defence against this charge, not least because it could be seen partly to deconstruct the difference between 'sin' and 'crime'. But the review says little about the novel itself, reiterating the kind of criticisms of Dickens's technique of characterisation that had been made the previous year by *The Spectator* and *The Saturday Review* (see pp. 17–18, 19), and praising the comic qualities of the tale, especially the conception of Wemmick. It sees these qualities, however, as no more than the remnants of the 'fires' that still live in Dickens's 'ashes' and advises him to 'lie fallow for a year or two' and 'eschew everything that is tragic, sentimental, or improving', so that he may have a chance of reproducing, in a more lively way, 'the delightful absurdities with which he charmed his readers a quarter of a century ago'.[83]

The final contemporary response to *Great Expectations* to be considered has been identified as the work of the novelist Margaret Oliphant.[84] Her account of the novel occurs in a long essay called 'Sensation Novels', which appeared in *Blackwood's Edinburgh Magazine* in May 1862. Turning to *Great Expectations* after discussing *The Woman in White*, she finds Dickens's novel sorely wanting in comparison with the latter novel, and with Dickens's own previous work. 'So far as *Great Expectations* is a sensation novel, it occupies itself with incidents all but impossible, and in themselves strange, dangerous, and exciting; but so far as it is one of the series of Mr. Dickens's works, it is feeble, fatigued, and colourless.' She praises Joe Gargery as a return to Dickens's 'ancient mood',[85] and commends the portrayal of Magwitch from his first 'vivid and effective' appearance in the churchyard, through the 'strange and frightening' quandary[86] in which his return places Pip, to the 'subdued pathos and tenderness' of his death.[87] On the other hand, all the Satis House scenes, and 'the entire connection between Miss Havisham, Pip, and Estella, is a failure',[88] while the 'secondary persons' of the novel, such as Mrs. Pocket and Wemmick, are, 'so far as they possess any character at all, specimens of oddity run mad'.[89] The 'sensation episode' in which Orlick imprisons Pip in the mill is 'the most arbitrary and causeless stoppage in the story', 'totally uncalled for, an interruption and encumbrance, interfering with the legitimate interest of the story, which is never so strong as to bear much trifling with'. Returning to the comparison with Collins, Oliphant acknowledges Dickens's superior gifts but finds that, because of laziness, caprice or complacency, *Great Expectations* is an inferior achievement to *The Woman in White*. 'In every way, Mr. Dickens's performance must yield precedence to the companion work of his disciple and assistant.'[90]

Margaret Oliphant's severe criticisms are a fitting point at which to conclude this chapter, for they stand at the opposite pole to H.F. Chorley's high praise of *Great Expectations* with which the chapter began. This first chapter has covered the scale of contemporary responses to the novel and discussed the wide divergence of opinion as to its merits. It is clear that, despite Dickens's fame and popularity, both his general critical standing, and the specific status of *Great Expectations*, were hotly contested in his own time. As this Guide proceeds, it will also become clear that the responses explored in this chapter raised many of the issues that future critics would later take up, debate and develop. These include the question of Pip's 'snobbery'; Dickens's methods of characterisation,

particularly his use of a 'labelling' or 'ticketing' technique; the representation of women, especially Miss Havisham and Estella; the role of Orlick
and the function of the scene in which he holds Pip prisoner in the
sluice-house; the effects of Dickens's linguistic exuberance; the questions
of unity and probability; the plot and structure of *Great Expectations*; the
impact of serial publication; the relation of the novel to the genres of the
romance and of sensation fiction; the absence within it of any attacks
upon specific social and political abuses; the novel's ambiguous ending.
But it would take some time before these questions would be thoroughly
pursued. In part, their pursuit had to await the development of a body of
academic critics who had the time, and the personal and professional
motivation, to devote themselves to the study of Dickens. But it would
also be necessary, before Dickens could be studied more deeply, to revive
his dishevelled reputation. In some of the reviews discussed in this
chapter, it is already possible to hear knives being sharpened; for the rest
of the nineteenth century, and well into the twentieth, they would be
plunged into Dickens's critical image remorselessly and repeatedly. Brave
attempts to fend off the attacks would be made around the turn of the
century by George Gissing and G.K. Chesterton; but it would not be until
the start of the 1940s that a Dickens revival would really start, and it
would then be led, not by academic critics, but by two freelance writers,
one English, one American: George Orwell and Edmund Wilson. The
next chapter of this Guide traces the story of the reputation of Dickens
and of *Great Expectations* from its decline in the late Victorian era, through
the turn-of-the-century defences by Gissing and Chesterton, to its
revival by Orwell and Wilson in a world at war.

CHAPTER TWO

Expectations Lost and Found: 1870–1949

THE DOMINANT visual image of Dickens that circulated in late June and in July 1870 was very different from the caricature that had appeared in shop windows in 1861, at the time of *Great Expectations*. Like that caricature, it showed Dickens's desk and chair; but the author himself was absent. The image was based on a picture that the artist Sir Luke Fildes had painted on the day that Dickens had died, 9 June 1870, and, in the weeks that followed, it was widely reproduced and embellished. Called *The Empty Chair*, it was a poignant symbol of the all-too-real death of the author.[1]

Dickens's death was both a national and international event. Benjamin Jowett, in his sermon at Dickens's funeral service at Westminster Abbey on 14 June 1870, said that 'he whose loss we now mourn occupied a greater space than any other writer in the minds of Englishmen during the last thirty-five years'.[2] In a letter to John Forster, Thomas Carlyle spoke of the death as 'an event world-wide, a *unique* of talents suddenly extinct'.[3] The flood of eulogies and obituaries was soon followed by biographies, the most important of which was John Forster's (1872–74). Its third volume made a momentous revelation about *Great Expectations*:

■ One other letter [of Dickens] throws light upon an objection taken not unfairly to the too great speed with which the heroine [Estella], after being married, reclaimed, and widowed, is in a page or two again made love to, and remarried by the hero. This summary proceeding was not originally intended. But, over and above its popular acceptance, the book had interested some whose opinions Dickens specially valued (Carlyle among them, I remember);[4] and upon Bulwer Lytton objecting to a close that should leave Pip a solitary man, Dickens substituted what now stands. 'You will be surprised' he wrote 'to hear that I have changed the end of *Great Expectations* from and after [*sic*] Pip's return to Joe's, and finding his little likeness there. Bulwer, who has been, as I think you know, extraordinarily taken by the book, so strongly urged it upon me, after reading the proofs, and supported his view with such good reasons, that I resolved to make the change. You shall have it when you come back to town. I have put in as pretty a little piece of writing as I could, and I have no doubt the story will be more acceptable through the alteration'. This turned out to be the case; but the first ending nevertheless seems to be more consistent with the drift, as well as natural working out, of the tale, and for this reason it is preserved in a note.[5] □

By revealing that – as the printed marginal notes in the original edition of Forster's life put it – the ending was '[n]ot as first written' and was '[c]hanged at Bulwer Lytton's suggestion', Forster provided readers and critics with a topic that is still hotly debated.[6] Chapter one of this Guide showed how one of the first reviewers of the novel, H. F. Chorley, had already drawn attention to the ambiguity of the ending as it had been printed (pp. 13, 15): the revelation of an earlier, alternative ending made matters even more complicated.

It also provided Dickens's enemies with ammunition. George H. Ford, in his study of the reception of Dickens's novels from 1836 to the 1940s, points out that Forster's biography had 'a mixed effect upon [Dickens's] reputation' in general,[7] and the specific revelation of the changed ending of *Great Expectations* was likely to lower his standing further among those who considered themselves 'cultivated and critical readers'. A writer who could change what Forster called a more 'consistent' ending for a more popular one on the basis of advice from a friend and perhaps partly for commercial reasons (Lytton was himself a bestselling author), might seem to lack the artistic integrity that was starting to be required of serious novelists. The revelation about *Great Expectations* may well have contributed to the decline of Dickens's reputation after his death.

But that decline would have happened in any case. Later nineteenth-century England saw a growing gulf between the common and 'cultivated' reader, and the development among 'cultivated' readers of a new ideology of the novel. That ideology has already been seen at work in some of the reviews of *Great Expectations* that were discussed in chapter one of this Guide. It was an ideology that required novelists to maintain a consistent illusion of reality in their fiction, to focus on the inner, psychological life of their characters, and to achieve an overall sense of organic coherence; Dickens, it seemed, often failed to meet these requirements. An index of the critical discomfort his fiction produced is G. H. Lewes's essay 'Dickens in Relation to Criticism', which appeared in 1872 in the influential journal he helped to found, the *Fortnightly Review*.

Lewes was a Victorian intellectual whose own work included writings on literature and theatre, biographies, ten plays, and two novels, *Ranthorpe* (1847) and *Rose, Blanche and Violet* (1847). He is best known, however, as the partner of the novelist George Eliot, whose own fiction seemed to be both displacing Dickens in terms of popularity and improving upon him in terms of literary quality.

In his essay, Lewes acknowledges Dickens's popularity and power, and implies that the requisite critical task is 'to exhibit the sources of that power'. He does not propose to undertake that task himself, but insofar as his essay does exhibit such sources, it suggests that they are profoundly compromised by their vulgarity and irrationality. His praise is hardly ever unqualified by negative criticism, as if he constantly feels impelled to demonstrate his anti-Dickensian credentials to the 'cultivated and critical' reader; he reiterates throughout the essay Dickens's 'undeniable defects'.[8] These defects include a deficiency in the 'higher faculties'[9] other than imagination; the presentation of 'types' that are 'fantastic', 'unreal' and 'impossible';[10] an absence of the 'ideal' and the 'heroic', and a limited horizon unable to encompass '[t]he world of thought and passion';[11] an incapacity to manage any logic except 'the logic of feeling'; an inability to connect 'his observations into a general expression'; and a lack of interest in the 'general relations of things'.[12] True, Dickens is credited with a sense of 'overflowing fun' that irresistibly provokes laughter, but, as Lewes reminds us, laughter at such 'preposterousness or extravagance' may produce a reaction afterwards of shame and 'revulsion'.[13] Lewes's observation, in 1872, that Dickens's capacity to provoke laughter may also produce a response of 'revulsion' was to be complemented, as will be seen later in this chapter, by Q.D. Leavis's remark, in 1932, that 'revulsion' may be the response of the 'alert critical mind'[14] to Dickens's capacity to provoke tears (see p. 52).

Lewes also grants the great fun-merchant 'an imagination of marvellous vividness, and an emotional, sympathetic nature capable of furnishing that imagination with elements of universal power';[15] but he soon after observes that 'in no other perfectly sane mind . . . have I observed vividness of imagination approaching so closely to hallucination'.[16] Dickens's power of imagination did mean that '[h]is types established themselves in the public mind like personal experiences';[17] but 'the public mind' is of coarser stuff than the discerning mind of 'the critic [who] is distressed to observe [in Dickens's novels] the substitution of mechanisms for minds, puppets for characters'. In what is perhaps the most memorable moment in the essay, Lewes observes that Dickens's '"catchwords" personified as characters' remind one 'of the frogs whose brains have been taken out for physiological purposes, and whose actions henceforth want the distinctive peculiarity of organic action, that of fluctuating spontaneity'.[18]

Lewes's condescending attitude to Dickens set the tone for the rest of the nineteenth century and persisted in some form well into the twentieth century – as is demonstrated by the attitude of Q. D. Leavis in 1932, as mentioned above and later in this chapter, and by the attitude of F. R. Leavis in 1948, which will be considered near the end of this chapter (pp. 67–68). Dickens continued to sell quite well, however, and around the turn of the century he did find three disparate defenders, each of whom made favourable mention of *Great Expectations*: Andrew Lang, George Gissing and Algernon Charles Swinburne. Lang was a poet and scholar best known for his collections of fairy tales, which appeared in twelve volumes whose titles were differentiated by colours, starting with *The Blue Fairy Book* (1889). Lang provided introductions and notes to the Gadshill edition of Dickens (1897–1908) and wrote an essay on Dickens for the *Fortnightly Review* in 1898.[19] This essay was by no means wholly flattering; for example, Lang echoes Lewes's partly pejorative notion of the hallucinatory capacity of Dickens's mind, saying that 'his imagination, at times, went back to what is probably the primitive condition of actual hallucination',[20] and he speaks of Dickens's 'congenital incapacity for composition, hardly overcome in *Bleak House* and *Great Expectations*'.[21] Nonetheless, *Great Expectations* emerges well from the essay. After what Lang calls the 'Sahara'[22] desert of *Little Dorrit* and the aberration ('hardly "the true Dickens"') of *A Tale of Two Cities*, it is the novel in which Dickens 'was his best self again, reminiscent, autobiographic, humorous, and furnished with perhaps the best of his plots, while his canvas was limited'.[23] In his introduction to the Gadshill edition of *Great Expectations*, also published in 1898,[24] Lang expands on his view of the novel in a largely favourable way, though he once again cites Lewes's point about 'hallucination'. Contending that the use of the first person was beneficial to Dickens because it prevented him from 'digressing into extravagance',[25] he judges that '[*David*] *Copperfield* and *Great Expectations* are his best novels . . . and, of the two, *Great Expectations* is the better constructed'. He goes on:

■ . . . There is a moral, not be a snob, when the temptation so to be is peculiarly strong, blending, as it does, with the ignorant diffidence of a boy born to be refined in intellect, but born among friends not, in a worldly sense, refined in manners. Not to be ashamed of them is no such light task, and we can sympathise with the erring Pip, if we cannot approve. Then, Joe Gargery is infinitely the most sympathetic of all Dickens's many sketches of humble worth, and moral dignity with a horny hand. . . . . . . The character of Pip chiefly resembles that of little David Copperfield in the elfin kind of fancies which occur to a small boy brought up among his seniors. Pip has not David's library, and knows not [Fielding's] *Tom Jones* (1749), but his mind is naturally imaginative and distinguished. He is an observer, as Dickens and David Copperfield were from infancy observers. His fancy is vivid almost to hallucination, in Mr. Lewes's phrase . . .

We may not be much in love with Estella, but . . . [her] education was so unique, and her fall from her high ideas of her social place so much deeper than even Pip's, that we can understand and partly sympathize with her . . . Miss Havisham . . . is not an inconceivable fantasy. The strange scene in which Pip sees her hallucinatory form hanging to [*sic*] a beam in the brewery (1:8, p.65) appears to lead to nothing, yet looks as if it had been intended to lead to something. Perhaps it is more 'eery' [*sic*] just as it stands, a shadow unrealized, a flicker risen out of an unconscious thought.

. . . Mr. Jaggers of the scented soap is perfectly original and interesting, while Wemmick's mannerisms are too kindly to be resented. 'Aged P.', too, is friendly . . . The convict, on his second avatar happily escapes the maudlin, into which a popular writer might so easily have declined [*Editor's Note*: the *Concise Oxford Dictionary* defines 'avatar' as the 'descent of deity to earth in incarnate form' in Hindu mythology and as 'incarnation', 'manifestation', or 'phase'. It is possible that Lang, especially in view of his interest in folk tale and fairy tale, used the term to imply that there is a 'supernatural' quality about Magwitch's return – compare the approach of Harry Stone's *Dickens and the Invisible World* (1979) discussed in chapter four of this Guide (pp.114–19).] . . . The muddy massive malignity of Orlick is very powerfully drawn, and there is much subtlety in the animal-like efforts to propitiate him made by Pip's paralyzed sister . . . we have a foolish liking for the invisible and obstreperous Old Bill Barley, not an eligible father-in-law.

The relatively happy conclusion was an afterthought. Bulwer Lytton, who knew the public, insisted on it, and, as a member of the public, one is glad that he carried his point . . . we rejoice that Estella did not marry 'a Shropshire doctor' [see Appendix A of this Guide], who, perhaps, is to be congratulated. Every one, like the hero of the ballad, would like 'to marry his old true love', and, as it seldom occurs in life, let the ceremony be performed in romance.[26] □

One of Dickens's other turn-of-the-century defenders, Swinburne, thought little of Lang's introductions, calling them 'the prefatory importunities of a writer disentitled to express and disqualified to form an opinion on the work of an English humorist' and comparing the 'intrusive condescension or adulation of such a commentator' to 'rubbish . . . shot down before the doorstep of Charles Dickens'.[27] But although Lang's introduction is relaxed, with a slightly rambling quality, it does present *Great Expectations* as a novel that has something to offer both the common and 'cultivated' reader and it makes a range of interesting points that will come on to the agenda of later critics – for example, that the portrayals of Pip, and even of Estella, are complex ones that can produce in the reader a response of both disapproval and sympathy. In drawing attention to the strange quality of Pip's vision of Miss Havisham hanging from the beam, he highlights a scene that future criticism will often discuss, and his charge that the scene is not fully integrated into the story implicitly challenges critics committed to demonstrating the organic unity of *Great Expectations* – how does Pip's vision form part of that unity?

The most substantial defence of Dickens at the turn of the century appeared in the same year as Lang's essay in the *Fortnightly Review* and his introduction to the Gadshill *Great Expectations*. George Gissing's *Charles Dickens: A Critical Study*[28] (1898) was and remains a major work of Dickens criticism by a perceptive critic and practising novelist with a wide knowledge of Dickens's work and of key developments in nineteenth-century fiction. As George H. Ford suggests, however, there is a tension in Gissing's study between his evident love of Dickens and the critical criteria to which he himself subscribed.[29] At times he sounds like a lawyer defending a large and unruly client, whom he himself mistrusts, in a courtroom where the judge, jury and a substantial portion of the spectators are hostile; he concedes most of the claims of the prosecution and thus increases his own difficulties when he wants to plead for Dickens's acquittal. He affirms that a large change has come about in 'the theory and practice of fiction' in late nineteenth-century England, in the light of which Dickens must seem 'in many respects, antiquated'. He acknowledges that Dickens 'had very little in common with the school of strict veracity, of realism'[30] to which Gissing was largely committed in his own novels and which, he believed, had 'directed fiction into a path it is likely to pursue for many a year to come'.[31] His defence thus involves an awkward attempt to argue that, although Dickens was constrained by his desires for money, praise and a harmonious relationship with his audience, he was nonetheless 'possessed with a sense of the absolute reality of everything he pictured forth' and therefore '[h]ad the word been in use he must necessarily have called himself a Realist'[32] – the capital R is Gissing's, perhaps with the double implication that Dickens is both the supreme Realist and not quite a realist in the later nineteenth-century sense. Gissing himself points to some of the limitations of realism as an ideology for the novel, and at times he glimpses the possibility of an anti-realist approach, as when he says: '[a]rt, for [Dickens], was art precisely because it was not nature'.[33] But he has no real doubt that realism is the dominant ideology for the novel of the present and future and that he must therefore mount his defence of Dickens primarily in realist terms. In this respect, of course, he does anticipate a key strand of twentieth-century criticism of Dickens, which will argue for the value of his novels on the grounds that they are, whatever appearances there may be to the contrary, true to life, even if their veracity is achieved more through symbolism than realism. Defences of Dickens in terms of an aesthetic of artificiality – notably, that of Robert Garis, in 1965 (see pp. 104–108) – remain comparatively rare. Gissing also anticipates an important subsidiary strategy of twentieth-century Dickens criticism when he devotes a chapter to comparisons between Dickens and a number of his foreign contemporaries, although of his chosen authors – Balzac, Victor Hugo, Dostoevsky and Daudet – it is Dostoevsky who has proved most fruitful.

Gissing's comments on *Great Expectations* are scattered throughout his study, but it is worth bringing some of them together both for their intrinsic interest and for their relation to the other criticism in this Guide. He does not appear to regard it as one of Dickens's most important works, but as a 'rich little book';[34] and he commends it for its disciplined use, in contrast to *David Copperfield,* of the first person 'which, granting to the narrator nothing less than Dickens's own equipment of genius, preserves verisimilitude with remarkable care, nothing being related, as seen or heard, which could not have been seen or heard by the writer'.[35] Moreover, Pip's narrative offers not merely verisimilitude but 'a true self-revelation';[36] it 'exhibits very well indeed the growth of a personality, the interaction of character and event'.[37] Gissing also registers, however, his sense that the illusion of Pip as narrator is not wholly sustained: '[o]ne is not permitted to lose sight of the actual author; though so much more living than Esther Summerson, Pip is yet embarrassed, like her, with the gift of humour. We know very well whose voice comes from behind the scenes when Pip is describing Mr. Wopsle's dramatic venture'.[38] He praises the portrayal of the Pocket family, comparing it favourably to the portrayal of the Jellybys in *Bleak House* as 'showing how well, when he chose, Dickens could satirize without extravagance', and he commends Dickens not only for his accurate rendering of Herbert – 'a capital specimen of the healthy, right-minded, and fairly-educated middle-class youth' – but also for the way in which he juxtaposes Herbert and Pip so that 'each throw[s] into relief the other's natural and acquired characteristics'.[39] Gissing also admires the portrait of Pumblechook, who is 'on the surface greatly amusing',[40] 'a source of inextinguishable laughter' exemplifying 'the preposterous self-esteem which always gave Dickens so congenial an opportunity'; but who, when examined more closely, 'is seen to be a very sordid creature', 'illustrative of a contemptible quality closely allied with the commercial spirit'.[41] Gissing's own intense dislike of 'trade' is perhaps revealed in these final comments; his best-known novel, *New Grub Street* (1891) dramatises the way in which 'the commercial spirit' has, he believes, corrupted the literature of his own day – '"Literature nowadays is a trade . . . your successful man of letters is your skilful tradesman"'.[42]

Gissing also intensely disliked what he saw as aggressive and domineering behaviour in women. This intense dislike – hatred might be a better word – surfaces in his approving account of Dickens's portrayal of Mrs. Joe in *Great Expectations*; he not only endorses the veracity of Dickens's representation of 'a shrew of the most highly developed order',[43] but also applauds the way in which Dickens ensures that she 'shall be brought to quietness . . . [b]y a half-murderous blow on the back of her head, from which she will never recover'.[44] Gissing elaborates remorselessly:

■ Dickens understood by this time that there is no other efficacious way with these ornaments of their sex. A felling and stunning and all but killing blow, followed by paralysis and slow death.[45] □

In his biography of Gissing, John Halperin suggests that this relish for violence is a projection of Gissing's own feelings towards the wife from whom he had recently parted and remarks that '[i]t is probably a good thing that Gissing left home when he did'.[46] It would be wrong, however, to interpret Gissing's observations on this aspect of *Great Expectations* solely in terms of his own psychology and of what his biography tells us about his tortuous and troubled relationships with women. He is also, it can be argued, responding to a violence that is indeed an element of the text of *Great Expectations* – and which some later criticism has tackled from psychoanalytic and feminist perspectives.[47]

Gissing has two major criticisms of *Great Expectations*. One is that the sections that deal with Miss Havisham and Estella are 'unsatisfactory', an unhappy survival of 'the old Dickens', 'unable to resist the lure of eccentricity, but no longer presenting it with [his former] gusto'. The other objection, more strongly expressed, is to the changed ending, which Gissing twice discusses, using a mechanical metaphor in the first instance and a musical metaphor in the second. In chapter three of his study, he claims that *Great Expectations* 'would be nearly perfect in its mechanism but for the unhappy deference to Lord Lytton's judgement, which caused the end to be altered. Dickens meant to have left Pip a lonely man, and of course rightly so'.[48] Later, in chapter eight, Gissing returns to the topic, contending that a grave, subtle, subdued pathos is 'the distinguishing note of *Great Expectations*'[49] and that therefore Dickens was correct in his original intention to end the book 'in the minor key'. By this time, the gloves are off; Lytton has been stripped of his title and what Gissing had earlier politely called 'Lord Lytton's judgement' about the ending is now roundly dismissed as 'Lytton's imbecile suggestion'.[50]

The third turn-of-the-century defender of Dickens was the poet Algernon Charles Swinburne. His essay on 'Charles Dickens' in *The Quarterly Review* in July 1902[51] tries to carry his case by extravagant praise rather than by the careful analysis found in Gissing or the relaxed but perceptive discussion offered by Lang; but his account of *Great Expectations* is significant in two respects. One is that he compares *Great Expectations* not only to nineteenth-century fiction – specifically, that of Thackeray – but also to eighteenth-century fiction – that of Fielding, and, more unexpectedly, Laurence Sterne, author of *Tristram Shandy* (1760–67). Swinburne makes the comparison with Fielding and Sterne in order to praise the character of Joe Gargery, and does not develop it any further; but it is, nonetheless, a comparison that opens up the possibility of placing Dickens in a context other than that of the kind of nineteenth-century realistic fiction, represented by George Eliot and Henry James, that tries to create a convincing illusion: both Fielding and Sterne, in their different ways, challenge the norms of the fictional illusion, draw attention to the fact that their books are constructions. Aspects of Dickens that may seem like faults if he is compared to Eliot and James do not necessarily seem like faults if he is compared to Fielding and Sterne.

The second significant aspect of Swinburne's essay is the major status he gives *Great Expectations*. In this, of course, he concurs with Lang, despite his aversion to Lang's introductions to the Gadshill Dickens; but he goes further than Lang in applauding the novel. Though conceding that it may possibly have no characters comparable to Sam Weller (in *The Pickwick Papers*) or Mrs. Gamp (in *Martin Chuzzlewit*), he suggests that it is superior to the earlier novels, even if it does not transcend 'the very best things' in those books. George J. Worth observes: 'Swinburne was one of the first critics to bestow such unalloyed praise on *Great Expectations* and to accord it so high a place among Dickens's novels'.[52] This is what Swinburne says:

■ Among the highest landmarks of success ever reared for immortality by the triumphant genius of Dickens, the story of *Great Expectations* must for ever stand eminent beside that of *David Copperfield*. These are his great twin masterpieces. Great as they are, there is nothing in them greater than the very best things in some of his other books: there is certainly no person preferable and there is possibly no person comparable to Samuel Weller or to Sarah Gamp. Of the two childish and boyish autobiographers, David is the better little fellow though not the more lifelike little friend; but of all first chapters is there any comparable for impression and for fusion of humour and terror and pity and fancy and truth to that which confronts the child with the convict on the marshes in the twilight? And the story is incomparably the finer story of the two; there can be none superior, if there be any equal to it, in the whole range of English fiction. And except in Thackeray's *Vanity Fair* (1847–48) and *The Newcomes* (1853–55), if even they may claim exception, there can surely be found no equal or nearly equal number of living and everliving figures. The tragedy and the comedy, the realism and the dreamery of life, are fused or mingled together with little less than Shakespearean strength and skill of hand. To have created Abel Magwitch is to be a god indeed among the creators of deathless men. Pumblechook is actually better and droller and truer to imaginative life than Pecksniff [in *Martin Chuzzlewit*]: Joe Gargery is worthy to have been praised and loved at once by Fielding and by Sterne: Mr. Jaggers and his clients, Mr. Wemmick and his parent and his bride, are such figures as Shakespeare, when dropping out of poetry, might have created, if his lot had been cast in a later century. Can as much be said for the creatures of any other man or god? The ghastly tragedy of Miss Havisham could only have been made at once credible and endurable by Dickens; he alone could have reconciled the strange and sordid horror with the noble and pathetic survival of possible emotion and repentance. And he alone could have eluded condemnation for so gross an oversight as the escape from retribution of so important a criminal as the 'double murderer and monster' [Orlick?] whose baffled or inadequate attempts are enough to make Bill Sikes [in *Oliver Twist*] seem comparatively the gentlest and Jonas Chuzzlewit [in *Martin Chuzzlewit*] the most amiable of men. I remember no such flaw in any other story I ever read. But in this story it may well have been allowed to pass unrebuked and unobserved; which yet I think it should not.[53] □

Swinburne goes on to pick out, from 'all the minor and momentary figures which flash into eternity across the stage of Dickens',[54] Bill Barley, another enthusiasm that he shares with Lang but which he takes much further, proposing that he is 'great among the greatest of the gods of comic fiction',[55] to be ranked with Francis the drawer (in Shakespeare's *Henry IV, Part II* (probably 1598)) and Cob the water-bearer (in Ben Jonson's play *Every Man in His Humour* (1598)). He concludes his account of *Great Expectations* by affirming that it 'was the author's last great work', the 'defects' of which 'are as nearly imperceptible as spots on the sun or shadows on a sunlit sea'.[56]

But Swinburne's case for Dickens was not argued through in a way that was likely to convince the sceptics. The most important defence of Dickens to appear after Gissing's was by the novelist, poet, essayist and polemicist G.K. Chesterton. His robust and perceptive study, *Charles Dickens*, proved popular, going through twenty-one editions between its first appearance in 1906 and 1946.[57] Like Gissing, Chesterton is well aware of the decline of Dickens's reputation, and he accounts for it first of all in terms of the difficulty that the later nineteenth and early twentieth century has in imagining the 'old atmosphere of a democratic optimism', 'a confidence in common men'[58] that, in Chesterton's view, characterised the early nineteenth century. Dickens 'was the voice in England of this humane intoxication and expansion, this encouraging of anybody to be anything. His best books are a carnival of liberty'[59] (it might be interesting to develop this idea today by drawing on the idea of the 'carnivalesque' in literature of the Russian theorist Mikhail Bakhtin). While Chesterton calls Gissing '[t]he soundest of the Dickens critics' and 'a man of genius',[60] he takes issue with Gissing's claim that Dickens grew up in a hard, cruel world. He concedes that it did contain hardness and cruelty, but charges that Gissing 'omits the wind of hope and humanity that was blowing through it'.[61]

The effect upon Dickens's reputation of the inability to imagine 'a democratic optimism' is linked by Chesterton to what he sees as the harm done to Dickens by 'the two last movements in literary criticism'. The first of these is realism. Like Gissing, Chesterton recognises that some of Dickens's 'scenes and types' do not meet realist criteria, that they are, indeed, 'wholly impossible',[62] and he also echoes Gissing in suggesting that literature need not copy life and in arguing that Dickens is, in his way, more lifelike than the realists: '[a]rt indeed copies life in not copying life, for life copies nothing. Dickens's art is like life because, like life, it is irresponsible, because, like life, it is incredible'. But Chesterton, in contrast to Gissing, identifies a second movement in literary criticism, which, in his view, has already displaced realism; this is a 'more symbolic school of criticism',[63] which deepens and refines the notion of 'real life', locating it internally, and seeing the external details on which the realists focused as imperfect symbols of – and, sometimes, disguises for – that inner life. Within this symbolist aesthetic, the faithful rendering of externals, as in strict realism, will fail to disclose anything of that inner life; in order to try to evoke it, exaggeration is essential. But modern symbolism has not benefited Dickens, because he exaggerates 'the wrong thing',[64] the 'mood our period does not understand', the 'old Revolution sense of infinite opportunity and boisterous brotherhood'.[65] Modern symbolists, Chesterton suggests, 'know what it is to feel a sadness so strange and deep that only impossible characters can express it: they do not know what it is to feel a joy so vital and violent that only impossible characters can express that'.[66]

Chesterton recognises, however, that the Dickens whom he constructs in the first chapter of his study is not quite the Dickens of *Great Expectations*. His specific discussion of the novel occurs later in his book, in the context of a more general argument that Dickens's later novels 'grow consistently graver, and as it were, more responsible' and that 'he improves as an artist if not always as a creator'.[67] This is what Chesterton says:

■ We see [this graver note] struck, I think, with particular and remarkable success in *Great Expectations*. This fine story is told with a consistency and quietude of individuality which is rare in Dickens. But so far had he travelled along the road of a heavier reality, that he even intended to give the tale an unhappy ending, making Pip lose Estella for ever; and he was only dissuaded from it by the robust romanticism of Bulwer Lytton. But the best part of the tale – the account of the vacillations of the hero between the humble life to which he owes everything, and the gorgeous life from which he expects something, touches a very true and somewhat tragic part of morals; for the great paradox of morality (the paradox to which only the religions have given an adequate expression) is that the very vilest kind of fault is exactly the most easy kind . . .

Dickens has dealt with this easy descent of desertion, this silent treason, with remarkable accuracy in the account of the indecisions of Pip. It contains a good suggestion of that weak romance which is the root of all snobbishness: that the mystery which belongs to patrician life excites us more than the open, even the indecent virtues of the humble. Pip is keener about Miss Havisham, who may mean well by him, than about Joe Gargery, who evidently does. All this is very strong and wholesome; but it is still a little stern. *Our Mutual Friend* brings us back a little into [Dickens's] merrier and more normal manner . . .[68] □

Chesterton returns to *Great Expectations* at greater length in an introduction to the 1907 Everyman edition of the novel, later collected in his *Appreciations and Criticisms of the Works of Charles Dickens* (1911).[69] Here he explores his sense of the novel as unique among Dickens's works in its 'serene irony and even sadness', its lack of a hero, and its similarity to Thackeray in its perspective on humankind. But Chesterton is also concerned to distinguish Dickens from Thackeray – and from George Eliot – by affirming Dickens's capacity to give 'the real unconquerable rush of energy in a character'. His account goes on to offer an explicit justification of symbolic or allegorical critical interpretation that does not depend upon a premise of conscious authorial intention – 'any great artist is symbolic without knowing it' – and then provides an allegorical reading of *Great Expectations* which is in part a political one: Joe Gargery and Trabb's boy epitomise the two poles of English democracy, one of long-suffering virtue, the other of assertion through sarcasm. The idea that Dickens should be interpreted symbolically was perhaps the most important development in Dickens criticism from 1940 to 1970; the idea that such interpretation should also have a political aspect was less central in that period, but reappeared from time to time, and has become more salient in the 1980s and 1990s. Chesterton's approach, in the extract that follows, thus anticipates both symbolic and political readings of *Great Expectations*:

■ *Great Expectations*, which was written in the afternoon of Dickens's life and fame, has a quality of serene irony and even sadness, which puts it quite alone among his other works. At no time could Dickens possibly be called cynical, he had too much vitality; but relatively to the other books this book is cynical; but it has the soft and gentle cynicism of old age, not the hard cynicism of youth . . . At no time could any books by Dickens have been called Thackerayan. Both of the two men were too great for that. But relatively to the other Dickensian productions this book may be called Thackerayan. It is a study in human weakness and the slow human surrender. It describes how easily a free lad of fresh and decent instincts can be made to care more for rank and pride and the degrees of our stratified society than for old affection and for honour. It is an extra chapter to Thackeray's *Book of Snobs* (1846–47).

The best way of stating the change which this book marks in Dickens can be put in one phrase. In this book for the first time the hero disappears . . . . . . *Great Expectations* may be called, like [Thackeray's] *Vanity Fair* (1847–48), a novel without a hero. [*Editor's Note*: The subtitle of *Vanity Fair* was *A Novel Without a Hero.*] Almost all Thackeray's novels except *The History of Henry Esmond* (1852) are novels without a hero, but only one of Dickens's novels can be so described. I do not mean that it is a novel without a *jeune premier*, a young man to make love; *Pickwick* is that and *Oliver Twist*, and, perhaps, *The Old Curiosity Shop*. I mean that it is a novel without a hero in the same far deeper and more deadly sense in which [Thackeray's] *The History of Pendennis* (1848–50) is also a novel without a hero. I mean that it is a novel which aims chiefly at showing that the hero is unheroic.

All such phrases as these must appear of course to overstate the case. Pip is a much more delightful person than Nicholas Nickleby [in *Nicholas Nickleby* (1838–39)]. Or to take a stronger case for the purpose of our argument, Pip is a much more delightful person than Sydney Carton [in *A Tale of Two Cities*]. Still the fact remains. Most of Nicholas Nickleby's personal actions are meant to show that he is heroic. Most of Pip's actions are meant to show that he is not heroic. The study of Sydney Carton is meant to indicate that with all his vices Sydney Carton was a hero. The study of Pip is meant to indicate that with all his virtues Pip was a snob. The motive of the literary explanation is different. Pip and Pendennis are meant to show how circumstances can corrupt men. Sam Weller and Hercules are meant to show how heroes can subdue circumstances.

This is the preliminary view of the book which is necessary if we are to regard it as a real and separate fact in the life of Dickens. Dickens had many moods because he was an artist; but he had one great mood, because he was a great artist. Any real difference therefore from the general drift, or rather (I apologise to Dickens) the general drive of his creation is very important. This is the one place in his work in which he . . . understands Thackeray . . . he considers mankind at somewhat the same angle as mankind is considered in one of the sociable and sarcastic novels of Thackeray. When he deals with Pip he sets out not to show his strength like the strength of Hercules, but to show his weakness like the weakness of Pendennis. When he sets out to describe Pip's great expectation he does not set out, as in a fairy tale, with the idea that these great expectations will be fulfilled; he sets out from the first with the idea that these great expectations will be disappointing . . . All [Dickens's] books might be called *Great Expectations*. But the only book to which he gave the name of *Great Expectations* was the only book in which the expectation was never realized. It was so with the whole of that splendid and unconscious generation to which he belonged. The whole glory of that old English middle class was that it was unconscious; its excellence was entirely in that, that it was the culture of the nation, and that it did not know it. If Dickens had ever known that he was optimistic, he would have ceased to be happy.

. . . in *Great Expectations* Dickens was really trying to be a quiet, a detached, and even a cynical observer of human life. Dickens was trying to be Thackeray. And the final and startling triumph of Dickens is this: that even to this moderate and modern story, he gives an incomparable energy which is not moderate and which is not modern . . . Compared to the rest of Dickens this is Thackeray; but compared to the whole of Thackeray we can only say in supreme praise of it that it is Dickens.

Take, for example, the one question of snobbishness. Dickens has achieved admirably the description of the doubts and vanities of the wretched Pip as he walks down the street in his new gentlemanly clothes, the clothes of which he is so proud and so ashamed. Nothing could be so exquisitely human, nothing especially could be so exquisitely masculine as that combination of self-love and self-assertion and even innocence with a naked and helpless sensibility to the slightest breath of ridicule. Pip thinks himself better than every one else, and yet anybody can snub him; that is the everlasting male, and perhaps the everlasting gentleman. Dickens has described perfectly this quivering and defenceless dignity. Dickens has described perfectly how ill-armed it is against the coarse humour of real humanity – the real humanity which Dickens loved, but which idealists and philanthropists do not love, the humanity of cabmen and costermongers and men singing in a third-class carriage; the humanity of Trabb's boy. In describing Pip's weakness Dickens is as true and as delicate as Thackeray. But Thackeray might have been easily as true and as delicate as Dickens. This quick and quiet eye for the tremors of mankind is a thing which Dickens possessed, but which others possessed also. George Eliot or Thackeray could have described the weakness of Pip. Exactly what George Eliot and Thackeray could not have described was the vigour of Trabb's boy . . . exactly what they could never have given, and exactly what Dickens does give, is the *bounce* of Trabb's boy. It is the real unconquerable rush and energy in a character which was the supreme and quite indescribable greatness of Dickens . . . the writer and reader rush with [Trabb's boy]. They start with him, they stare with him, they stagger with him, they share an inexpressible vitality in the air which emanates from this violent and capering satirist. Trabb's boy is among other things a boy; he has a physical rapture in hurling himself like a boomerang and in bouncing to the sky like a ball. It is just exactly in describing this quality that Dickens is Dickens and that no-one else comes near him . . . This quality, whether expressed intellectually or physically, is the profoundly popular and eternal quality in Dickens; it is the thing that no one else could do. This quality is the quality which has always given its continuous power and poetry to the common people everywhere. It is life; it is the joy of life felt by those who have nothing else but life. It is the thing that all aristocrats have always hated and dreaded in the people. And it is the thing which poor Pip really hates and dreads in Trabb's boy.

A great man of letters or any great artist is symbolic without knowing it. The things he describes are types because they are truths . . . It may be a reasonable question whether the artist should be allegorical. There can be no doubt among sane men that the critic should be allegorical . . . Hence it is unavoidable in speaking of a fine book like *Great Expectations* that we should give even to its unpretentious and realistic figures a certain massive mysticism. Pip is Pip, but he is also the well-meaning snob. And this is even more true of those two great figures in the tale which stand for the English democracy. For, indeed, the first and last word upon the English democracy is said in Joe Gargery and Trabb's boy. The actual English populace, as distinct from the French populace or the Scotch or Irish populace, may be said to lie between those two types. The first is the poor man who does not assert himself at all, and the second is the poor man who asserts himself entirely with the weapon of sarcasm. The only way in which the English now ever rise in revolution is under the symbol and leadership of Trabb's boy . . .

. . . Joe Gargery must stand as he stands in the book, a thing too obvious to be understood. But this may be said of him in one of his minor aspects, that he stands for a certain long-suffering in the English poor, a certain weary patience and politeness which almost breaks the

heart. One cannot help wondering whether that great mass of silent virtue will ever achieve anything on this earth.[70] □

Chesterton's defence was not enough to turn the tide, however, not least because Chesterton himself came to be identified with the forces of reaction against the new developments in literature and criticism – associated with T. S. Eliot, Ezra Pound, James Joyce, Virginia Woolf – that have since come to be known as Modernism. For those who were enthusiastic about these new developments, Chesterton, like Dickens himself, was old hat: to defend Dickens was to be associated with an Edwardian and Victorian past that had to be vigorously rejected in order to move forward. Of course, Dickens still had plenty of readers and admirers: this was demonstrated by the founding of the Dickens Fellowship in the UK in 1902 and its launching in 1905 of *The Dickensian: A Magazine for Dickens Lovers*. By 1926, G. K. Chesterton could write of the Fellowship as 'a body whose buoyant vitality was once sufficient even to support the incubus of myself as a president'.[71] Both the Fellowship, which now has branches worldwide, and *The Dickensian*, are still going strong.[72] Writing on *Great Expectations* in *The Dickensian* in February 1913, Willoughby Matchett contended that '[n]o book of Dickens has of late years risen so rapidly in critical estimation', though he acknowledged that 'the big public' – as distinct from 'the special Dickens public' – was 'still apparently labouring under the idea that the novel is for Dickens quite a second-rate affair'.[73] Matchett affirmed, however, that the novel has 'the merit of a great creation of theme' and he detected an element in it that, while it might not appeal to the 'big public' of 1913, could, as we can see with hindsight, strike a chord with a mid-twentieth-century mood: '[d]isillusion, unsatisfied desires, character warped by circumstance give the tale a touch of bitterness'.[74]

But it would take time before *Great Expectations* won wider acceptance. General studies of Dickens's work, and of specific aspects of it, continued, of course, to appear in the first quarter of the twentieth century – for example, W. Walter Crotch's three books *The Pageant of Dickens* (1915), *The Secret of Dickens* (revised edition, 1919) and *The Soul of Dickens* (1916), which contain a range of scattered references to *Great Expectations*, and William S. Holdsworth's *Charles Dickens as a Legal Historian* (1928), which, among other topics related to the law, discusses Jaggers. In 1922, the critic John Middleton Murry could even write an article in *The Times* called 'The Dickens Revival', in which he argued that a proper appreciation of Dickens was a test of superior taste.[75] But Murry's notion of a 'revival' was premature. The later 1920s were to see, especially at the University of Cambridge, the development in the UK of a stringent approach to the criticism and evaluation of literature: an approach based on rigorous close reading and on a strong concern to uphold certain literary and ethical standards such as coherence, organic unity, moral poise, and the eschewal of what was seen as emotional indulgence. In such a perspective, Dickens, certainly at that time, was likely to be found wanting; indeed there is a sense in which the development of academic literary criticism in twentieth-century England was based on a rejection of Dickens.

In 1932, one of the leading figures in the new Cambridge criticism, Q. D. Leavis, produced a celebrated and influential book, based on her PhD thesis, called *Fiction and the Reading Public*, in which she analysed what she saw as the decline of literary standards from the mid-nineteenth-century onwards under the pressure of commercialism. In her analysis, Dickens is seen as a key figure in this decline, with *Nicholas Nickleby* marking the inauguration of the modern kind of bestseller. Q. D. Leavis affirms that 'Dickens stands primarily for a set of crude emotional exercises' and is the dishonourable discoverer of 'the formula "laughter and tears" that has been the foundation of practically every popular success ever since (Hollywood's as well as the bestseller's)'. No 'intellectual stimulus'[76] is needed to provoke such tears, which are of the kind 'that rise in the heart and gather to the eyes involuntarily or even in spite of the reader, though an alert critical mind may cut them off at the source in a revulsion to [*sic*] disgust'. As mentioned earlier in this chapter, this 'revulsion' at the 'disgust' produced by Dickens's capacity to provoke tears complements G. H. Lewes's remark in 1872 that Dickens's capacity to provoke laughter may produce a response of 'revulsion' (see p. 38).

Q. D. Leavis goes on to claim that Dickens's 'originality is confined to recapturing a child's outlook on the grown-up world'; 'emotionally he is not only uneducated but also immature'. Lacking the 'mature, discreet, well-balanced personality' of the eighteenth-century novelist, he is, in what is clearly a bad sense, 'one with his readers; they enjoyed exercising their emotional responses, he laughed and cried aloud as he wrote'.[77] These assaults, with their accusations of immaturity and emotional indulgence, anticipate the devastating dismissal of Dickens by Q. D. Leavis's husband and fellow-critic, F. R. Leavis, sixteen years later in *The Great Tradition* (1948) (see pp. 67–68). It is also interesting to note, however, especially in view of her later strong endorsement of *Great Expectations* (see pp. 109–11), that *Fiction and the Reading Public*'s condemnation of Dickens is qualified at one point; despite his serious flaws, Dickens 'has a personal outlook and idiom which, though elsewhere only present in patches, succeed in getting the upper hand in *David Copperfield* and *Great Expectations* sufficiently for these novels to be called literature'.[78] This grudging concession, however, was unlikely, in 1932, to encourage young critics committed to a stringent approach to spend much time on Dickens.

In a sense, however, *Great Expectations* fared better in the robust hands of Q. D. Leavis than it did in the limp palms of one of Dickens's professed admirers in the 1930s, Stephen Leacock. Since Leacock himself was best known as a writer of humorous sketches, it is no surprise that he preferred the earlier to the later Dickens: but it is interesting that in his book on Dickens's life and work, first published in 1933, he claims (though he gives no supporting evidence) that it is not merely his view but 'the opinion of the many' that the novels of the 1860s, of which *Great Expectations* was the first, 'cannot rank among the great works of Dickens'. *Our Mutual Friend* is 'the weakling of a robust family'[79] and 'even *Great Expectations* . . . could hardly have survived except for its cousinship to still greater [novels]'.[80] Leacock continues:

■ The opening of the book . . . is as wonderful an opening as only Dickens could make. But the story is throughout on a lower level than the greater books, the characters less convincing, the nullities more null, the plot more involved, the fun, what there is of it, apt to sound forced and mechanical. One looks in vain in its pages for world-famous characters. The ending, – unexpectedly altered from tragedy to relief at the suggestion of Bulwer Lytton, – is as unconvincing as any end must be when fitted on to the beginning of something else.[81] □

It is a judgement that, to some extent, echoes some of the negative responses to *Great Expectations* in the early reviews, for example that of Margaret Oliphant (see p. 34). From Edmund Wilson onwards, a key strategy of the Dickens critical revival of the 1940s and 1950s would be to counter this supposed 'opinion of the many' by promoting the later novels as superior to the earlier in terms of artistry and maturity.

That revival was yet to come. One stimulus to it was a biographical revelation about Dickens. In the *Daily Express* of 3 April 1934, an article by Thomas Wright appeared, headed '98 Years Ago To-day – Charles Dickens Began His Honeymoon'. As K. J. Fielding points out, it had long been known that, after the break with his wife, Dickens's name had been linked with that of a young actress, Ellen Lawless Ternan; but up to this point biographers had accepted Dickens's public denial that there was anything improper about the relationship. Wright did not call Dickens a liar; he conceded that the denial was true when it was first made, just after he had separated from his wife: but he went on to affirm: 'I can state positively . . . that Miss Ternan did later become Dickens's mistress'.[82] More details about the relationship emerged in Wright's *Life of Charles Dickens* (1935), his *Autobiography* (1936) and Gladys Storey's *Dickens and Daughter* (1939) – Storey had been a close friend of Kate Perugini, Dickens's second daughter.[83] The full truth of the relationship between the ageing author and the young actress remains obscure, and may never be known; but it has continued to fascinate biographers and critics (sometimes in spite of themselves), and prompted an interest in Ellen Ternan's own life, which has recently resulted in a full-length biography by Claire Tomalin, *The Invisible Woman: The Story of Nelly Ternan and Charles Dickens* (1990).

The question of the relevance of biography to literary criticism has been hotly debated in the twentieth century, and most critics will use biographical material, if at all, with great caution. There can be no doubt, however, that such material has an effect upon interpretation, even if only by prompting a strenuous effort to exclude it. The immediate effect of the revelation was to make Dickens into a much more *interesting* figure – much more complex and, in a sense, much more modern; and this new image of Dickens could be linked, as it would be in Edmund Wilson's famous 1941 essay, with the search for complexity and modernity in his novels. Moreover, the relationship could be seen as especially relevant to *Great Expectations*, since he had been writing the novel at that time, and it was possible to suggest elements of Ellen in Estella – not least in the fact that the Christian name of the latter could be seen as a partial anagram of Ellen Lawless Ternan.

A further stimulus to the Dickens revival, and especially to the discussion of *Great Expectations*, came in 1937 from an ancient but still vigorous voice: that of the world-famous playwright, Bernard Shaw, who had himself, in his early days, been a novelist. Shaw's 'Preface' appeared in a 'Limited Editions Club' edition of *Great Expectations*, and was to circulate more widely when republished in a revised and compressed form as the 'Introduction' to the 'Novel Library' edition of 1947. The 1947 version will be considered here as it is more concise and may also have been the version that Shaw originally intended to publish.[84] Shaw's account of *Great Expectations* is informed by his evident love of Dickens, his acknowledged debt to Dickens in his plays,[85] his personal knowledge of the Victorian era, and his political commitment. In his general comments on Dickens, he points out that 'Marx and Dickens were contemporaries living in the same city and pursuing the same profession of literature' and provocatively classes them both as 'revolutionist[s]',[86] with the difference that 'Marx knew that he was a revolutionist whilst Dickens had not the faintest suspicion of that part of his calling'.[87] Nonetheless, '*Little Dorrit* is a more seditious book than *Das Kapital* [(1867–94)]'.[88] He calls *Great Expectations* itself Dickens's 'most compactly perfect book', 'all-of-one-piece and consistently truthful as none of the other books are', and he registers its seriousness – 'life is no laughing matter in *Great Expectations*'.[89] He makes some criticisms of the novel; taking up the question of the two endings, he contends that Dickens 'made a mess of both': the original ending 'is much too matter-of-fact to be the right ending to a tragedy',[90] and the 'conventional happy ending is an outrage' in a book into which 'Dickens put nearly all his thought' and which is 'too serious . . . to be a trivially happy one'. Estella is seen as 'a curious addition to the gallery of unamiable women painted by Dickens',[91] 'a born tormentor' of Pip who never shows 'a moment of kindness' to others. Like the *British Quarterly Review* writer back in 1862 (see p. 33) and like George Gissing (in regard to Mrs. Joe) in 1898 (see p. 43), Shaw legitimises violence against women, or at least against dominant women like Estella; he sees Drummle as more of a victim than a bully, 'obliged to defend himself from her clever malice with his fists' and thus, by his violence, offering the reader 'a consolation . . . for Pip's broken heart', even if it is 'not altogether a credible one' because 'the real Estellas can usually intimidate the real Bentley Drummles'. In common with the *British Quarterly Review* writer, Shaw is unconvinced by the idea that Estella is, as he puts it, 'redeemed by Bentley's thrashings', and sees it as part of 'the final sugary suggestion' that the novel's conclusion constitutes.[92] As shall be seen in the extract below, Shaw makes further criticisms of *Great Expectations* by means of interesting comparisons between Dickens, H. G. Wells and Victor Hugo; but he first of all puts his positive case for the novel:

■ Apart from this [final sugary suggestion] the story is the most perfect of Dickens's works. In it he does not muddle himself with the ridiculous plots that appear like vestiges of the stone age in many of his books, from *Oliver Twist* to the end. The story is built round a single and simple catastrophe: the revelation to Pip of the source of his great expectations. There is, it is true, a trace of the old plot superstition in Estella turning out to be Magwitch's daughter; but it provides a touchingly happy ending for that heroic Warmint. Who could have the heart to grudge it to him?

As our social conscience expands and makes the intense class snobbery of the nineteenth century seem less natural to us, the tragedy of *Great Expectations* will lose some of its appeal. I have already wondered [in the first paragraph of the 'Foreword'][93] whether Dickens himself ever came to see that his agonizing sensitiveness about the blacking bottles and his resentment of his mother's opposition to his escape from them was not too snobbish to deserve all the sympathy he claimed for it. Compare the case of H. G. Wells, our nearest to a twentieth-century Dickens. Wells hated being a draper's assistant as much as Dickens hated being a warehouse boy; but he was not in the least ashamed of it, and did not blame his mother for regarding it as the summit of her ambition for him. I cannot help speculating on whether if Dickens had not killed himself prematurely to pile up money for that excessive family of his, he might not have reached a stage at which he could have got as much fun out of the blacking bottles as Mr. Wells got out of his abhorred draper's counter.

Dickens never reached that stage; and there is no prevision of it in *Great Expectations*; for in it he never raises the question why Pip should refuse Magwitch's endowment and shrink from him with such inhuman loathing. Magwitch no doubt was a Warmint from the point of view of the genteel Dickens family and even from his own; but Victor Hugo would have made him a magnificent hero, another Valjean [the central figure of Hugo's novel *Les Misérables* (1862)]. Inspired by an altogether noble fixed idea, he had lifted himself out of his rut of crime and honestly made a fortune for the child who had fed him when he was starving. If Pip had no objection to be a parasite instead of an honest blacksmith, at least he had a better claim to be a parasite on Magwitch's earnings than, as he imagined, on Miss Havisham's property. It is curious that this should not have occurred to Dickens; for nothing could exceed the bitterness of his exposure of the futility of Pip's parasitism. If all that came of sponging on Miss Havisham (as he thought) was the privilege of being one of the Finches of the Grove, he need not have felt his dependence on Magwitch to be incompatible with his entirely baseless self-respect. But Pip – and I am afraid Pip must to this extent be identified with Dickens – could not see Magwitch as an animal of the same species as himself or Miss Havisham. His feeling is true to the nature of snobbery; but his creator says no word in criticism of that ephemeral limitation.

The basic truth of the situation is that Pip, like his creator, has no culture and no religion. Joe Gargery, when Pip tells a monstrous string of lies about Miss Havisham, advises him to say a repentant word about it in his prayers; but Pip never prays; and church means nothing to him but Mr. Wopsle's orotundity. In this, he resembles David Copperfield, who has gentility but neither culture nor religion. Pip's world is therefore a very melancholy place, and his conduct, good or bad, always helpless. This is why Dickens worked against so black a background after he was roused from his ignorant middle-class cheery optimism by Carlyle. When he lost his belief in bourgeois society and with it his lightness of heart he had neither an economic Utopia nor a credible religion to hitch on to. His world becomes a world of great expectations cruelly disappointed.[94] □

Shaw's revolutionary Dickens resembles in key respects the proto-Marxist Dickens of T. A. Jackson's full-length study, which appeared in the same year as Shaw's original 'Preface'. Jackson's *Charles Dickens: The Progress of a Radical* (1937) highlights, in its 'Foreword', the diversity of Dickens's admirers and the paradox in the nature of his readership that this produces. It links this paradox with the critical debate about Dickens's work:

■ The antinomical [contradictory] character of his popularity – among State officials, bourgeois moralists, Communists, convicts, and the unlettered generally – is emphasized by the sharp division which persists, and has from the first persisted, among literary critics as to Dickens's true place in the hierarchy of his art [that is, the art of the novel]. For some he is far and away the supreme *English* novelist. For others he is the supreme example of English incapacity for High Art. He is, say these latter, thin, banal, grotesque, maudlin, exaggerated, extravagant . . . . . . His very popularity is, to these critics, a proof of his inferiority . . . No man, they say, could become so instantly and remain so widely popular and be really great.

To which another school, headed by G.K. Chesterton, makes the obvious reply – that his abiding popularity proves that, for good or ill, he struck a chord which never fails to excite a response in the emotions of common humanity everywhere . . .[95] □

After this shrewd summary of the debate, which shows a clear grasp of some of its major aspects, Jackson decides that he will not pursue it directly – '[l]et us leave this critical problem to the critics' – but will instead investigate 'the relation of Dickens's work to the period in which it was produced'.[96] His analysis of this relation is a bold and dogmatic one, as we can see in the following extract from his account of *Great Expectations*:

■ Self-satisfied, mid-Victorian, British society buoyed itself up with as great 'expectations' of future wealth and glory as did poor, deluded Pip. If it had but known, its means of ostentation came from a source (the labour of the depressed and exploited masses) to which it would have been as shocked to acknowledge indebtedness as Pip was to find he owed all his acquired gentility to the patronage of a transported felon. Magwitch differed little from the uncouth monster which respectable society envisaged to itself as the typical 'labouring man'. And in literal truth, good, respectable society owed as much to these working men, and was as little aware of it, as was Pip of the source of his advantages. And respectable society is as little grateful as Pip, whenever the truth is revealed.

Great Expectations shows Dickens in the trough of the wave, his optimism shattered, and his Radicalism nonplussed in consequence. He had not reached a conception of any revolutionary role open to the proletariat. But, if the bourgeoisie is, after all, made up of nothing but Bentley Drummles, Compeysons, Pumblechooks and their like, even another September 1792, and another Reign of the Guillotine, would be preferable to the continuance of their role in perpetuity. No inference but this is possible from a novel which preaches so clearly the folly and worse of a refusal to face the ugly actualities of life.[97] □

As this shows, Jackson's approach is short on a sense of historical and literary detail and complexity;[98] but his trenchant attempt to relate Dickens to his time may have helped to stimulate more nuanced and informed versions of that relationship – it is significant that the pioneering accounts of George Orwell, Edmund Wilson and Humphry House all cite Jackson, even when dissenting from him.[99] Moreover, Jackson's political concerns do not prevent him from discussing other features of *Great Expectations*, and, after his vigorous exposition of its supposed political allegory, he goes on to discuss some of its psychological, ethical and universal aspects. He praises Dickens's rendering of Pip for its 'child-psychology' in the early chapters of the novel,[100] and for its 'delineation of [his] turning . . . into an appalling little snob' in scenes that 'strike home to the streak of snobbery in every one of us'.[101] In his conclusion to his account of the novel, he contends that 'the pathetically-painful story of Pip's cruel awakening' irresistibly reveals 'the pith and marrow of the author's purpose – that Pip, here, like David Copperfield in another sense, stands for Everyman'.[102] As shall be seen in the next chapter of this Guide, the interpretation of Pip as 'Everyman' will be made in 1953 by a rather different critic, Dorothy Van Ghent (see pp. 75, 76, 78). Jackson does not ask, in fact, how Pip as an 'Everyman' who exemplifies the 'snobbery in all of us' relates to the Pip whom he has compared to a specific historical moment, that of '[s]elf-satisfied, mid-Victorian, British society'; and this exemplifies a more general reluctance to make links between the political aspect of his account and its psychological, ethical and universal dimensions – dimensions that would be acceptable topics in mainstream 1950s criticism as the political aspect would not.

Jackson's work – perhaps written deliberately in a populist spirit – was too simplistic, however, to feed directly into a critical revival. The key sources of that revival were to be two essays by freelance writers, one English, one American, who shared some of Jackson's political concerns, but who engaged with Dickens in a way that was sufficiently complex and perceptive to allow academic critics to take them seriously. These essays were 'Charles Dickens', by George Orwell, and 'Dickens: The Two Scrooges' by Edmund Wilson.

Orwell's essay, written in 1939,[103] first appeared in his *Inside the Whale* in 1940. Clear, lively, perceptive and wide-ranging, it is full of forceful, concise formulations that are thought-provoking even when they do not command complete assent. The essay is not academic but nonetheless provides a host of topics that could be explored by academic critics and researchers. Orwell covers many aspects of Dickens, but has two main concerns that are considered here: to define Dickens's attitude to society and politics, and to identify his qualities as a writer. Orwell takes issue with what he sees as Chesterton's attempt to turn Dickens into an incarnation of Chestertonian medievalism, and T.A. Jackson's attempt to make Dickens 'a bloodthirsty revolutionary';[104] he also dissents from an implication that he attributes to both Chesterton and Jackson, that Dickens was 'a "proletarian" writer'.[105] Dickens, Orwell argues, wrote mostly about the middle class; and he was not a 'revolutionary' writer 'in the ordinarily accepted sense of the word'.[106] But, 'even if Dickens was a bourgeois, he was certainly a subversive writer, a radical, one might truthfully say a rebel',[107] every page of whose work displays 'a consciousness that society is wrong somewhere at the root'.[108] His 'criticism of society' is, however, 'almost exclusively moral';[109] 'in every attack [he] makes upon society he is always pointing to a change of spirit rather than a change of structure'; '[e]ssentially . . . he is always saying' that it is '[u]seless to change institutions without a "change of heart"'. But Orwell, after affirming that '[a] "change of heart" is in fact *the* alibi of people who do not wish to endanger the *status quo*', goes on to ask whether 'a merely moral criticism of society may not be just as "revolutionary" – and revolution, after all, means turning things upside down – as the politico-economic criticism which is fashionable at this moment'.[110] There is an interesting oscillation in Orwell's essay between a diagnosis of Dickens's limitations from a radical left-wing political viewpoint and a sense that it might be possible to regard a 'moral' viewpoint as, in its way, no less 'revolutionary'. This swaying between the 'political' and the 'moral' is understandable in 1940, at the end of a decade that had seen both fervent political commitments and massive political disappointments in which Orwell himself had been intensely involved; and his suggestion of a possible radicalism in a 'moral' approach anticipated some of the literary criticism of the 1950s, which would distance itself from politics and focus its dissent in a moral critique of society.

Orwell makes three major references to *Great Expectations* in his essay. One is when he is trying to define Dickens's social attitudes, and contends that 'in spite of his generosity of mind, he is not free from the special prejudices of the shabby-genteel'.[111] As a result of this he is repelled by slum-dwellers and 'shows less understanding of criminals than one would expect of him'; he is 'well aware of the social and economic causes of crime' but 'often seems to feel that when a man has once broken the law he has put himself outside human society'.[112] In Orwell's view, the limitations of Dickens's attitude to crime are illustrated by *Great Expectations*:

■ As soon as he comes up against crime or the worst depths of poverty, he shows traces of the 'I've always kept myself respectable' habit of mind. The attitude of Pip (obviously the attitude of Dickens himself) towards Magwitch in *Great Expectations* is extremely interesting.

Pip is conscious all along of his ingratitude towards Joe, but far less so of his ingratitude towards Magwitch. When he discovers that the person who has loaded him with benefits for years is actually a transported convict, he falls into frenzies of disgust: 'The abhorrence in which I held the man, the dread I had of him, the repugnance with which I shrank from him, could not have been exceeded if he had been some terrible beast', etc., etc. (2:20, p.317). So far as one can discover from the text, this is not because when Pip was a child he had been terror-ized by Magwitch in the churchyard; it is because Magwitch is a criminal and a convict. There is an even more 'kept-myself-respectable' touch in the fact that Pip feels as a matter of course that he cannot take Magwitch's money. The money is not the product of a crime, it has been honestly acquired; but it is an ex-convict's money and therefore 'tainted'. There is nothing psychologically false in this either. Psychologically the latter part of *Great Expectations* is about the best thing Dickens ever did; throughout this part of the book one feels 'Yes, that is just how Pip would have behaved'. But the point is that in the matter of Magwitch, Dickens identifies with Pip, and his attitude is at bottom snobbish. The result is that Magwitch belongs to the same queer class of characters as Falstaff and, probably, Don Quixote – characters who are more pathetic than the author intended.[113] □

We can see that in this passage Orwell combines a biographical and sociological approach to Dickens, in which he uses *Great Expectations* to illustrate and analyse further its author's social attitudes, with an approach that is of a more strictly literary-critical kind, in which he analyses the attitudes of a *fictional* character and praises the psychological accuracy of the representation of that character. This praise for the latter part of *Great Expectations* is complemented elsewhere in his essay by his admiration for its earlier part, which he uses to demonstrate Dickens's incomparable 'power of entering into the child's point of view':

■ Dickens [is] able to stand both inside and outside the child's mind, in such a way that the same scene can be wild burlesque or sinister reality, according to the age at which one reads it. Look, for instance, at . . . the scene in which Pip, in *Great Expectations*, coming back from Miss Havisham's house and finding himself completely unable to describe what he has seen, takes refuge in a series of outrageous lies – which, of course, are eagerly believed. All the isolation of childhood is there. And how accurately he has recorded the mechanisms of the child's mind, its visualizing tendency, its sensitiveness to certain kinds of impression [as when] Pip relates how in his childhood his ideas about his dead parents were derived from their tombstones.[114] □

Orwell's third major reference to *Great Expectations* in his essay occurs when he is trying to define Dickens's distinctiveness as a writer. As *The Eclectic Review* had done at the time of the first appearance of *Great Expectations* in 1861 (see p.28), Orwell highlights Dickens's 'fertility of invention, which is invention not so much of characters, still less of "situations", as of turns of phrase and concrete details'. In one of those formulations that make Orwell's essay itself so fertile, he says: 'The outstanding, unmistakable mark of Dickens's writing is the *unnecessary detail* [Orwell's italics]'.[115] In his work, '[e]verything is piled up, detail on detail'. According to Orwell, this is something you either like or do not like; but he goes on to suggest, taking an example from *Great Expectations*, that Dickens's 'profuse, overflowing quality'[116] may have its drawbacks:

■ As a novelist [Dickens's] natural fertility greatly hampers him, because the burlesque which he is never able to resist is constantly breaking into what ought to be serious situations. There is a good example of this in the opening chapter of *Great Expectations*. The escaped convict, Magwitch, has just captured the six-year-old Pip in the churchyard. The scene starts terrifyingly enough, from Pip's point of view. The convict, smothered in mud and with his chain trailing from his leg, suddenly starts up among the tombs, grabs the child, turns him upside down and robs his pockets. Then he begins terrorizing him into bringing food and a file:

> . . . [H]e held me by the arms, in an upright position on the top of the stone, and went on in these fearful terms:
> "You bring me, to-morrow morning early, that file and them wittles. You bring the lot to me, at that old Battery over yonder. You do it, and you never dare to say a word or dare to make a sign concerning your having seen such a person as me, or any person sumever, and you shall be let to live. You fail, or you go from my words in any partickler, no matter how small it is, and your heart and your liver shall be tore out, roasted and ate. Now, I ain't alone, as you may think I am. There's a young man hid with me, in comparison with which young man I am a Angel. That young man hears the words I speak. That young man has a secret way pecooliar to himself, of getting at a boy, and at his heart, and at his liver. It is in wain for a boy to attempt to hide himself from that young man. A boy may lock his door, may be warm in bed, may tuck himself up, may draw the clothes over his head, may think himself comfortable and safe, but that young man will softly creep and creep his way to him and tear him open. I am a keeping that young man from harming of you at the present moment, with great

difficulty. I find it wery hard to hold that young man off of your inside. Now, what do you say?" (1:1, p. 6)

Here Dickens has simply yielded to temptation. To begin with, no starving and hunted man would speak in the least like that. Moreover, although the speech shows a remarkable knowledge of the way in which a child's mind works, its actual words are quite out of tune with what is to follow. It turns Magwitch into a sort of pantomime wicked uncle, or, if one sees him through the child's eyes, into an appalling monster. Later in the book he is to be represented as neither, and his exaggerated gratitude, on which the plot turns, is to be incredible because of just this speech. As usual, Dickens's imagination has overwhelmed him. The picturesque details were too good to be left out.[117] □

In this passage, we see Orwell working as a literary critic in the 'strict' sense, rather than in biographical or sociological terms; he identifies what he sees as a key general feature of Dickens's writing – the unnecessary detail – and seeks to demonstrate how that feature may be harmful with specific reference to a particular passage from *Great Expectations*. It is not necessary to agree either with his general point or with his criticism of the specific passage to appreciate the value of his method – indeed, it is a method that, by combining general argument and specific example, makes fruitful disagreement possible. But it is also important that his strictly 'literary' criticism of Dickens is not, in the overall context of his essay, hermetically sealed from biographical, sociological and political considerations; these considerations and the 'strictly literary' ones enrich each other. Orwell shows how to coordinate a range of approaches – biographical, sociological, political, and literary-critical. Both as an example of how to conduct criticism, and in its general and specific analyses of Dickens, his essay is truly seminal. In its compact compass, it sows seeds that in later years will bring a rich critical harvest.

The same is true of Edmund Wilson's essay on Dickens, which featured as the first of seven 'studies in literature' in his book *The Wound and the Bow* (1941). Like Orwell's essay, it is lucid, vigorous, wide-ranging, insightful and immensely stimulating, packed with propositions for future critics to challenge and develop. Wilson constructs a Dickens who is both a deeply self-divided human being and a serious symbolist artist. Affirming that '[i]t is necessary to see [Dickens] as a man in order to appreciate him as an artist',[118] Wilson skilfully draws on biographical material – in particular the 'trauma' of the blacking factory episode,[119] and the relationship with Ellen Ternan – to build up a picture of a manic-depressive Dickens, alternating, like Scrooge, between merriment and moroseness. Indeed, Wilson suggests that if it were possible to imagine following Scrooge beyond the end of *A Christmas Carol*, the reader would soon find that he would relapse from his festive cheerfulness into his former gloom. This dualism in Dickens's life also runs through his work. At first it takes the form of 'good' and 'bad' contrasts, for instance, by means of counterbalancing characters within and between novels – 'an affable lawyer who is really unscrupulous, Vholes [in *Bleak House*], and a kindly lawyer who pretends to be unfeeling, Jaggers [in *Great Expectations*]';[120] later the dualism grows more complex as the novels try to explore the combination of good and bad in one character.

Wilson is writing, like Orwell, at the end of a decade in which political commitment in writing had been strongly emphasised but was now starting to fall into discredit; and he shares Orwell's desire to define Dickens's attitude to society and politics. He asserts that '[f]undamentally, [Dickens] was not interested in politics'[121] and that he was 'sometimes actually stupid about politics'.[122] But, like Orwell, he is concerned to rescue a subversive if not revolutionary Dickens, arguing that Dickens's lack of interest in, or intelligence about, politics did not entail conformity. In imagination, Wilson suggests, Dickens played the two roles that were 'natural' to him as a 'man of spirit whose childhood ha[d] been crushed by the cruelty of organized society' – the roles of criminal and rebel – and he continued until his death 'to put into them all that was most passionate in his feeling'.[123] Dickens was 'almost invariably *against* institutions'. We can see that here Wilson is developing a version of Dickens which accords with some of the biographical and textual evidence and which could also prove congenial to the major form of cultural dissidence that would emerge in the UK, Europe and the USA in the next decade, the 1950s – a form represented, in different aspects, by Albert Camus's preference for rebellion over revolution, by the anarchic anti-institutionalism of the American beat writers, by the partial romanticisation of crime in the work of Norman Mailer, and by the vehement self-assertion of some of the British Angry Young Men. Wilson's modernised Dickens is not divorced from the nineteenth century; indeed, Wilson locates him in his times with some skill; but in doing so he provocatively inverts the stereotype of Dickens as the quintessential Victorian: '[o]f all the great Victorian writers, he was probably the most antagonistic to the Victorian Age itself'.[124]

Wilson combines his portrayals of Dickens the divided man and Dickens the anti-Victorian with a portrait of the middle-aged artist as a major dramatic symbolist. He endorses Chesterton's view that Dickens was the greatest English writer of his time and Shaw's linking of Dickens's name with Shakespeare's (Wilson does not mention that for Shaw such a link might be a dubious compliment). Though not of 'the rank where Shakespeare has few companions', Dickens is, Wilson affirms, 'the greatest dramatic writer that the English had had since Shakespeare, and he created the largest and most varied world'. His work, moreover, has 'a complexity and a depth' to which previous critics, such as Gissing and Shaw, have hardly done justice,[125] and which, Wilson hints, might be better understood through comparison with Kafka, Mann and Joyce – writers who would become, in the 1950s, modernist icons. Wilson finds this complexity and depth particularly in his work from *Dombey and Son* onwards, when Dickens finally sheds picaresque looseness and mechanical plot: 'now he is to organize his stories as wholes, to plan all the characters as symbols, and to invest all the details with significance'.[126] With this claim, Wilson outlines the basis for many subsequent critical readings of Dickens's later novels, especially in the 1950s and 1960s, which will proceed on the assumption that these novels are to be read as organised wholes in which the characters function symbolically and in which every detail is significant (see, in this Guide, Dorothy Van Ghent, pp. 74–79). Such an assumption could, and in some cases did, lead to a psychological and/or formalist emphasis that largely excluded social and political questions. Wilson also argues, however, that Dickens's concern with unity and symbolism from *Dombey* onwards, was combined with an attempt 'to trace an anatomy of [contemporary] society', although he emphasises that this was always conducted dramatically rather than didactically, 'through the observed interrelations between highly individualized human beings rather than through political or economic analysis'.[127] He thus provides both a rationale, and a restrictive clause, for critics who still want to concern themselves with the political and social significance of Dickens's novels; they may certainly do so, but they must explore that significance as it is embodied in the human relationships represented in the fiction.

In his specific comments on *Great Expectations*, Wilson links the novel with *Little Dorrit* as having some similarities in theme, as being 'full of the disillusion and discomfort of this period of Dickens's life', and as showing a 'distinctly new' turn in its treatment both of social situations and of individual psychology.[128] Both novels offer 'a great deal more psychological interest than . . . Dickens's previous books', telling us 'what the characters think and feel, and even something about how they change'.[129] The presentation of Pip, in particular, is judged by Wilson to be 'a great advance'[130] because he incorporates those 'good' and 'bad' elements that had often been divided between different characters in Dickens's previous fiction. Although Wilson has said earlier in his essay that Pip, once he gets the chance to become a gentleman, 'straightaway turns into a mean little snob',[131] he later provides this more nuanced summary:

■ In *Great Expectations* we see Pip pass through a whole psychological cycle. At first, he is sympathetic, then by a more or less natural process he turns into something unsympathetic, then he becomes sympathetic again.[132] □

Turning from the character of Pip himself, Wilson goes on to propose that, following a development first evident in *Bleak House*, the solution of the mystery in *Great Expectations* – that is, the revelation of the source of the 'expectations' – is also Dickens's moral. He then posits the 'great expectations' themselves as the later novel's key symbol and reaffirms T. A. Jackson's view that they represent Victorian mid-century optimism (see p. 57). In this perspective, he judges the original ending 'perfect in tone and touch' and condemns the changed ending because it damages the moral, symbolic and historical significance of the novel. The reason Dickens yielded to Bulwer Lytton, Wilson suggests, was that he 'was still a public entertainer who felt that he couldn't too far disappoint his audience.'[133] In this respect, at least, Dickens does not quite measure up to the standards of the great modernists.

The essays of Orwell and Wilson were complemented and extended in some respects by Humphry House's important book *The Dickens World* (1941). House notes how in recent years – he is referring to the later 1930s – literary criticism, and especially literary history, have become more 'sociological', more concerned with 'the social and economic environment'.[134] He contends, however, that 'nearly all' the writers who have dealt with Dickens as a social historian and a reformist in his novels have 'interpreted Dickens more through their own beliefs than through the beliefs of his time'.[135] House declares that his own aim is 'to show in a broad and simple way the connexion between what Dickens wrote and the times in which he wrote it, between his reformism and some of the things he wanted reformed, between the attitude to life shown in his books and the society in which he lived'. House, clearly unafraid of resembling Mr. Gradgrind in *Hard Times* (1854), affirms that his book will be much concerned with facts, 'and illustrated with quotations from miscellaneous sources'. House's willingness to employ 'miscellaneous sources' anticipates the critical movement that began in the 1980s, known as the 'New Historicism', which also draws on a variety of 'miscellaneous sources' in its discussion of texts. House, however, has a more traditional notion of the value of such sources than the New Historicists, seeing them as the only means by which one can accurately envisage a writer's environment and grasp his purposes: 'the exact language of contemporaries alone can have the authentic tone and idiom necessary to conviction'.[136]

House is thus, like Shaw, Jackson and Wilson, one of those critics who see *Great Expectations* as expressive of its age – the age in which it was written, the 1850s, rather than the age in which it was set, the 1820s and 1830s. He believes, however, that his view of the age is more accurate than that of earlier critics because it is based on contemporary documentary sources. He argues that Dickens's novel expresses a belief in the power of money, for good and ill, which was only possible in a country with a stable domestic economy and expanding foreign markets; in this respect, House, although not writing as a Marxist, shows a quasi-Marxist sense of the importance of the 'economic base', and, while the existence of the Empire is not explicitly mentioned, it is perhaps implicit in the mention of those expanding foreign markets. House also shows a quasi-Marxist sense of the importance of class; *Great Expectations* is not so much expressive of its age in a universal sense as expressive of the attitudes and concerns of a particular class in a particular age, who, because of their dominance, are able to present their values as universal: '[t]he book is the clearest artistic triumph of the Victorian bourgeoisie on its own special ground'.[137]

This extract joins House at the beginning of the paragraph in which he sums up Pip's story as 'a snob's progress' – a pithy phrase that would acquire wide currency:

■ In the last resort [Dickens] shared Magwitch's belief that money and education can make a 'gentleman', that birth and tradition count for little or nothing in the formation of style. The final wonder of *Great Expectations* is that in spite of all Pip's neglect of Joe and coldness towards Biddy and all the remorse and self-recrimination that they caused him, he is made to appear at the end of it all a really better person than he was at the beginning. It is a remarkable achievement to have kept the reader's sympathy throughout a snob's progress. The book is the clearest artistic triumph of the Victorian bourgeoisie on its own special ground. The expectations lose their greatness, and Pip is saved from the grosser dangers of wealth; but by the end he has gained a wider and deeper knowledge of life, he is less rough, better spoken, better read, better mannered; he has friends as various as Herbert Pocket, Jaggers, and Wemmick; he has earned in his business abroad enough to pay his debts, he has become third partner in a firm that 'had a good name, and worked for [its] profits, and did very well' (3:20, p. 476). Who is to say that these are not advantages? Certainly not Dickens. But he shirks the implications of the reconciliation with Joe and Biddy: there is one emotional scene with friendliness all round, which shows that in spite of his new accent and new manners Pip is the same decent little fellow after all: but what if he had had no Herbert to fall back on, and had been forced to build his fortunes again from scratch in the old village with Gargerys and Wopsles? Dickens does not face this: he takes Pip's new class position as established, and whisks him off to the East, where gentlemen grow like mushrooms. Yet we do not feel that this is artistically wrong, as the final marriage to Estella is wrong: for the book is the sincere, uncritical expression of a time when the whole class-drift was upwards and there was no reason to suppose that it would ever stop being so. The social ideals of

Pip and Magwitch differ only in taste. Though Pip has shuddered at the convict for being coarse and low, he consoles him on his death-bed with the very thought that first fired him and then kept alive his own love for Estella: '"You had a child . . . She is a lady and very beautiful"' (3:17, p.456) . . . . . . *Great Expectations* is the perfect expression of a phase of English society: it is a statement, to be taken as it stands, of what money can do, good and bad; of how it can change and make distinctions of class; how it can pervert virtue, sweeten manners, open up new fields of enjoyment and suspicion. The mood of the book belongs not to the imaginary date of its plot, but to the time in which it was written; for the unquestioned assumption that Pip can be trans-formed by money and the minor graces it can buy, and that the loss of one fortune can be repaired on the strength of incidental gains in voice and friends, were only possible in a country secure in its internal economy, with expanding markets abroad: this could hardly be said of England in the 'twenties and 'thirties.[138] □

The work of House, Wilson and Orwell comprised the most important contribution to the Dickens revival in the 1950s. But that revival met a major obstruction in the UK. The most influential critic in postwar England was F.R. Leavis – whose wife and fellow-critic, Q.D. Leavis, had largely dismissed Dickens back in 1932, as was observed earlier in this chapter (see p.52). In 1948 Leavis published *The Great Tradition*, a book that was significantly to affect the attitudes of English critics to Dickens over the next two decades. Leavis's first sentence throws down the gauntlet: '[t]he great English novelists are Jane Austen, George Eliot, Henry James, and Joseph Conrad – to stop for the moment at that com-paratively safe point in history'.[139] Dickens is excluded, and later in his first chapter, Leavis tells us why:

■ That Dickens was a great genius and is permanently among the classics is certain. But the genius was that of a great entertainer, and he had for the most part no profounder responsibility as a creative artist than this description suggests. Praising him magnificently in *Soliloquies in England* (1922), [George] Santayana says: 'In every English-speaking home, in the four quarters of the globe, parents and children [will] do well to read Dickens aloud of a winter's evening'.[140] This note is right and significant.[141] The adult mind doesn't as a rule find in Dickens a challenge to an unusual and sustained seriousness.[142] □

For Leavis, the only exception to this is *Hard Times*, which is unique in Dickens's work because of its 'perfection as a work of art' and its 'sus-tained and complete seriousness'.[143] Leavis's general judgement on Dickens develops a line of criticism that, as was seen earlier in this Guide, had begun to emerge in the later nineteenth century, for example in the criticism of G. H. Lewes (see pp. 37–39); but Leavis's powerful cultural position and memorable phrasing gave his words special weight. Until post-structuralism and deconstruction began to transform literary studies in the UK in the 1980s, much British academic criticism of Dickens was to take place in Leavis's long shadow, and often took the form of attempts by critics to demonstrate that Dickens met Leavisian criteria such as maturity and seriousness. Ironically, these critics eventually included the Leavises themselves, in their *Dickens the Novelist* (1970).

Leavis had much less influence in the USA, however. There was, in fact, no one North American critic in the immediate postwar era who defined the function of criticism for the USA as Leavis did for the UK, and the critic who perhaps came closest to doing so, Lionel Trilling, was no detractor of Dickens. His most significant contribution to the Dickens revival was his introduction to a 1953 edition of *Little Dorrit*;[144] his most important mention of *Great Expectations*, however, is in his essay 'Manners, Morals, and the Novel', first published in the *Kenyon Review* in 1948 and given wider currency by its inclusion in his influential book *The Liberal Imagination* (1950).[145] In that essay, he makes the general claim that the 'characteristic work' of novels 'is to record the illusion that snobbery generates and to try to penetrate to the truth which, as the novel assumes, lies hidden beneath all the false appearances'. He cites *Great Expectations* as an example:

■ The greatness of *Great Expectations* begins in its title: modern society bases itself on great expectations which, if ever they are realized, are found to exist by reason of a sordid, hidden reality. The real thing is not the gentility of Pip's life but the hulks and the murder and the rats and decay in the cellarage of the novel.[146] □

Trilling's summary of Dickens's novel is brief but potent. Not only does it, within the context of his essay, make *Great Expectations* an exemplar of the 'characteristic work of the novel' and thus enhance its status; it also, especially when it floats free of its original context as memorable critical comments tend to do, makes the novel seem vividly relevant to the post-war world. Whereas House, Wilson, Orwell, Jackson and Shaw all, in their respective ways, make specific links between *Great Expectations* and *Victorian* society, Trilling makes a much more general link with what he calls 'modern' society. He thus gives the novel a far wider general application; it could apply, not only to mid-nineteenth-century British society, but also to twentieth-century American society. In such a perspective, *Great Expectations* might even be seen as a complement to F. Scott Fitzgerald's *The Great Gatsby* (1925), a novel that Trilling would play a major part in promoting.[147] By setting *Great Expectations* free of its

Victorian moorings, and implying its appeal to a modern American audience living in a society of great expectations and great fears, Trilling anticipates and helps to stimulate the powerful readings of Dickens's novel that will emerge from the USA in the following decade. This decade will be explored in the next chapter of this Guide.

CHAPTER THREE

Expanding Expectations: The 1950s

THE CRITICAL reputation of *Great Expectations* rose throughout the 1950s. This was not because Dickens had been wholly rehabilitated; his fiction, in general terms, still posed a problem for many critics, especially those who worked in the expanding field of literary study in the universities. He was too large a figure to be ignored, despite F.R. Leavis; but he could not easily be made to conform with the critical criteria associated with 'Leavisism' in the UK and the New Criticism in the USA that were then becoming dominant. These criteria derived from the new aesthetics implied and sometimes explicitly promoted in the later nineteenth and early twentieth century by writers such as James, Conrad, Eliot, Lawrence and Joyce. They were congenial to a postwar culture that, in the UK and the USA, was wary of the political commitments of the 1930s and which sought an imaginative refuge from the spectres of the Cold War – as well as, perhaps, an oblique and muted reflection of those spectres. The criteria in question included organic unity; psychological depth and complexity; 'showing' through dramatisation and indirection rather than 'telling' in a direct and didactic way; the subordination of language to unity, complexity and 'showing'; and an eschewal of explicit political concerns. In such a climate, some novels of Dickens were easier to assimilate than others; *Great Expectations* was one of them.

At the start of the 1950s, however, some of the old radical fires still burned, and their flames warm the large critical biography of Dickens published in 1950 by the prolific Australian novelist, poet and critic, Jack Lindsay. By his own account Lindsay's reasons for writing his study included 'a great love of Dickens',[1] the apparent absence of a book that seriously tried to grapple with Dickens's creative processes, and a desire to relate Dickens's work to the processes of history – processes that Lindsay saw in terms of a humanistic Marxism. He acknowledges the stimulus provided by Edmund Wilson's essay, and, like Wilson, he tries, as the extract below shows, to integrate literary criticism, biographical material, and a sense of historical context. Lindsay also shares with

Wilson a willingness to employ Marxist and Freudian terminology, but he does so much more emphatically than the American critic, in a manner that to some extent recalls that of T. A. Jackson but which is less simplistic. It is interesting to compare the account below both with Jackson's in the previous chapter of this Guide (see pp. 56–58), and with later interpretations informed by Marx and Freud such as Steven Connor's in chapter five of this Guide (see pp. 130–36).

■ [*Great Expectations*] showed the result of the effort of concentration made in *A Tale* [*of Two Cities*]; its theme was worked out with a new economy and a new precision in the definition of entangled relationships . . . [Dickens] wrote in the first person as in *David Copperfield* but his power of dramatic translation of the day-dream had greatly increased since 1849, and the personal material is much more surely controlled, related in a masterly way throughout to the social issue and the artistic problem.

. . . From one angle the book records the sharp turn into disillusion that the great expectations of his love for Ellen [Ternan] have taken. 'Is this cold and scheming creature the love which has haunted me all my life?' he asks. But in asking that question he inevitably asks a lot more questions. If the principle of love has deceived him, his whole attitude to himself and to society has been based on untenable conclusions. His whole life has been based on an illusion.

Hence the book becomes a thorough attempt at self-examination. 'All other swindlers upon earth,' says Pip, 'are nothing to the self-swindlers, and with such pretences did I cheat myself' (2:9, p. 225). The pretences were the day-dream that the lovely girl haunting the house of mysteriously accursed wealth was destined for him and that he was chosen out of the ruck by the mistress of the house for the inheritance of higher things. In attacking these pretences, in revealing their falsehood, their basis in a distorted view of reality, he is attacking the heart of the day-dream which had carried him through his early years and had persisted to some extent right up to *A Tale*. In *Nickleby* he had assumed the romantic right of the hero to a life of unearned leisure; in *Chuzzlewit* the crisis of Martin was in some sort a crisis in the notion of the heritage. *Bleak House* showed in Richard Carstone the effects of living on hope to get an unearned place in life; and in *Little Dorrit* the sudden accession to unearned wealth devastates Amy's hopes, till the Merdle collapse releases her. A new type of hero slowly appears: the worried hard-working Arthur Clennam.

But now Dickens sharply turns back and confronts fully the basis of the romantic solution, the gaining of wealth and position by some chance event which reveals the 'true heir'. He declares it false from every aspect. The romantic heroine is, in fact, in his world, a vicious

careerist, and the romantic hero is a good fellow vitiated by his unjus-
tified claims on life. He is a man who seeks to deny his origins in
common life.

Once again Dickens, who in his own life was so deeply agitated by
desire and fear of the past, desires to relive the Edenic day-dream and
to show up the fear of exposure as unworthy and contaminated; on[c]e
again he attempts to evalu[at]e the agitating thing. The shame of
Dorrit, the deep terror of Manette [in *A Tale of Two Cities*], here becomes
the day-dream evasion of Pip, who builds his life on a set of false
assumptions which, if persisted in, mean the loss of manhood and
honour, despair and perversion.

Thus, beginning as an image of Dickens himself, Pip becomes the
emblem of his age. Once again Dickens fuses his inner conflict with
the conflict of the world around him. Pip turns into an emblem of the
deep and hopeless falsity of the Victorian world, the Great Expectations
that throve so loudly after the Great Exhibition [of 1851]. Behind all the
hopes of rising in the world, Dickens insists, there lies a murder of love,
a degradation of human relationships. The term Great Expectations,
indeed, has a dual reference – to the lie-based hopes of the post-1850
situation and to the defeated hopes of the [eighteen-] forties . . .

Unfortunately Bulwer Lytton argued Dickens out of the 'unhappy
ending' which he had intended; and Dickens imposed the romantic
solution in modified form on a book which throughout was based on
an unrelenting attack on such solutions. But this deformation of the
end cannot [a]ffect the creative impact of the novel as a whole. Dickens
in concise uncompromising terms sets out the moral that has kept
growing ever stronger since the flight of Little Nell with the Old
Gambler: [t]he system of capitalist society is based on the denial and
distortion of human values. True, human beings are not everywhere
broken down into money values, into things of the market; that is
because the system cannot swallow everything. But the individual,
insofar as he is a member of such a society, is distorted and internally
rotted.

Here lies Dickens's greatness, in his capacity to grasp and understand this fact in all its fullness. Only Shakespeare before him had
been able to live at this intense heart of the struggle of values. *Dickens
maintains an unbroken faith in people with an entire pessimism as to capitalist
society* [Lindsay's italics].

. . . we find in *Great Expectations* many symbols carried over from *A
Tale*. Manette, haunted into madness by the injustice of the past, is
close to Miss Havisham, haunted into madness by the injustice of the
past. Both are closed away from the world . . . Both are driven into the
creation of a curse that they end by fearing and wishing to end, in vain
. . . . . . The curse of Manette, which, by its working out, symbolizes

the contradictions of the Revolution, is thus one with the curse of Miss Havisham, which, by its working out, symbolizes the contradictions of capitalist society. In that society the primal curse of unlove works in a complex way, breaking some, partially distorting others, strengthening those who rebel or dissent. The struggle of Manette or Miss Havisham to break through the benumbing curse with its repetition-compulsions is one aspect of the whole struggle of life to renew itself despite the hell of capitalist relations. It conditions, it is an integral part of, the struggle of Darnay or Pip for love and self-respect . . .

The fact that [Pip's] inheritance turns out to be the gift of a ferocious criminal is an ironic twist; the discovery of the fact is a spasmic moment in the drive to self-consciousness. But there is a deeper irony in the fact that Pip the gentleman had been quite content to inherit, as he thought, from the crazed woman of the curse, and it is only when the contaminated money takes on an obviously reprobated social tint that he is driven into realization of the curse's effect upon him. His passion for Estella is thus revealed as the sexual form of the deep, evil, perverting society; and his masochistic self-immolation on her disdain becomes the expression both of his fall from human dignity and of his desire to save the suffering soul of humanity at whatever personal cost. For the person whose power of love has been murdered is the worst sufferer of all, has endured the worst wrong; and the impulse to accept pain from him or her is at least in part based in a wish to atone – to bring the sufferer to the point of awakening from the evil spell, the point of self-knowledge where the cruel act is confronted and acknowledged.

The wronged and suffering soul in the beautiful desired body – there seems the deepest possible contradiction, the most potent image of both the evil thing and the thing to be saved . . . . . . That . . . is why in the novel [Dickens] gives Estella as mother a murderess. From no other womb could have been born the girl whose suffering soul seems to hold the fiercest contradictions of the contemporary world. And as a final touch of allegory he makes Magwitch, Pip's convict benefactor, her father. She is the child of murder and rapacious greed. Yet, in the story, her mother is shown as a woman whom we feel to have great depths of suffering, pride and strength; and her father owns elements of good nature and gratitude which make him in the long run a more sympathetic character than the law-abiding citizens who wish to hound him down. In the tensions between the allegorical meaning of the characters in the story and their complexities as real people there develops a full dialectical sense of the process of transformation continually going on in society.[2] □

The most influential critical biography of Dickens in the 1950s was, however, the two-volume life by the American writer and academic

Edgar Johnson, *Charles Dickens: His Tragedy and Triumph* (1952). Johnson's account of *Great Expectations* is close to Lindsay's in that it links the novel to Dickens's personal development, to his earlier fiction, and to a wider social critique, but Johnson does not use Marxist and Freudian terminology, and he offers a somewhat distanced and softened version of Lindsay's interpretation. *Great Expectations*, which in Lindsay's view was an uncompromising critique of capitalist society with an immediate relevance to the postwar cultural and political crisis, becomes, with Johnson, a criticism of 'a pecuniary society' of the Victorian past 'dedicated to selfish ends'.[3] It could be argued that Johnson's interpretation was closer to Dickens's own understanding of his novel; but it was also an index of what was becoming a more general reluctance, in the Cold War climate of the 1950s, to emphasise the anti-capitalist implications of Dickens's fiction.

1953 saw the publication of Dorothy Van Ghent's *The English Novel: Form and Function*, which looks at eighteen novels, from Cervantes' *Don Quixote* (1605, 1615) to Joyce's *A Portrait of the Artist as a Young Man* (1916). Although Van Ghent claims that her book is designed for the general reader as well as the student, it is more weighted towards an audience of students and teachers than are the studies of George Orwell, Edmund Wilson, Humphry House, Jack Lindsay or Edgar Johnson. Springing partly, as Van Ghent's introduction tells us, from courses on the novel given at Kansas University from 1948 to 1951, it includes, for each novel, both an analysis and a set of 'Problems for Study and Discussion' that could clearly be used for teaching.[4] Van Ghent's work is significant, however, because it identifies and explores, in an insightful way, a range of key aspects of *Great Expectations* and because it combines this specific analysis with a more general view of the nature and function of the novel as a form. Although Van Ghent does not herself use the term 'theory', she is a kind of proto-theorist, trying to elaborate a broad notion of the novel that will classify and help to explain the specific novels she studies.

For Van Ghent, the 'primary interest' of the novel as a form is its illumination of life, but it can only provide this illumination insofar as it is a coherent work of art.[5] The coherence is a matter of pattern, structure and unity. A novel is 'one complex pattern, or Gestalt [German for 'form', 'figure', 'shape'], made up of component [patterns]' and it must have 'integral structure'.[6] It also has individual character – 'its own tensions, physiognomy, and atmosphere'. The novel can express the deepest ideas, but its nature as a medium entails that it best conveys ideas implicitly, through its patterning and structure. We judge the quality of a novel by its unity, by the 'concreteness, distinctness, and richness' of its 'character', its world, and by 'its meaningfulness – its ability to make us more aware of the meaning of our lives'.[7]

In her chapter on *Great Expectations,* Van Ghent marshals a range of topics that will be taken up and developed by future critics. She identifies and illustrates some key devices in Dickens's novel, relates those devices to its metaphysical, ethical and social themes, defends Dickens against the charges that his characters lack inner life and that he uses coincidence in an arbitrary way, and explores the overall imaginary world that he constructs in this work, and, she implies, in his other novels. She thus follows Humphry House in her assumption that there is a 'Dickens world', an overall imaginative vision that is specific to Dickens; but although she does relate that world in broad terms to the historical context in which it emerged, her emphasis is more aesthetic, ethical and metaphysical, less sociological, than that of House; in that respect, it exemplifies a more general tendency of Anglo-American literary criticism in the 1950s. Pip is seen, not as House sees him, as the representative of a specific, if dominant class, nor, as Lindsay sees him, as 'the emblem of his age' (see p. 72), but as an 'Everyman' – a notion that will be taken up by a number of subsequent critics.

Some of the technical devices Van Ghent identifies might be given other names in more recent criticism. For example, she says that in Dickens 'people are described by nonhuman attributes, or by such an exaggeration of or emphasis on one part of their appearance that they seem to be reduced wholly to that part, with an effect of having become "thinged"'.[8] Today, a critic might speak of such devices as 'reification' – the term borrowed from Marxism to denote the process of turning people into things; as 'metonymy' – the rhetorical feature in which a person or thing is indicated by the use of a term associated with that person or thing; and as synecdoche – the rhetorical feature in which a whole is indicated by the name of a part (or sometimes *vice versa*). The absence of such terms in Van Ghent sometimes results in a certain awkwardness – as her use of the word 'thinged' demonstrates – but it also, at times, seems to compel her to explore more widely, and to express herself more fully, than she might have done had such terms been easily to hand in the critical lexicon of the 1950s. Furthermore, for today's readers, it reinforces a sense of the pioneering quality of her work, conducted without the battery of critical terms and concepts that are now available.

Considering the charge that Dickens's characters lack a complex inner life, Van Ghent suggests, acutely, that the '"inner life"' of *Great Expectations* is not merely 'inside' its characters but is distributed across other elements in the novel: the 'moral dialectic . . . arises not solely from the "characters" . . . but from all the elements in the aesthetic structure'.[9] She also addresses the objections to Dickens's use of coincidence, arguing that his coincidences are orderly rather than arbitrary within the imaginary world he creates, that they are a product of its 'moral dynamics'.[10]

With her belief that the primary interest of novels is their illumination of life, Van Ghent relates her explorations of technique in *Great Expectations* to its themes and to their wider social, ethical and metaphysical significance. Thus she identifies its 'subject' as the 'etiology' – the exploration of the causes – 'of guilt and of atonement'[11] and charges that the 'generic crime' in the novel is that 'of using people as means to personal ends'.[12] The crime of using people may be committed on both an individual and a social level; Van Ghent explores how Pip is both victim and perpetrator of such a crime and how he performs an act of redemption both for himself and for society as a whole. As a child, he is subject to the abuse of power by adults who use him for their own ends; as he grows up, he himself seeks, and partly finds, the power to use others for his own ends. Van Ghent shares Humphry House's view that Pip is representative of his society; but, in a striking reinterpretation, she argues that Pip is representative, not only because he is, on the literal level, a snob, but more significantly because he is, on the symbolic level, a 'murderer' in that he dehumanises the weak, in a manner typical of the society of which he is a member. Such dehumanisation is most powerfully symbolised in his rejection of Magwitch after the old convict's return; when he finally accepts Magwitch, takes responsibility for him, and learns to love him, he symbolically redeems not only himself but also his society. In Van Ghent's reading, Pip comes close, not only to Everyman – a comparison that she makes explicitly at one point[13] – but also to Christ, a comparison that she does not make explicitly, but which is implied in her idea of a figure who suffers and atones for the sins of a society.

The extract below joins Van Ghent's essay as she homes in on the significance of crime in *Great Expectations*:

■ Two kinds of crime form Dickens's two chief themes, the crime of parent against child, and the calculated social crime. They are formally analogous, their form being the treatment of persons as things; but they are also inherent in each other, whether the private will of the parent is to be considered as depraved by the operation of a public institution, or the social institution is to be considered as a bold concert of the depravities of individual 'fathers'. In *Great Expectations* the private crime against the child is Mrs. Joe's and Pumblechook's and Wopsle's, all 'foster parents' either by necessity or self-conceit; while the social crime is the public treatment of Magwitch. That the two kinds of crime are inherent in each other we are made aware of as we are led to identify Magwitch's childhood with Pip's; the brutality exercised towards both children was the same brutality, though the 'parents' in the one case were private persons, and in the other, society itself. Complicating the meaning of 'the crime' still further, Magwitch also has taken upon himself the role of foster parent to Pip, and whether, as parent, he acts in charity or impiousness, or both, is a major ambiguity which the drama sets out to resolve.

'The crime', in Dickens, is evidently a permutation of multiple motivations and acts, both public and private, but always with the same tendency to convert people into things, and always implying either symbolically or directly a child–parent situation. The child–parent situation has been disnatured, corrupted, with the rest of nature; or rather, since the child–parent situation is the dynamic core of the Dickens world, the radical disnaturing here is what has corrupted the rest. His plots seldom serve to canalize, with the resolution of the particular set of plotted circumstances, the hysteria submerged in his vision of a nature gone thoroughly wrong; the permutations of the crimes are too many, and their ultimate cause or root is evasive, unless one would resort to some dramatically unmanageable rationale such as original sin. The Dickens world requires an act of redemption. A symbolic act of this kind is again and again indicated in his novels. . . . But the redemptive act should be such that it should redeem not only the individual 'fathers', but society at large. . . . *Great Expectations* is an exception among his novels in that here the redemptive act is adequate to and structural for both bodies of thematic material – the sins of individuals and the sins of society.

Pip first becomes aware of the 'identity of things' (1:1, p.3) as he is held suspended heels over head by the convict; that is, in a world literally turned upside down. Thenceforth Pip's interior landscape is inverted by his guilty knowledge of this man 'who had been soaked in water, and smothered in mud, and lamed by stones, and cut by flints, and stung by nettles, and torn by briars' (1:1, p.4). The apparition is that of all suffering that the earth can inflict, and that the apparition presents itself to a child is as much as to say that every child, whatever his innocence, inherits guilt (as the potential of his acts) for the condition of man. The inversion of natural order begins here with first self-consciousness: the child is heir to the sins of the 'fathers'. Thus the crime that is always pervasive in the Dickens universe is identified in a new way – not primarily as that of the 'father', nor as that of some public institution, but as that of the child – the original individual who must necessarily take upon himself responsibility for not only what is to be done in the present and the future, but what has been done in the past, inasmuch as the past is part and parcel of the present and the future. The child is the criminal, and it is for this reason that he is able to redeem his world; for the world's guilt is his guilt, and he can expiate it in his own acts.

The guilt of the child is realized on several levels. Pip experiences the psychological *form* (or feeling) of guilt before he is capable of voluntary evil; he is treated by adults – Mrs. Joe and Pumblechook and

Wopsle – as if he were a felon, a young George Barnwell (a character in the play which Wopsle reads on the night when Mrs. Joe is attacked) wanting only to murder his nearest relative, as George Barnwell murdered his uncle. This is the usual nightmare of the child in Dickens, a vision of imminent incarceration, fetters like sausages, lurid accusatory texts. He is treated, that is, as if he were a thing, manipulable by adults for the extraction of certain sensations: by making him feel guilty and diminished, they are able to feel virtuous and great. But the psychological *form* of guilt acquires spiritual *content* when Pip himself conceives the tainted wish – the wish to be like the most powerful adult and to treat others as things. At the literal level, Pip's guilt is that of snobbery towards Joe Gargery, and snobbery is a denial of the human value of others. Symbolically, however, Pip's guilt is that of murder; for he steals the file with which the convict rids himself of his leg iron, and it is this leg iron, picked up on the marshes, with which Orlick attacks Mrs. Joe; so that the child does inevitably overtake his destiny, which was, like George Barnwell, to murder his nearest relative. But the 'relative' whom Pip, adopting the venerable criminality of society, is, in the widest symbolic scope of intention, destined to murder is not Mrs. Joe but his 'father', Magwitch – to murder in the socially chronic fashion of the Dickens world, which consists in the dehumanization of the weak, or in moral acquiescence to such murder. Pip is, after all, the ordinary mixed human being, one more Everyman in the long succession of them that literature has represented, but we see this Everyman as he develops from a child; and his destiny is directed by the ideals of his world – towards 'great expectations' which involve the making of Magwitches – which involve, that is, murder . . .

In Dickens's modification of the folk pattern of the fairy wishing, Magwitch is Pip's 'fairy godfather' who changes the pumpkin into a coach. Like all the 'fathers', he uses the child as a thing in order to obtain through him vicarious sensations of grandeur. In relation to society, however, Magwitch is the child, and society the prodigal father; from the time he was first taken for stealing turnips, the convict's career has duplicated brutally and in public the pathos of the ordinary child. Again, in relation to Pip, Magwitch is still the child; for, spiritually committed by his 'great expectations' to that irresponsibility which has accounted for the Magwitches, Pip is projectively, at least, answerable for Magwitch's existence and for his brutalization. Pip carries his criminal father within him; he is, so to speak, the father of his father. The ambiguities of each term of the relationship are such that each is both child and father, making a fourfold relationship; and the act of love between them at the end is thus reinforced fourfold, and the redemption by love is a fourfold redemption: that is to say, it is symbolically infinite, for it serves for all the meanings Dickens finds it possible to attach to the central child–father situation, the most profound and embracing relationship that, in Dickens's work, obtains among men.

As the child's original alienation from 'natural' order is essentially mysterious, a guilty inheritance from the fathers which invades first awareness, so the redemptive act is also a mysterious one. The mysterious nature of the act is first indicated, in the manner of a motif, when Mrs. Joe, in imbecile pantomime, tries to propitiate her attacker, the bestial Orlick. In Orlick is concretized all the undefined evil of the Dickens world, that has nourished itself underground and crept along walls, like the ancient stains on the house of Atreus [*Editor's Note*: the house of Atreus was the royal family of Mycenae whose bloody story was dramatised in ancient Greek tragedies such as Aeschylus' trilogy *Oresteia* (458 B.C.), Euripides' *Electra* (413 B.C.) and *Orestes* (408 B.C.), and Sophocles' *Electra* (date uncertain).]. He [Orlick] is the lawlessness implied in the unnatural conversions of the human into the non-human, the retributive death that invades those who have grown lean in life and who have exercised the powers of death over others. He is the instinct of aggression and destruction, the daemonism of sheer external Matter as such; he is pure 'thingness' emerging without warning from the ooze where he has been unconsciously cultivated. As Orlick is one form of spiritual excess – unmotivated hate – Joe Gargery is the opposed form – love without reservation. Given these terms of the spiritual framework, the redemptive act itself could scarcely be anything but grotesque – and it is by a grotesque gesture, one of the most profoundly intuitive symbols in Dickens, that Mrs. Joe is redeemed. What is implied by her humble propitiation of the beast Orlick is a recognition of personal guilt in the guilt of others, and of its dialectical relationship with love. The motif reappears in the moment of major illumination in the book. Pip 'bows down', not to Joe Gargery, towards whom he has been privately and literally guilty, but to the wounded, hunted, shackled man, Magwitch, who has been guilty towards himself. It is in this way that the manifold organic relationships among men are revealed, and that the Dickens world – founded in fragmentariness and disintegration – is made whole.[14] □

Van Ghent opens up so many aspects of *Great Expectations* that her theoretical framework can hardly contain them; but this makes her interpretation faithful to the richness and complexity of Dickens's novel and deeply fertile for future critics. A more elegant and economical account – which is also, in its way, deeply fertile – is G. Robert Stange's essay 'Expectations Well Lost: Dickens'[s] Fable for His Time'. Stange, in an often-cited remark, sums up *Great Expectations* as 'the classic legend of the nineteenth century'; his own essay is perhaps the classic essay of the 1950s on *Great Expectations*. His reading constructs a novel that satisfies all the then-dominant criteria: it has an 'organic' pattern and a 'unifying centre'; it has a 'natural' theme and 'an elemental form'; it is 'an art form that belongs to an ancient type', the 'moral fable', and it thus 'concentrates on permanently significant issues'. It has a 'dialectic progression' that involves a 'negation' and a 'partial synthesis', but this progression is mythical and individual more than Marxist. In its 'moral of the return to Joe' at the end of the novel, it 'sharply contradicts the accepted picture of Dickens as a radical critic of society'. Stange is alluding here to the view promoted, in different ways, by Shaw, Jackson and Lindsay, and it is interesting that he does characterise it, in 1954, as an 'accepted picture'; it suggests that, at this time, the rejection of political concerns in literary criticism could be seen as a radical and refreshing challenge to a dominant orthodoxy, even though, in historical hindsight, it seems likely that what Stange saw as 'the accepted picture' was already on the way out and that it was his own kind of ostensibly non-political approach that was becoming the orthodoxy.

In this respect, it is perhaps significant that, according to Stange, *Great Expectations* falters when it tries to present a 'social message' (though hardly a very radical one) of the dangers of idleness. Stange diagnoses the weakness as a technical flaw; it occurs because the 'message' is presented with 'didactic intent' rather than 'moral insight', through 'statement, rather than as experience or dramatized perception', displaying 'the Dickens who *professes*' rather than 'the Dickens who *sees*'. These are key oppositions for 1950s criticism, and in bringing them to bear on *Great Expectations*, Stange both reinforces the relevance of such criteria and implicitly emphasises how well the rest of the novel satisfies them.

The failure of this attempt to convey a 'social message', the contradiction offered by the portrayal of Joe to the idea of Dickens as a radical social critic, and the engagement of *Great Expectations* with 'permanently interesting . . . human concerns', do not mean, for Stange, that the novel is disengaged from history. As his essay title states, *Great Expectations* is 'Dickens'[s] fable for his time', and it 'is as interesting for its historical as for its timeless aspects'. It does raise questions that are, on some level, social and political, such as the one that Stange, in an interesting mixture of legal, ethical, religious and faintly Marxist language, defines in this way: '[w]e find Magwitch guilty of trying to own another human being, but we ask whether his actions are any more sinful than those of the wealthy *bourgeois*'.

Two other aspects of this concise, lucid and perceptive essay, which is so much of its time and which yet has significant implications well beyond it, should be noted. One is the very interesting suggestion that

Jaggers is to be seen as a 'surrogate of the artist' – or of a certain kind of artist. The other is Stange's description of Pip in his London days as a *'flâneur'* (idler, loafer), which might merit development today in the light of the notion of the *flâneur* in the criticism of Walter Benjamin.[15]

Stange starts by affirming the exceptional accomplishment of Dickens's novel:

■ *Great Expectations* is a peculiarly satisfying and impressive novel. It is unusual to find in Dickens's work so rigorous a control of detail, so simple and organic a pattern. In this very late novel the usual features of his art – proliferating sub-plots, legions of minor grotesques – are almost entirely absent. The simplicity is that of an art form that belongs to an ancient type and concentrates on permanently signifi-cant issues. *Great Expectations* is conceived as a moral fable; it is the story of a young man's development from the moment of his first self-awareness, to that of his mature acceptance of the human condition.

So natural a theme imposes an elemental form on the novel: the overall pattern is defined by the process of growth, and Dickens employs many of the motifs of folklore. The story of Pip falls into three phases which clearly display a dialectic progression. We see the boy first in his natural condition in the country, responding and acting instinctively and therefore virtuously. The second stage of his career involves a negation of child-like simplicity; Pip acquires his 'expecta-tions', renounces his origins, and moves to the city. He rises in society, but since he acts through calculation rather than through instinctive charity, his moral values deteriorate as his social graces improve. This middle phase of his career culminates in a sudden fall, the beginning of a redemptive suffering which is dramatically concluded by an attack of brain fever leading to a long coma. It is not too fanciful to regard this long illness as a symbolic death; Pip rises from it regener-ate and percipient. In the final stage of growth he returns to his birthplace, abandons his false expectations, accepts the limitations of his condition, and achieves a partial synthesis of the virtue of his inno-cent youth and the melancholy insight of his later experience.

Variants of such a narrative are found in the myths of many heroes. In Dickens'[s] novel the legend has the advantage of providing an action which appeals to the great primary human affections and serves as unifying centre for the richly conceived minor themes and images which form the body of the novel . . . . . . The particular fable that Dickens elaborates is as interesting for its historical as for its timeless aspects. In its particulars the story of Pip is the classic legend of the nineteenth century: *Great Expectations* belongs to that class of education or development-novels which describe the young man of talents who progresses from the country to the city, ascends in the social hierarchy, and moves from innocence to experience . . . . . . *Great Expectations* is not more profound than other development-novels, but it is more mysterious. The recurrent themes of the genre are all there: city is posed against country, experience against innocence; there is a search for the true father; there is the exposure to crime and the acceptance of guilt and expiation. What Dickens's novel lacks is the clarity, and, one is tempted to say, the essential tolerance of the French. He could not command either the saving ironic vision of Stendhal or the disenchanted practicality and secure Catholicism of Balzac. For Dickens, always the Victorian protestant, the issues of a young man's rise or fall are conceived as a drama of the individual conscience; enlightenment (partial at best) is to be found only in the agony of personal guilt.

Great Expectations . . . is interesting for many reasons: it demonstrates the subtlety of Dickens's art; it displays a consistent control of narrative, imagery, and theme which gives meaning to the stark outline of the fable, and symbolic weight to every character and detail. It proves Dickens's ability (which has frequently been denied) to combine his genius for comedy with his fictional presentation of some of the most serious and permanently interesting of human concerns.

The principal themes are announced and the mood of the whole novel established in the opening pages . . . The first scene with the boy Pip in the graveyard is one of the best of the superbly energetic beginnings found in almost all Dickens's mature novels. In less than a page we are given a character, his background, and his setting; within a few paragraphs more we are immersed in a decisive action. Young Pip is first seen against the background of his parents' gravestones – monuments which communicate to him no clear knowledge either of his parentage or his position in the world. He is an orphan who must search for a father and define his own condition. The moment of this opening scene, we learn, is that at which the hero has first realized his individuality and gained his 'first most vivid and broad impression of the identity of things' (1:1, p. 3). This information given the reader, the violent meeting between Pip and the escaped convict abruptly takes place.

The impression of the identity of things that Pip is supposed to have received is highly equivocal. The convict rises up like a ghost from among the graves, seizes the boy suddenly, threatens to kill him, holds him upside down through most of their conversation, and ends by forcing the boy to steal food for him. The children of Dickens's novels always receive rather strange impressions of things, but Pip's epiphany is the oddest of all, and in some ways the most ingenious [*Editor's Note*: An 'epiphany' is a manifestation, an appearance, of a supernatural or divine being – Christ or God in Christian theology – but Stange is probably using the word in a sense derived from James Joyce, whose *Stephen Hero* (first published 1944) defined an 'epiphany' more in aesthetic than in religious terms, as 'a sudden spiritual manifestation' of the unique quality of a thing, that thing's 'soul' or 'whatness'.[16]]. This encounter in the graveyard is the germinal scene of the novel. While he is held by the convict, Pip sees the world upside-down; in the course of Dickens's fable, the reader is invited to try the same view. This particular change of viewpoint is an ancient device of irony, but an excellent one: Dickens's satire asks us to try reversing the accepted senses of innocence and guilt, success and failure, to think of the world's goods as the world's evils.

A number of ironic reversals and ambiguous situations develop out of the first scene. The convict, Magwitch, is permanently grateful to Pip for having brought him food and a file with which to take off his leg-iron. Years later he expresses his gratitude by assuming in secrecy an economic parenthood; with the money he has made in Australia he will, unbeknownst to Pip, make 'his boy' a gentleman. But the money the convict furnishes him makes Pip not a true gentleman, but a cad. He lives as a *flâneur* in London, and when he later discovers the disreputable source of his income is snobbishly horrified.

Pip's career is a parable which illustrates several religious paradoxes: he can gain only by losing all he has; only by being defiled can he be cleansed. Magwitch returns to claim his gentleman, and finally the convict's devotion and suffering arouse Pip's charity; by the time Magwitch has been captured and is dying Pip has accepted him and come to love him as a true father. The relationship is the most important one in the novel: in sympathizing with Magwitch Pip assumes the criminal's guilt; in suffering with and finally loving the despised and rejected man he finds his own real self.

Magwitch did not have to learn to love Pip. He was naturally devoted to the 'small bundle of shivers' (1:1, p.4), the outcast boy who brought him the stolen food and the file in the misty graveyard. There is a natural bond, Dickens suggests, between the child and the criminal; they are alike in their helplessness; both are repressed and tortured by established society, and both rebel against its incomprehensible authority. In the first scene Magwitch forces Pip to commit his first 'criminal' act, to steal the file and food from his sister's house. Though this theft produces agonies of guilt in Pip, we are led to see it not as a sin but as an instinctive act of mercy. Magwitch, much later, tells Pip: "'I first become aware of myself, down in Essex, a thieving turnips for my living'" (3:3, p.344). Dickens would have us, in some obscure way, conceive the illicit act as the means of self-realization.

In the opening section of the novel the view moves back and forth between the escaped criminal on the marshes and the harsh life in the house of Pip's sister, Mrs. Joe Gargery. The 'criminality' of Pip and the convict is contrasted with the socially approved cruelty and injustice of Mrs. Joe and her respectable friends. The elders who come to the Christmas feast at the Gargerys' are pleased to describe Pip as a criminal: the young are, according to Mr. Hubble, "'[n]aterally wicious'" (1:4, p.26). During this most bleak of Christmas dinners the child is treated not only as outlaw, but as animal. In Mrs. Joe's first speech Pip is called a "'young monkey'" (1:2, p.9) [*Editor's Note*: This in fact occurs on the day before the Christmas dinner.]; then the spirits of the revellers rise, more and more comparisons are made between boys and animals. Uncle Pumblechook, devouring his pork, toys with the notion of Pip's having been born a "'Squeaker'" (1:4, p.27–8) . . . . . .

This identification of animal and human is continually repeated in the opening chapters of the novel, and we catch its resonance throughout the book. When the two convicts – Pip's 'friend' and the other fugitive, Magwitch's ancient enemy [Compeyson] – are captured, we experience the horror of official justice, which treats the prisoners as if they were less than human . . . And the prison ship, lying beyond the mud of the shore, looked to Pip 'like a wicked Noah's ark' (1:5, p.41).

The theme of this first section of the novel – which concludes with the capture of Magwitch and his return to the prison ship – might be called 'the several meanings of humanity'. Only the three characters who are in some way social outcasts – Pip, Magwitch, and Joe Gargery the child-like blacksmith – act in charity and respect the humanity of others. To Magwitch Pip is distinctly not an animal, and not capable of adult wickedness: "'You'd be but a fierce young hound indeed, if at your time of life you could help to hunt a wretched warmint'" (1:3, p.19). And when, after he is taken, the convict shields Pip by confessing to have stolen the Gargerys' pork pie, Joe's absolution affirms the dignity of man:

> 'God knows you're welcome to it – so far as it was ever mine,' returned Joe, with a saving remembrance of Mrs. Joe. 'We don't know what you have done, but we wouldn't have you starved to death for it, poor miserable fellow-creatur. – Would us, Pip?' (1:5, p.41).

The next section of the narrative is less tightly conceived than the introductory action. Time is handled loosely; Pip goes to school, and becomes acquainted with Miss Havisham of Satis House and the beautiful Estella. The section concludes when Pip has reached early manhood, been told of his expectations, and has prepared to leave for London. These episodes develop, with variations, the theme of childhood betrayed. Pip himself renounces his childhood by coming to accept the false social values of middle-class society. His perverse development is expressed by persistent images of the opposition between the human and the non-human, the living and the dead.

On his way to visit Miss Havisham for the first time, Pip spends the night with Mr. Pumblechook, the corn-chandler, in his lodgings behind his shop. The contrast between the aridity of this old hypocrite's spirit and the viability of his wares is a type of the conflict between natural growth and social form. Pip looks at all the shop-keeper's little drawers filled with bulbs and seed packets and wonders 'whether the flower-seeds and bulbs ever wanted of a fine day to break out of those jails and bloom' (1:8, pp.54–55). The imagery of life repressed is developed further in the descriptions of Miss Havisham and Satis House. [There is, for example,] the abandoned brewery where the once active ferment has ceased; no germ of life is to be found in Satis House or in its occupants . . . . . . [When Pip enters the empty building where beer was once made, he] fancies that he sees a figure hanging by the neck from a wooden beam, 'a figure all in yellow white, with but one shoe to the feet; and it hung so, that I could see that the faded trimmings of the dress were like earthy paper, and that the face was Miss Havisham's' (1:8, p.65).

Miss Havisham *is* death. From his visits to Satis House Pip acquires his false admiration for the genteel; he falls in love with Estella and fails to see that she is the cold instrument of Miss Havisham's revenge on human passion and on life itself. When Pip learns he may expect a large inheritance from an unknown source he immediately assumes (incorrectly) that Miss Havisham is his benefactor; she does not undeceive him. Money, which is also death, is appropriately connected with the old lady rotting away in her darkened room.

Conflicting values in Pip's life are also expressed by the opposed imagery of stars and fire. Estella is by name a star, and throughout the novel stars are conceived as pitiless . . . Estella and her light are described as coming down the dark passage of Satis House 'like a star' (1:8, p.60), and when she has become a woman she is constantly surrounded by the bright glitter of jewellery.

Joe Gargery, on the other hand, is associated with the warm fire of the hearth or forge . . . . . . At the end of the novel Pip finds the true light on the homely hearth, and in a last twist of the father–son theme, Joe emerges as a true parent – the only kind of parent that Dickens could ever fully approve, one that remains a child. The moral of this return to Joe sharply contradicts the accepted picture of Dickens as a radical critic of society. Joe is a humble countryman who is content with the place in the social order he has been appointed to fulfil. He fills it '"well and with respect"' (2:19, p.148); Pip learns that he can do no better than to emulate him.

The second stage of Pip's three-phased story is set in London, and the moral issues of the fiction are modulated accordingly. Instead of the opposition between custom and the instinctive life, the novelist treats the conflict between man and his social institutions. The topics and themes are specific, and the satire, some of it wonderfully deft, is more social than moral. Not all Dickens's social message is presented by means that seem adequate. By satirizing Pip and his leisure class friends (The Finches of the Grove, they call themselves) the novelist would have us realize that idle young men will come to a bad end. Dickens is here expressing the Victorian Doctrine of Work – a pervasive notion that both inspired and reassured his industrious contemporaries.

The difficulty for the modern reader, who is unmoved by the objects of Victorian piety, is that the doctrine appears to be the result, not of moral insight, but of didactic intent; it is presented as statement, rather than as experience or dramatized perception, and consequently it never modifies the course of fictional action or the formation of character. The distinction is crucial: it is between the Dickens who *sees* and the Dickens who *professes*; often between the good and the bad sides of his art.

The novelist is on surer ground when he comes to define the nature of wealth in a mercantile society. Instead of moralistic condemnation we have a technique that resembles parable. Pip eventually learns that his ornamental life is supported, not by Miss Havisham, but by the labour and suffering of the convict Magwitch:

> 'I swore arterwards, sure as ever I spec'lated and got rich, you should get rich. I lived rough, that you should live smooth; I worked hard that you should be above work. What odds, dear boy? Do I tell it fur you to feel an obligation? Not a bit. I tell it, fur you to know as that there hunted dunghill dog wot you kep life in, got his head so high that he could make a gentleman – and, Pip, you're him!' (2:20, p. 317)

The convict would not only make a gentleman but own him. The blood horses of the colonists might fling up the dust over him as he was walking but, '"I says to myself, 'If I ain't a gentleman, nor yet ain't got no learning, I'm the owner of such. All on you owns stock and land; which on you owns a brought-up London gentleman?'"' (2:20, p. 319).

In this action Dickens has subtly led us to speculate on the connections between a gentleman and his money, on the dark origins of even the most respectable fortunes. We find Magwitch guilty of trying to own another human being, but we ask whether his actions are any more sinful than those of the wealthy *bourgeois*. There is a deeper moral in the fact that Magwitch's fortune at first destroyed the natural gentleman in Pip, but that after it was lost (it had to be forfeited to the state when Magwitch was finally captured) the '"dunghill dog"' (2:20, p.317) did actually make Pip a gentleman by evoking his finer feelings. This ironic distinction between 'gentility' and what the father of English poetry [Chaucer] meant by 'gentilesse' [gentleness, nobility, courtesy, delicacy] is traditional in our literature and our mythology. In *Great Expectations* it arises out of the action and language of the fiction; consequently it moves and persuades us as literal statement never can.

The middle sections of the novel are dominated by the solid yet mysterious figure of Mr. Jaggers, Pip's legal guardian. Though Jaggers is not one of Dickens's greatest characters he is heavy with implication; he is so much at the centre of this fable that we are challenged to interpret him – only to find that his meaning is ambiguous. On his first appearance Jaggers strikes a characteristic note of sinister authority . . .
. . . Pip wonders at first if Jaggers is a doctor. It is soon explained that he is a lawyer – what we now ambiguously call a *criminal* lawyer – but he is like a physician who treats moral malignancy, with the doctor's necessary detachment from individual suffering. Jaggers is interested not in the social operations of the law, but in the varieties of criminality. He exudes an antiseptic smell of soap and is described as washing his clients off as if he were a surgeon or a dentist.

Pip finds that Jaggers has 'an air of authority not to be disputed . . . with a manner expressive of knowing something secret about every one of us that would effectually do for each individual if he chose to disclose it' (1:18, p.135). When Pip and his friends go to dinner at Jaggers's house Pip observes that he 'wrenched the weakest part of our dispositions out of us' (2:7, p.213). After the party his guardian tells Pip that he particularly liked the sullen young man [he] called Spider [Drummle]: '"Keep as clear of him as you can. But I like the fellow, Pip; he is one of the true sort. Why if I was a fortune-teller . . . But I am not a fortune-teller," he said . . . "You know what I am, don't you?"' (2:7, p.217). This question is repeated when Pip is being shown through Newgate Prison by Jaggers's assistant, Wemmick. The turnkey says of Pip: '"Why then . . . he knows what Mr. Jaggers is"' (2:13, p.262).

But neither Pip nor the reader ever fully knows what Mr. Jaggers is. We learn, along with Pip, that Jaggers has manipulated the events which have shaped the lives of most of the characters in the novel; he has, in the case of Estella and her mother, dispensed a merciful but entirely personal justice; he is the only character who knows the web of secret relationships that are finally revealed to Pip. He dominates by the strength of his knowledge the world of guilt and sin – called *Little Britain* – of which his office is the centre. He has, in brief, the power that an artist exerts over the creatures of his fictional world, and that a god exerts over his creation.

As surrogate of the artist, Jaggers displays qualities of mind – complete impassability, all-seeing unfeelingness – which are the opposite of Dickens's, but of a sort that Dickens may at times have desired. Jaggers can be considered a fantasy figure created by a novelist who is forced by his intense sensibility to relive the sufferings of his fellow men and who feels their agonies too deeply ... ... Jaggers has a complete understanding of human evil but, unlike the living artist, can wash his hands of it. He is above ordinary institutions; like a god he dispenses justice, and like a god displays infinite mercy through unrelenting severity ... ...

The final moral vision of *Great Expectations* has to do with the nature of sin and guilt. After visiting Newgate Pip, still complacent and self-deceived, thinks how strange it was that he should be encompassed by the taint of prison and crime. He tries to beat the prison dust off his feet and to exhale its air from his lungs; he is going to meet Estella, who must not be contaminated by the smell of crime. Later it is revealed that Estella, the pure, is the bastard child of Magwitch and a murderess. Newgate is figuratively described as a greenhouse, and the prisoners as plants carefully tended by Wemmick ... These disturbing metaphors suggest that criminality is the condition of life. Dickens would distinguish between the native, inherent sinfulness from which men can be redeemed, and that evil which destroys life: the sin of the hypocrite or oppressor, the smothering wickedness of corrupt institutions. The last stage of Pip's progression is reached when he learns to love the criminal and to accept his own implication in the common guilt ... ... The patterns of culpability in *Great Expectations* are so intricate that the whole world of the novel is eventually caught in a single web of awful responsibility.[17] □

Stange's essay concludes by hinting at a more profound metaphysical dimension in *Great Expectations*, finding in the 'remoter implications' of its 'treatment of guilt and expiation ... something excessive and idio-syncratic' which is analogous to Dostoevsky.[18] Like George Gissing and Edmund Wilson, Stange calls on a comparison with Dostoevsky to enhance Dickens's stature; but the comparison also enables Stange to register an aspect of *Great Expectations* that his overall critical ideology cannot wholly contain. The limits of such an ideology were highlighted by J. Hillis Miller's *Charles Dickens: The World of His Novels* (1958). This book is probably the most substantial study of Dickens produced in the 1950s, and it shows the value of an alternative critical approach informed by European philosophy. Although Miller was to become celebrated in the 1980s as a practitioner of deconstruction and a close associate of the leading deconstructionist Paul de Man, his Dickens study adopts the phenomenological perspective of a critic who, like de Man, was working in the USA but was originally from Europe: this was Georges Poulet. In contrast to his later deconstructionist emphasis on the ways in which texts undermine themselves and escape from their authors, Miller affirms that 'all the works of a single writer form a unity, a unity in which a thousand paths radiate from the same centre'. Every detail of a writer's work thus leads back to the 'centre' and the nature of that centre – which is not so much an accessible location as what Miller calls 'an impalpable organizing form'[19] – can be more fully grasped by selecting and bringing together salient details from the text, the words of which constitute 'the primary datum, a self-sufficient reality beyond which the critic need not go'. Thus, while Miller does sometimes draw on biographical and historical detail and make reference to the society out of which Dickens's novels emerged, his main focus is, like that of the American New Criticism, on the texts themselves. Miller also shares the New Critical emphasis on unity, but his phenomenological perspective means that he posits unity as inhering not so much in individual texts as in the whole body of a writer's work, which uniquely expresses that writer's way of relating to and experiencing the world.

His study of Dickens thus aims to explore 'the imaginative universe of Dickens, and the revelation of that presiding unity hidden at the centre, but present everywhere within his novels and partially revealed there in the embodied disguises of particular characters, actions, interiors, land-scapes, and cityscapes'. Acknowledging that Dickens's imaginative universe, like that of any great writer, is 'infinite' and might profitably be explored by any number of critical paths, he opts for what he feels to be a salient approach, 'the theme of the search for a true and viable identity'.[20] To take this approach is to discover that *Great Expectations* is the most unified and concentrated expression of Dickens's abiding sense of the world, and [that] Pip might be called the archetypal Dickens hero',[21] in his lack of and quest for an authentic and independent identity '[i]n a world where the only possible relation to other people seems to be that of oppressor to oppressed, or oppressed to oppressor'.[22] In these respects, Pip also sounds like an archetypal existential hero, in the sense popularised by the French writer Jean-Paul Sartre in the 1950s, who emphasised the necessity of individual self-creation in a hostile world; and it is certainly possible to add existentialism to phenomenology and the New Criticism as influences upon Miller's 1950s interpretation of Dickens. Miller also draws, as shall be seen in the extract below, on the Christian existentialism of the nineteenth-century Danish thinker Søren Kierkegaard to define Pip's final relationship to Magwitch.

Miller analyses a number of means by which, in *Great Expectations*, characters who are oppressed in one or more ways try to achieve a position of dominance. One can dominate those beneath one in the social chain, as Wemmick, victimised himself by the legal apparatus that he serves, dominates the prisoners whom he visits in Newgate; or, in a more complex move, one can try to 'enjoy the power of the oppressor without being guilty of having unjustifiably seized that power', as both Magwitch and Miss Havisham do: 'No one will be able to blame Magwitch for the arrogance of Pip the gentleman, and no one will blame Miss Havisham for the cruelties Estella practices on her suitors'.[23] Miller's analysis of the inevitable failure of these attempts anticipates, to some extent, his later deconstructive interest in irresolvable paradoxes. It leads on to his analysis of Pip himself, which begins his account below:

■ Neither way out of alienation will work, neither the attempt to become an oppressor of those below even while being oppressed from above, nor the attempt to endow someone else with the power to be an oppressor while one remains innocently passive oneself. One other way remains, a way that even more subtly than the others hides its radical defect: [t]he disinherited one may accept 'great expectations'. That is, he may believe that, in spite of his apparent lack of status and of any real reason for existing, there is a hidden place for him, a destined role among those who enjoy the dignity and security of becoming masters. Pip repudiates what he is now with the utmost horror: [h]e denies that he is an orphan, 'brought up by hand' (1:2, p.8), destined to be apprenticed to Joe and to spend the rest of his life as a country blacksmith. No, he is not what he appears to be. He is really the secret self which lies unfulfilled in the future, beyond the shadowy mists of his great expectations. Now, he is not what he is, and he is what he is not. Pip's acceptance of great expectations does not mean seizing recognition of his usefulness by force. It means believing that he will be miraculously given a place in society as though it were his natural right, as though the world had for some unaccountable reason conspired to keep his real place hidden, only to bestow it at last as a free gift . . . He believes that Estella and all the privileges possessed by a gentleman are destined for him by Miss Havisham. He will not need to dirty his hands with the crime of appropriating a place among the oppressors. He will suddenly be transformed from the class of the exploited to the class of the exploiters. There will be an absolute discontinuity between his initial given condition of alienation and isolation, and the suddenly attained possession of a secure place in society. The new man will be both free (cannot Pip buy anything he wants?), and at the same time wholly consecrated in his new role by the approval of society . . . .

It is at first difficult to see why Pip's great expectations do not seem to him another form of the degrading manipulation by society, another subtler form of alienation. They do appear that way to Joe and Biddy, who accept their status with the proud independence of the lower class . . . Why . . . does Pip accept so readily a change in status which to Joe seems an affront to his pride and independence? It is a very different thing to have as one's given place in society the status of a gentleman rather than the status of a blacksmith. It approaches the reconciliation of freedom and security which Pip seeks. Moreover, the circumstances of mystery which surround the great expectations make it possible to manipulate their meaning ambiguously. Pip thinks they come from Miss Havisham, but he is not certain, and this uncertainty allows him to interpret them as at once a wilful choice on someone's part to change his place in society, or as a reward for faithful service, or as recognition that he has too noble a nature to be a blacksmith. Because of the mystery about the gift Pip can look upon his great expectations as at once earned and gratuitously bestowed. The more pleasant interpretation is the one which makes them the recognition by society of what his inmost nature has been all along . . . .

But Pip finds that being a gentleman is no escape from uncertainty and guilt. One of the conditions of his great expectations is that he shall still go by the name of Pip, the name he gave himself in his early childhood. This is a symbol of the fact that he cannot make a full break with the past, and in a way hints of the terrible revelation which will shatter his expectations. But even when he has received his expectations, is living as a gentleman in London, and has not received the blow which will destroy his hopes, he is not at peace . . . This is partly, no doubt, because of [his] uncertainty about Estella, but it is also part of the very condition of being a gentleman – as Dickens showed in his other portraits of idle and uneasy aristocrats (such as Eugene Wrayburn [in *Our Mutual Friend*] or Henry Gowan [in *Little Dorrit*]). These young gentlemen all suffer from ennui, and from an inability to choose a course of action. Paralysis of will seizes them precisely because they have unlimited possibilities. There are so many courses open to them that they are wholly unable to choose one. Far from realizing the peace of a reconciliation of freedom and security, Pip's transformation into a gentleman only plunges him into deeper disquietude and weariness of spirits – deeper because he is even further than ever away from the discovery of some externally imposed duty which will tell him what to do and who he is . . . .

Finally, Pip discovers the emptiness of his hope of being given a justified place in the ruling class. He discovers that his real benefactor is not Miss Havisham, the representative of society, but the pariah Magwitch, '"hunted dunghill dog"' (2:20, p. 317). This discovery is really a discovery of the self-deception of his great expectations, his recognition that they were based on an irreconcilable contradiction.

Pip has been climbing slowly towards Estella and towards the freedom and security of gentility. Now the ladder has collapsed, and he finds himself back at his origin again, back where he was at the opening of the story. Then he had received his 'first most vivid and broad impression of the identity of things' (1:1, p.3), including himself, on the day he stole food from his home to feed an escaped convict. Now he has discovered that the source of his 'expectations' is not Miss Havisham, but that same convict. Moreover, he has discovered that Estella, the star of his expectations and the symbol of his desire for gentility, is really the daughter of Magwitch. All that he thought was taking him further and further from his shameful beginning has only been bringing him inexorably back to his starting point . . .

But Pip's return is to an origin which has been transformed into its opposite. Then the tie to Magwitch was repudiated as sinful, as the guilty secret of a crime against home, as a shameful bond to the dregs of society, and as the pain of moral isolation. Now that same tie is about to be revalued. As Pip starts down the Thames on the desperate attempt to save the life of the convict who has broken parole to return to him . . . [he] stands ready to face the truth which lies at the very centre of *Great Expectations*: all the claims made by wealth, social rank, and culture to endow the individual with true selfhood are absolutely false. However far he apparently travels from his origin he will still be akin to the mud and briars of the marshes and to the terrible man he met there on the day he became aware of himself as Pip . . . And, at the same time, Pip discovers that he himself has initiated the series of events which he believed were descending on him from the outside through a mysterious grace. He it was who committed the act of aggression against his family, stole for the convict, did not give him up to the soldiers, and formed the secret 'taint of prison and crime' (2:13, p.263) which has stuck to him all his life. He it is who is himself the source of all that has happened to him, all that he has believed was not his responsibility. The appearance of Magwitch to claim the 'gentleman what he has made' reveals to the horrified Pip that he has not been free, that he has been secretly manipulated as though he were a passive tool, or puppet, or a mechanical man created for Magwitch's revenge on society. But it also reminds him that he has himself been guilty of the act of kindness, outside the bounds of all socially approved morality, which formed his tie to the convict. Moreover, he has also been Miss Havisham's 'tool' . . .

Pip's life as a gentleman turns out to have combined the worst possible aspects of both sides of the human condition: its unjustifiable freedom, and its imprisonment in a given situation. On the one hand, Pip's life as a gentleman has been a fraud practised on society. He has in effect pushed and elbowed his way into a place in the upper class –

gratuitously and under false pretences. He must experience the bad conscience of the social climber, the parvenu. Pip is thrown back, therefore, on his initial isolation. There is nothing outside himself that judges, approves, consecrates his existence. On the other hand, Pip discovers that his life as a gentleman has been unwittingly a return to the life of a manipulated object he had so hated when he was a child being brought up 'by hand' (1:2, p. 8). He is returned to his alienation, and to his submission to what is imposed on him by force from the outside, and determines his actions, his place in the world, and even his nature . . . From the height of his great expectations, Pip is cast down again into the depths of disinheritance. He has indeed acted freely in forming his filial bond to Magwitch, freely in the sense that he has acted outside every social law. His freedom has been horrifyingly transformed into a wholesale assault and fraud on society. He is, in fact, even more disinherited than he was at the beginning, for now he knows the full meaning of his state, and he is able to compare this realization that he is nothing except what he has made himself with the self-deceiving hope of the great expectations he has so recently lost . . .

The third part of 'Pip's Expectations' traces the slow rise of the hero's fortunes. He moves out of the depths of despair in which he finds himself at the end of the second part. Love is the cause of this reversal of fortune. For Dickens, as for the general tradition of ethical thought, love is the only successful escape from the unhappiness of singularity, the unhappiness of being this unique and isolated person, Pip.

For Dickens, as for generations of Christian moralists, love means sacrifice. Pip must abandon all the proud hopes which have formed the secret core of his life. He must abandon forever his project of being a gentleman, the belief that somewhere there is a place for him which he can possess by right. He must accept the fact that he can in no way transcend the gap between 'the small bundle of shivers growing afraid of it all and beginning to cry' (1:1, p. 4) and the wind, sea, sky, and marshland, the alien universe – in no way, that is, but by willingly accepting this separation. And to accept this means to accept Magwitch, who springs up with 'a terrible voice' (1:1, p. 4) from the marshes at the moment Pip becomes aware of his separateness.

Pip learns about love, then, not through Estella, but through the slow change in his relation to Magwitch. Only this change makes possible a transformation of his relation to Estella. Otherwise, Pip would have remained, even if he had possessed Estella, the submissive worshipper of a cold and distant authority . . . . . .

By choosing his servitude to Magwitch, Pip transforms it into freedom. The dialectic of love in Dickens is more like the Kierkegaardian choice of oneself than like Sartre's endlessly frustrated conflict between two freedoms striving to be both free and secure at the same time. In place of the self-assertive love which requires the other to make himself the basis of one's selfhood, there is substituted by Magwitch and Pip the mutual sacrifice of their dearest claims to self-hood. For Dickens, as for Kierkegaard, the self can only affirm itself through self-sacrifice. But what was for Kierkegaard the relation of man to God becomes in Dickens the relation of man to man. No charac-ter in Dickens finally achieves authentic selfhood by establishing direct relation to God. Only the mutually self-denying, self-creating relationship of love succeeds, whereas the active assertion of will and the passive hope of great expectations both fail.[24] □

Miller's book put Dickens's work, and *Great Expectations*, firmly on the critical map, showing how the kind of fiction despised by a Victorian intellectual like G.H. Lewes could sustain a sophisticated critical approach drawing on important European thinkers of the nineteenth and twentieth centuries. In a sense, however, Miller's study was ahead of its time, not so much in the specific phenomenological perspective that it employed as in its willingness to engage with Dickens on a high level of philosophical seriousness. Mainstream literary criticism in the UK and the USA was not quite ready for that, and while Miller's book could not be ignored, it did not appear in a context where it could have changed the broad direction of Dickens studies. As far as critical readings of *Great Expectations* were concerned, the next two decades were to see consolida-tion and further exploration within a broadly agreed consensus, generating some remarkably rich criticism but also resulting in a growing sense, especially as the 1970s advanced, of the need for change. The story of these decades is traced in the next chapter.

CHAPTER FOUR

Consolidating Expectations: The 1960s and 1970s

BY 1960, *Great Expectations* was established as a major novel. The analyses of Van Ghent, Stange and Miller, considered in the last chapter, had amply demonstrated its richness and complexity, and the work of a number of other critics in the 1950s had confirmed that it was worthy of serious attention.[1] Dickens criticism in general had made great strides in the USA, though it still lagged behind in the UK, partly as a result of the inhibiting influence of the Leavises, who had not yet publicly reversed their dismissive judgement on the great entertainer. In the 1960s, however, British critics, notably Barbara Hardy, would start to catch up. The new decade would see a period of consolidation in which the 1950s critical interpretations of *Great Expectations* and of other Dickens novels would be taken up, developed, refined, redefined and disputed. There would also be some important new departures.

At the very start of the decade, in the January 1960 issue of the UK journal *Essays in Criticism*, an essay on *Great Expectations* appeared that was to prove very influential: Julian Moynahan's 'The Hero's Guilt: the Case of *Great Expectations*'.[2] Citing the analyses of Van Ghent and Stange, Moynahan focuses on a 'discrepancy' in Dickens's novel 'between the hero's sense of guilt and the actual amount of wrong-doing for which he may be said to be responsible'. Pip, Moynahan contends, 'has certainly one of the guiltiest consciences in literature', but his feelings of guilt hardly seem justified by what he does or even intends to do. Pip's may be, as Humphry House said, 'a snob's progress' (see p.66), but, as Moynahan points out, '[s]nobbery is not a crime. Why should Pip feel like a criminal?'[3] He observes that both Van Ghent and Stange try to account for Pip's apparently excessive sense of guilt in metaphysical terms, by arguing that he takes on a common guilt, the guilt of the world; they attempt, that is, to bridge the gap between Pip's snobbery and what Moynahan calls the 'more drastic phenomena of criminality' displayed in the novel by 'making criminal guilt a universal condition'. To challenge this kind of approach, Moynahan adopts an idea of Van Ghent's, which he sums up as the idea of 'implicit relations between character and character'[4] in the novel; but whereas Van Ghent focuses on the implicit relation between Pip and Magwitch, Moynahan detects another implicit relation, which in 1960 was rather surprising, between Pip and Orlick.

From the first reviews of the novel, as was seen in chapter one, Orlick had not found favour with critics (see pp. 19, 29–30, 32, 34); but from the late 1940s he had begun to emerge as a source of possible fascination. Humphry House, for example, in an essay first published in *The Dickensian* in 1948 and collected in his book *All in Due Time* (1955), had claimed that Orlick was 'far more interesting than Compeyson or Magwitch'.[5] Moynahan's essay offers an elaborated account of the function of this awkward figure, seeing him as the 'objective correlative' of Pip's sense of guilt. The notion of the 'objective correlative' had been proposed by T. S. Eliot in his 1919 essay '*Hamlet*', and it was to become widely influential in Anglo-American literary criticism in the mid-twentieth century: Eliot saw the 'objective correlative' as 'a set of objects, a situation, a chain of events' in a work of art that could represent and evoke a particular emotion:[6] seen in this way, Orlick and his activities stand for Pip's sense of guilt. By suggesting that Orlick functions as an 'objective correlative' in *Great Expectations*, Moynahan is raising the status of the novel by claiming that it exemplifies one of the key aesthetic notions of a major Modernist author.

The extract below begins at the start of the second section of Moynahan's essay, where he takes issue with Van Ghent's view (see pp. 75, 76, 78) of Pip as an 'Everyman':

■ . . . Pip's relation to the criminal milieu of *Great Expectations* is not that of an Everyman to a universal condition. It is rather a more concrete and particularised relation than the metaphysical approach would indicate, although the novel defines that relation obliquely and associatively, not through discursive analysis. Miss Van Ghent has suggested a metaphoric connection between Magwitch and Pip [see pp. 76–79]. Her proposal of such implicit relations between character and character, even though they do not become rationalised anywhere, is an illuminating insight into the artistic method of the mature Dickens. But her principle can be applied differently and yield rather different results.

I would suggest that Orlick rather than Magwitch is the figure from the criminal milieu of the novel whose relations to him come to define Pip's implicit participation in the acts of violence with which the novel abounds. Considered by himself, Orlick is a figure of melodrama. He is unmotivated, his origins are shrouded in mystery, his violence is unqualified by regret. In this last respect he is the exact opposite of Pip, who is, of course, filled with regret whenever he remembers how he has neglected his old friends at the forge.

On the other hand, if we consider Orlick in his connections with Pip, some rather different observations can be made. In the first place, there is a peculiar parallel between the careers of the two characters. We first encounter Orlick as he works side by side with Pip at the forge. Circumstances also cause them to be associated in the assault on Mrs. Joe. Orlick strikes the blow, but Pip feels, with some justification, that he supplied the assault weapon. Pip begins to develop his sense of alienation from the village after he has been employed by Miss Havisham to entertain her in her house. But Orlick too turns up later on working for Miss Havisham as gatekeeper. Finally, after Pip has become a partisan of the convict, it turns out that Orlick also has become a partisan of an ex-convict, Compeyson, who is Magwitch's bitter enemy.

Up to a point, Orlick seems not only to dog Pip's footsteps, but also to present a parody of Pip's upward progress through the novel, as though he were in competitive pursuit of some obscene great expectations of his own. Just as Pip centres his hopes successively on the forge, Satis House, and London, so Orlick moves his base of operations successively from the forge, to Satis House, and to London. From Pip's point of view, Orlick has no right to interest himself in any of the people with whom Pip has developed close ties. For instance, he is appalled when he discovers that his tender feeling for Biddy is given a distorted echo by Orlick's obviously lecherous interest in the same girl. And when he discovers that Orlick has the right of entry into Satis House he warns Jaggers to advise Miss Havisham to get rid of him. But somehow he cannot keep Orlick out of his affairs. When Magwitch appears at Pip's London lodging half-way through the novel, Orlick is crouching in darkness on the landing below Pip's apartment. And when Pip is about to launch the escape attempt down the Thames, his plans are frustrated by the trick which brings him down to the marshes to face Orlick in the hut by the limekiln. Its lurid melodrama and the awkwardness of its integration with the surrounding narrative has made many readers dismiss this scene as a piece of popular writing aimed at the less intelligent members of Dickens's audience. But the confrontation of Orlick and Pip on the marshes is crucial for an understanding of the problem I am discussing, because it is the scene in which Dickens comes closest to making explicit the analogy between the hero and the novel's principal villain and criminal.

Orlick inveigles Pip to the limepit not only to kill him but to overwhelm him with accusations. Addressing Pip over and over again as "'Wolf'" (3:14, pp. 421, 422, 423, 424, 425), an epithet he might more readily apply to himself, he complains that Pip has cost him his place, come between him and a young woman in whom he was interested, tried to drive him out of the country, and been a perpetual obstacle in the path of his own uncouth ambitions. But the charge he makes with the greatest force and conviction is that Pip bears the final responsibility for the assault on Mrs. Joe:

> 'I tell you it was your doing – I tell you it was done through you,' he retorted, catching up the gun, and making a blow with the stock at the vacant air between us. 'I come upon her from behind, as I come upon you to-night. *I* giv' it her! I left her for dead, and if there had been a limekiln as nigh her as there is now nigh you, she shouldn't have come to life again. But it warn't old Orlick as did it; it was you. You was favoured, and he was bullied and beat. Old Orlick bullied and beat, eh? Now you pays for it. You done it; now you pays for it.' (3:14, p.423)

The entire scene has a nightmare quality. This is at least partly due to the weird reversal of roles, by which the innocent figure is made the accused and the guilty one the accuser. As in a dream the situation is absurd, yet like a dream it may contain hidden truth. On the one hand Orlick, in interpreting Pip's character, seems only to succeed in describing himself – ambitious, treacherous, murderous, and without compunction. On the other hand, several of Orlick's charges are justified, and it is only in the assumption that Pip's motives are as black as his own that he goes wrong. We know, after all, that Pip is ambitious, and that he has repudiated his early associates as obstacles to the fulfilment of his genteel aspirations. Another interesting observation can be made about Orlick's charge that '"[i]t was you as did for your shrew sister"' (3:14, p.423). Here Orlick presents Pip as the responsible agent, himself merely as the weapon. But this is an exact reversal of Pip's former assumptions about the affair. All in all, Orlick confronts the hero in this scene, not merely as would-be murderer, but also as a distorted and darkened mirror-image. In fact, he presents himself as a monstrous caricature of the tender-minded hero, insisting that they are two of a kind with the same ends, pursued through similarly predatory and criminal means. This is what his wild accusations come down to . . . . . .

. . . In *Great Expectations* . . . the theme of ambition is treated under the two aspects of desire and will, the search for a superabundance of love and the drive for power. And it is in his presentation of the theme in the latter aspect that Dickens makes the more profound analysis of the immoral and criminal elements in his hero's (and the century's) favourite dream.

But Pip's ambition is passive. He only becomes active and aggressive after he has ceased to be ambitious. How then does *Great Expectations* treat the theme of ambition in terms that are relevant to the total action of which Pip is the centre? I have already begun to suggest an answer to the question. Ambition as the instinct of aggression, as the pitiless drive for power directed against . . . authority-figures is both coalesced and disguised in the figure of Orlick. And Orlick is bound to the hero by ties of analogy as double, *alter ego* and dark mirror-image. We are dealing here with an art which simultaneously disguises and reveals its deepest implications of meaning, with a method which apparently dissociates its thematic materials and its subject matter into moral fable-*cum*-melodramatic accompaniment, yet simultaneously presents through patterns of analogy a dramatic perspective in which the apparent opposites are unified. In *Great Expectations* criminality is displaced from the hero on to a melodramatic villain. But on closer inspection that villain becomes part of a complex unity – we might call it Pip-Orlick – in which all aspects of the problem of guilt become interpenetrant and co-operative. The only clue to this unity which is given at the surface level of the narrative is Pip's obsession of criminal guilt. Pip tells us over and over again that he feels contaminated by crime. But we do not find the objective correlative of that conviction until we recognize in the insensate and compunctionless Orlick a shadow image of the tender-minded and yet monstrously ambitious young hero . . . .

. . . Dickens's novel defines its hero's dream of great expectations and the consequences stemming from indulgence in that dream under the two aspects of desire and will, of regressive longing for an excess of love and of violent aggressiveness. In the unfolding of the action these two dramas are not presented separately. Instead they are combined into Dickens's most complex representation of character in action. Pip is Dickens's most complicated hero, demonstrating at once the traits of criminal and gull, of victimizer and victim. He is victimized by his dream[,] and the dream itself, by virtue of its profoundly anti-social and unethical nature, forces him into relation with a world in which other human beings fall victim to his drive for power. He is, in short, a hero sinned against and sinning: sinned against because in the first place the dream was thrust upon the helpless child by powerful and corrupt figures from the adult world; a sinner because in accepting for himself a goal in life based upon unbridled individualism and indifference to others he takes up a career which *Great Expectations* repeatedly, through a variety of artistic means, portrays as essentially criminal.[7] □

Moynahan's approach depends on going beyond or beneath what he calls, in the above extract, 'the surface level of the narrative' to a supposedly deeper, partly hidden pattern of connections and correspondences. This approach provoked a strong riposte from another critic who would produce influential interpretations of Dickens in the 1960s, Barbara Hardy, then teaching at Birkbeck College in London. In a short, polemical article that appeared in *Essays in Criticism* a year after Moynahan's, in January 1961, she charged Moynahan with 'exaggerations' that stemmed from 'a neglect of critical decorum' and indicted him for making 'a very sudden swoop beneath the literal level'.[8] In a more extended essay, she demonstrated her own approach to *Great Expectations*; her lucid, concise and perceptive analysis of the role of food in *Great Expectations*, first published in *Essays in Criticism* in October 1963,[9] aims to stay closer to the literal level, the surface narrative. The analysis was revised slightly when it was incorporated into Hardy's book *The Moral Art of Dickens* (1970), and it is the later version that is quoted below.

Like Van Ghent and Moynahan, Hardy is concerned to point to patterns of recurrence and analogy in the novel and to suggest that these patterns have moral significance; but she contends that the patterns connected with eating that she highlights do not need to be interpreted in specialised metaphysical or psychological terms, or translated into a more abstract conceptual vocabulary, as do the wild waves in *Dombey and Son*, the fog in *Bleak House*, or the prison in *Little Dorrit*: '[t]he meals in Dickens convey no more . . . than the elementary implications of natural domestic and social order, given particularity by the context of the novel'. That is to say, the meals in *Great Expectations* are already significant in the ways in which meals are in everyday life, but their significance is extended by their associations with different characters and events in the novel to show 'the irony and necessity of [its] internal moral pattern'.[10] In particular, food is seen in relation to ceremony and to love.

Hardy's essay is an excellent example of a humanist reading of *Great Expectations* that is both accessible and sophisticated and which skilfully relates specific events in the novel to its broader themes. In the extract below, Hardy discusses three key meals in the novel – the first, frantic feed of Magwitch on the marshes; Pip's first meal at Satis House; and his doleful breakfast with Magwitch on the morning after the transport's return from Australia:

■ The first meal in *Great Expectations* is *demanded* in the first chapter. Magwitch in desperate hunger terrifies Pip into stealing food: '"you know what wittles is . . . you get me wittles"' (1:1, pp.5, 6). In the third chapter Pip brings the food, and Magwitch makes the first response of gratitude which begins the long chain of obligation, illusion, pride, and love. It is necessary to see what moves his gratitude: it is not the mere provision of food, important though this is. Pip is doing more than satisfy the physical need, he is allowing nature more than nature needs [*Editor's Note*: In Shakespeare's *King Lear*, Scene 7, lines 425–26 (Quarto Text, 1608), the King says to Regan: 'Allow not nature more than nature needs,/Man's life is cheap as beast's.'[11]]. Magwitch is eating like a beast but Pip treats him as a guest and makes him respond as a guest . . . . . . Pip is no more in the conventional position of host than Magwitch is in the conventional position of guest, but the very lack of ceremony moves Pip to do more than steal and give in terror and in minimal satisfaction of need. Pity moves him to sauce the meat with ceremony and turn it into something more than Lady Macbeth's 'bare meeting' [*Editor's Note*: In Shakespeare's *Macbeth* (1606), Act 3, Scene 4, lines 34–36, Lady Macbeth says: 'To feed were best at home./From thence the sauce to meat is ceremony,/Meeting were bare without it'.[12]]. Just as Lady Macbeth's rebuke has special point because it is made at a great feast to the host who is a guest-murderer, so Pip's ceremony has special point in this bare rough meeting where the guest is desperate and the host terrorized:

> Pitying his desolation . . . I made bold to say, 'I am glad you enjoy it.'
> 'Did you speak?'
> 'I said I was glad you enjoyed it.'
> 'Thankee, my boy. I do.' (1:3, p. 19)

The child's civility and pity take no offence from his guest's table-manners. These are carefully observed, without revulsion:

> I had often watched a large dog of ours eating his food; and I now noticed a decided similarity between the dog's way of eating, and the man's. The man took strong sharp sudden bites, just like the dog. He swallowed, or rather snapped up, every mouthful, too soon and too fast; and he looked sideways here and there while he ate, as if he thought there was danger in every direction of somebody's coming to take the pie away. He was altogether too unsettled in his mind over it, to appreciate it comfortably, I thought, or to have anybody to dine with him, without making a chop with his jaws at the visitor. In all of which particulars he was very like the dog. (1:3, p. 20)

The detached account makes the politeness more marked. It is apparent that Pip's naive comparisons, to the dog and to more comfortable meals, imply no sense of social superiority, though the social implications are plain to the reader. Pip is not repelled by the resemblance to the dog, but is sorry for it, and instead of treating the man like a dog, gives with love. The "'I am glad you enjoy it'" and the "'Thankee'" (1:3, p.19) turn the rudest meal in the novel into an introductory model of ceremony. What makes the ceremony is love, generosity, and gratitude. I need not labour the attachment of this scene to the main themes of the novel.

This meal acts as a model of ceremony, and controls our response to the many related descriptions of meals which succeed it. The gratitude and compassionate love are both present in Chapter 5, when Magwitch lies about stealing the food, to protect Pip, and is answered by Joe: "'God knows you're welcome to it – so far as it was ever mine . . . We don't know what you have done, but we wouldn't have you starved to death for it, poor miserable fellow-creatur. – Would us, Pip?'" (1:5, p.41).

This in its turn evokes another response of gratitude – an inarticulate working of the throat – from Magwitch. The first small links are forged in Pip's chain 'of iron or gold, of thorns or flowers' (1:9, p.73).

It is not until much later . . . that Pip sees that this is where his chain really begins, 'before I knew that the world held Estella' (2:19, p.309). The actual image is narrowed down, in the next chapter, to the 'wretched gold and silver chains' with which Magwitch has loaded him (2:20, p.320). [*Editor's Note*: This is a variant reading; in the Clarendon Dickens, it is Pip who is wretched, not the chains: the passage reads: 'loading wretched me with his gold and silver chains' and the version Hardy uses is given in a footnote.] When the image of the chain first appears (in the singular) it has no connection with the convict for Pip sees its beginning in his encounter with Miss Havisham and Estella, in Satis House. The beginning of his illusory great expectations, like the beginning of the real ones, is marked by a significant meal. Estella is the hostess, Pip the guest. The meal is less grotesque than the meal with Magwitch but it too lacks the ceremonious cover of a roof, for Estella tells Pip to wait in the yard:

> She came back, with some bread and meat and a little mug of beer. She put the mug down on the stones of the yard, and gave me the bread and meat without looking at me, as insolently as if I were a dog in disgrace. I was so humiliated, hurt, spurned, offended, angry, sorry – I cannot hit upon the right name for the smart – God knows what its name was – that tears started to my eyes. (1:8, p.63)

The contrast is clinched by the comparison with the dog. Pip's full wants are not satisfied, even though this is the hospitality of Satis House, but in terms of physical need he is given enough. He is treated like a dog, given no more than nature needs, but he does not lose his appetite, any more than Magwitch, treated with courtesy, stops eating like a dog. Dickens makes this distinction unsentimentally and truthfully, merely allowing Pip to observe that '[t]he bread and meat were acceptable, and the beer was warming and tingling, and I was soon in spirits to look about me' (1:8, p.64). Like Magwitch, and for similar reasons of protective love, Pip lies about this meal. His sense of humiliation and his desire to protect Estella from 'the contemplation of Mrs. Joe' (1:9, p.67) makes him elaborate the marvellous childish fantasy about the '"cake and wine on gold plates"' which Pumblechook and Joe and Mrs. Joe, in their social innocence, accept. Pip invents a meal appropriate to Satis House, and hides his shame, but he preserves both the hierarchy and the bizarre quality of his encounter by placing the meal in a coach, and saying that he '"got up behind the coach to eat mine, because she told me to"'. Even the dog comes back, magnified into four '"[i]mmense"' dogs who come off rather better than Pip since they fight '"for veal cutlets out of a silver basket"' (1:9, p.68). On his next visit to Satis House we return briefly to the dog: 'I was taken down into the yard to be fed in the former dog-like manner' (1:11, p.90). The two meals respond in perfect antithesis.

The first ceremony of love finds another responsive scene when Magwitch discloses his responsibility and motivation to Pip. We are carefully reminded of the first meal on the marshes: '"I drops my knife many a time in that hut when I was a eating my dinner or my supper, and I says to myself, 'Here's the boy again, a looking at me whiles I eats and drinks!'"' (2:20, p.317).

It is to this actual memory of the meal that he attaches his plan to '"make that boy a gentleman"' (2:20, p.317) but when the gentleman serves him with a meal he does not look at him as the boy did:

> He ate in a ravenous manner that was very disagreeable, and all his actions were uncouth, noisy, and greedy. Some of his teeth had failed him since I saw him eat on the marshes, and as he turned his food in his mouth, and turned his head sideways to bring his strongest fangs to bear upon it, he looked terribly like a hungry old dog. If I had begun with any appetite, he would have taken it away, and I should have sat much as I did – repelled from him by an insurmountable aversion, and gloomily looking át the cloth. (3:1, p.329)

The uncouth eating, the hunger, the sideways movement, and the comparison with the dog are repetitions from the early scene which emphasize the distance between the child and the man. This time the observation is full of revulsion, the food is not sauced with ceremony. But if the host has changed, the guest has not, and he apologizes for his doglike eating with undoglike courtesy:

> 'I'm a heavy grubber, dear boy,' he said, as a polite kind of apology
> when he had made an end of his meal, 'but I always was. If it had
> been in my constitution to be a lighter grubber, I might ha' got into
> lighter trouble.' (3:1, p.329)

The apology is made without shame or self-pity on the part of
Magwitch, and provokes no sympathy on the part of Pip. In the early
scene the child's pity was impulsive and provoked simply by the desperate eating and panic. In the later scenes, Pip is in a position to see
the connection between the heavy grubbing and the heavy trouble,
but describes without pity the roughness and greed: 'there was
Prisoner, Felon, Bondsman, plain as plain could be'. (3:1, p.336)[13] □

In this interpretation of *Great Expectations*, Barbara Hardy takes her
distance from what might be called the 'symbolic realist' approach to
Dickens by playing down the novel's symbolism, effectively making
Dickens into more of a realist. But it is not a very great distance; she
remains very close to a 'symbolic realist' perspective and her reading is
easily compatible with it. A much more drastic challenge to this perspective was mounted in Robert Garis's *The Dickens Theatre* (1965). Garis
points out that critics from Edmund Wilson to J. Hillis Miller and beyond
have tried to rehabilitate Dickens by arguing that, at his best, and
especially in his later novels, he did fulfil 'symbolic realist' criteria; that
his 'darker novels do in fact turn out to be coherent complex organisms
when they are properly identified as symbolic in method'.[14] Garis
contends, however, that these interpretations will not, in the end, hold
water, because 'Dickens characteristically worked in a literary and moral
mode that ordinarily is taken by readers seriously interested in art to be
incapable of producing "high art"'.[15] This literary and moral mode is a
theatrical one; Dickens's art is a 'theatrical art'[16] in which we are constantly aware of Dickens as 'the performer', 'the artificer':[17] '[t]he first
impression, and a continuing one, in Dickens's prose is of a voice manip-
ulating language with pleasure and pride in its own skill'.[18] Dickens 'is an
illusionist in the sense that the creation of an illusion is something he
does only at certain moments, and with spectacular effect; he is not
producing a *continuous* illusion of reality'.[19]

Garis's original approach to Dickens is undoubtedly able to account for
aspects of his work that cannot easily be accommodated in a 'symbolic
realist' perspective. It may, however, seem to be an approach that is
rather more applicable to a novel like, say, *Bleak House*, which mixes first-
person narration by one of the characters with bravura performances by
the omniscient author, than to *Great Expectations*, where the omniscient
author gives way throughout to a first-person narrator who is not
Dickens. Garis argues, however, that this is not the case. Robert B.

Partlow, Jr., in an essay of 1961 on 'point of view' in *Great Expectations*, had contended that the narrator of *Great Expectations* was 'neither Pip nor Mr. Pip, but Mr. Pirrip, a moderately successful, middle-aged businessman, a *petit bourgeois* who has risen in life by his own exertions and a fine bit of luck'.[20] Garis caps this by claiming that the narrator is not Pip, Mr. Pip, *or* Mr. Pirrip; the narrator is *Dickens,* and we know it. The reader is always aware that Dickens is conducting a sustained impersonation of 'Pip', 'Mr. Pip', and 'Mr. Pirrip' and that, at certain moments, the theatrical mask will be set aside so that Dickens himself can take the stage. Once Garis has made this argument, he goes on to highlight what he sees as a disparity between the explicit moral concern of the book – Pip's snobbery and penitence – and the lack of dramatic pressure in Dickens's rendering of the scenes in which this moral aspect might have been dramatised. He then turns to what he sees as the real meaning of *Great Expectations,* which he relates to Freud's *Civilization and its Discontents.* The extract below begins as he focuses on the presentation of Pip's 'snobbery':

■ 'Pip the Snob' appears mostly when Pip is dealing with people associated with his past and with the forge; this is the whole point about his snobbishness, of course. And we are never surprised to find him being merely an audience for Mr. Jaggers or Mr. Wemmick in the city. But when Mr. Wopsle comes to town, and calls himself in his new role as actor to the attention of Pip in his new role as young gentleman, we might expect a comic duet between these two pretenders. Instead, Dickens chooses to let Mr. Wopsle give a solo performance, to cast Pip in the role of discreet, decent, and kind observer, and to render the performance of *Hamlet* in his own loud and brilliant professional manner. These seem sound and intelligent professional choices, but another similar instance is perhaps less successful. When Joe comes to town and is, as Pip's voice tells us, made uncomfortable and awkward by Pip's city manners, these manners are not themselves rendered concretely but only asserted. We actually see and hear very little to criticize in Pip's behaviour, since our attention is fully occupied by Joe and his hat. That this should be so, that we should not be allowed really to experience Pip's 'betrayal' of Joe at this moment, is understandable in view of the nature of theatrical art and is not felt to be a weakness in the scene. But it is at such moments that one realizes that, judged by the standards of non-theatrical art, Dickens's achievement is of a very special kind. Consider how intensely painful the scene would be if Pip's snobbishness were concretely rendered, how deep the shame that could have been communicated to us by setting out the scene dramatically; and then how mild, in comparison, the emotions are in the scene as it is, how easy, how familiar, how undisturbing the shame actually expressed.

The truth is that there is no very great dramatic pressure in the entire rendering of Pip's betrayal of Joe through snobbery, his realization of that snobbery and his penitence. Yet this is the explicitly stated moral burden of the whole novel. *Great Expectations* is a novel in which the official meaning is not rendered from the inside and is not present before us continuously in a dramatic illusion of reality: it is merely one of the many routines out of which the novel is constructed and is really on a par in that respect with the description of Mrs. Gargery's funeral and Mr. Wopsle's *Hamlet*. It is a performance, an impersonation, a mimicking of moral self-discovery to which the natural theatrical response is one of pleasure in the tact and delicacy of tone with which the whole enterprise is carried out. I do not mean to suggest that one observes and assesses the performance callously, without being moved by the sentiments which are given so refined a theatrical embodiment . . . we can acknowledge and share the explicit emotional and moral 'meaning' of *Great Expectations*, while at the same time recognizing that our mode of response to these humane and familiar sentiments is a theatrical one . . . . . .

But the theatrical story and the theatrical meaning which make up the surface of *Great Expectations* is not the whole story nor the whole meaning of this curiously resonant novel . . . . . . [Its meaning is] different from the meaning of the other mature novels. *Bleak House, Hard Times, Little Dorrit, Our Mutual Friend* – all these portray a world in which human freedom and happiness is threatened by wrong systems, wrong institutions, bad habits, bad values, bad people. And the portrait of this world becomes Dickens's rhetorical instrument for attacking these wrongs. But *Great Expectations* offers a new portrait. Dickens's new insight discovers a world in which human freedom and happiness are frustrated not by social wrongs, not by bad habits, but by the opposite, by the best and most demanding ideals of society. Pip is frustrated by people and by habits and by values which he, Dickens, and the reader all take to be good rather than bad. Moreover, the final statement of the significance of Pip's experiences articulates a moral attitude which we agree is good. Yet we feel that it is also a frustrating attitude and the tone of the whole work confirms us in this opinion. Dickens's new insight into his world, in short, is an embodiment of Freud's theme in one of his most important works, *Civilisation and its Discontents*.

. . . if we should stop to think about the curious emptiness of Pip's response to Biddy's marriage, it would immediately occur to us that the response is not in the least surprising, since we have known all along that Pip is like that, that something is missing in him. We have also known the identity of that something, though we may never have named it consciously. One name for it would be 'force of will', but a more accurate and illuminating word is 'libido' [psychological drive or energy, especially of a sexual kind]. We have known from the beginning of the novel that what is missing from Pip's life is any free expression of libido, and that it is missing because it is held in contempt and horror by the ideals of the civilization within which Pip tries to make a life for himself. It must have been for this reason that Dickens was drawn to the characterization, as he was earlier drawn to Arthur Clennam [in *Little Dorrit*] and was later to Eugene Wrayburn [in *Our Mutual Friend*]. But *Great Expectations* differs from the novels which surround it. Although Pip is, beneath the surface of the novel, known to us as 'the man without will, the man who cannot act', yet on the surface of the novel he is defined as 'the man who wanted and acted wrongly'. *Great Expectations* is the deepest of Dickens's visions of the discontents of civilization because of this unemphasized contradiction: the traditional moralization of its surface allowed Dickens unconsciously to render in the structure of his story itself that final pessimism about the possibility of human happiness which, in combination with his regretfully humorous acceptance of this condition, is his deepest criticism of life . . . . . .

Here, then, is the basic fable of *Great Expectations* and the vision of life and criticism of life which it embodies. It is the story of a hopeful young man with a strong animal body and powerful desires who is called on at every turn to display, in the commonest actions of his everyday life, the ideals of the civilization into which he was born: continual self-restraint, self-control, forgiveness of enemies, fortitude in withstanding – not heroic combat, which would be invigorating – but boredom and frustration and insult. He is this perfect model of moral deportment because he is 'morally timid and very sensitive' – because he is so utterly persuaded of the validity of these ideals that he never finds any adequate opportunity for expressing, or even recognizing, his own interests and his own self. Although he has within himself 'sustained . . . a perpetual conflict with injustice', this conflict, because his civilization never offered him a vocabulary for articulating it, was always turned against himself. In his youth it took the form of 'kicking [his injured feelings] into the brewery-wall, and twisting them out of [his] hair' (1:8, p. 64); when he grows up he inevitably turns his frustrations against himself in the form of continual remorse and guilt. Looking everywhere about him and in particular at the people responsible for his continued frustrations, he can find no one to blame: but this is true only because he is imbued with the moral obligation of understanding and forgiving. Moreover, there is no conceivable alternative to his sense of horror and repulsion about the one source of power apparently available in this civilization: blood, wildness, and violence. It never occurs to him that these horrors are really 'human', that they are in any way worthy of respect. Pip is an obedient child of civilization; the fact that he is also a human animal, with many and complex impulses which breed animal needs and glamorous hopes and great expectations – this fact leads to the melancholy, mildly humorous acceptance of the world's insufficiency which is the novel's guiding tone and final meaning.[21] □

Garis's book was quite well received but his radical approach was not really taken up. For most Dickens critics, it was 'business as usual' – and *Great Expectations* was a thriving business. In 1966, Philip L. Marcus began an essay by observing: '[i]n recent years, *Great Expectations* has been perhaps more exhaustively studied than any other of Dickens's novels: modern critics have perceptively analyzed its social satire, psychological import, structure and symbolism'. But there were also signs that the *Great Expectations* industry was starting to seem rather predictable. Marcus's essay is a case in point: claiming that critics, despite their exhaustive studies, have neglected the element of plot, he attempts 'to satisfy the need for a modern analysis of the handling of plot in *Great Expectations*' by relating it both to 'the mid-Victorian genre of "sensation fiction"' and to recent critical accounts of the 'rich thematic significance' of the novel.[22] The result is competent but not pathbreaking. A more innovative approach to the matter of plot in Dickens's novel can be found in Peter Wolfe's 1974 essay discussed later in this chapter (pp. 111–14); but a truly 'modern' analysis of plot in *Great Expectations* would not appear until Peter Brooks's essay in 1980, which is explored in the next chapter of this Guide (see pp. 122–30).

The sense, from the later 1960s, that criticism of Dickens, and of *Great Expectations*, had entered a more predictable phase was confirmed by the appearance in 1970 of *Dickens the Novelist*, by F. R. and Q. D. Leavis. The book had been eagerly awaited, both because of the prestige that the Leavises still enjoyed and because it appeared to be a reversal of their earlier dismissals of Dickens. In an essay on F. R. Leavis in *Language and Silence* (1969), George Steiner – who judged *Great Expectations*, along with *Bleak House*, as 'manifestly ampler achievements' than *Hard Times*, the one novel approved of in *The Great Tradition* – observed in a footnote that the 'full-scale critical study of Dickens's major novels' on which Leavis was 'reportedly, at work . . . will not only be of very great interest in itself, but as constituting one of the rare instances in which Dr. Leavis has "revalued" one of his own, and most influential, dismissals'.[23] But the great expectations the book aroused were not fulfilled. The Leavises did not explain their earlier dismissal but projected it onto others; for example, their preface asserts that they 'should like to make it impossible . . . for any intellectual . . . to tell us with the familiar easy assurance that Dickens of course was a genius, but that his line was entertainment, so that an account of his art that implies marked intellectual powers . . . is obviously absurd'.[24] But this 'genius-but' dismissal of Dickens had been very much the line of F. R. Leavis himself in *The Great Tradition*.

The desire to 'make it impossible' to express certain attitudes to Dickens is also evident in the title of Q. D. Leavis's chapter on *Great Expectations*, 'How We Must Read *Great Expectations*'. As John Lucas points out in his *Charles Dickens: The Major Novels* (1992) – and as the examples in this Guide amply demonstrate – 'the insistence [in Leavis's title] on a "correct" interpretation [is] doomed to failure . . . [t]here is no one way in which we *must* read the novel'.[25] (This is not to deny that some ways of reading it are better than others.) Q. D. Leavis's essay is, as George J. Worth observes, '[g]enerally . . . far more in the critical mainstream of her generation than she finds it convenient to acknowledge',[26] but it does offer some worthwhile suggestions. Two interesting comparisons are made in the essay. One is between *Great Expectations* and Hawthorne's *The Scarlet Letter*, which, according to Q. D. Leavis, resembles Dickens's novel in its 'highly stylized settings', its 'schematic technique', 'its salvationist outcome' and 'its exploration of the effects of guilt'.[27] The other is between *Great Expectations* and John Bunyan's *The Pilgrim's Progress* (Part 1, 1678; Part 2, 1684), particularly with regard to the scene in which Pip returns to the marshes and is captured by Orlick. She suggests that this echoes 'Christian's pilgrimage through the Valley of the Shadow of Death' and that Orlick is Apollyon: 'in Bunyan's allegory Christian had had to meet and overcome the Devil's advocate in the Valley of Humiliation'.[28]

The most substantial part of Q. D. Leavis's essay is her consideration of the parts that guilt and shame play in the novel. It is notable that she is one of the large company of critics – including, in this Guide, Bernard Shaw, T. A. Jackson, Humphry House, Jack Lindsay and G. Robert Stange – who take Pip as representative of his society, although each critic has her or his own view of the specific ways in which Pip is representative. For Q. D. Leavis, his representativeness lies in his guilt and his class-based shame, as can be seen in the following extract:

■ Dickens's preoccupations in *Great Expectations* are with the fundamental realities of his society and focus on two questions: how was it that a sense of *guilt* was implanted in every child, and with what consequences? And what part does *Class* play in the development of such a member of that society? The novelist is concerned with the effects of these two sanctions, guilt and shame, and it is an inseparable feature of this concern that he continually insinuates the question: what is 'real' in such a context? for Pip is continually in doubt and perplexity as to whether the real life is that social one with its rules of right and wrong, into which he was born, or the life of the imagination that grows out of natural feeling, into which he was inducted from the opening chapter, his first distinct memory. Of course it is in the working out and presentation of these inquiries that the value of the novel lies, in the minute particularities of the individual life which are yet so skilfully presented as to carry overtones of allegory and to be exemplary. The pertinacity and concentration of Dickens's mind on his theme has made the two questions, in which the third is implied, so interwoven as to be inseparable eventually, and his Shakespearean genius as a creator has produced the wonderful plot which is not only exciting to read and faultless in execution but strikingly classical in its perepeteia [sudden change, reversal[29]]. Every detail of the plot, moreover, expresses some aspect, some further aspect, of the theme, and one that is necessary for its full apprehension by the reader. A remarkable feature of the novel is the complexity of the irony which informs the plot from beginning to end (the rewritten end which is demonstrably superior to the one first intended and which perfectly completes the intention and meaning of the novel) – an irony which inheres in the title; yet the novel is affirmative and constructive, not, like other novels shot through with irony (e.g., [Mark Twain's] *Huckleberry Finn* (1884), [Herman Melville's] *The Confidence-Man* (1857), [Stendhal's] *Le Rouge et Le Noir* [(*The Red and the Black*)] (1830)), pessimistic or nihilistic.

And whereas Dickens's difficulties, ever since they first appeared in *Oliver Twist*, in reconciling the reader's demands for realism with his own need, for his creative intentions, of a non-rational symbolism of situation and action, a freer form of dealing with experience than his inheritance from the eighteenth-century novelists provided, he has at last, in *Great Expectations*, managed to reconcile realism and symbolism so that in this novel we move without protest, or uneasiness even, from the 'real' world of everyday experience into the non-rational life of the guilty conscience or spiritual experience, outside time and place and with its own logic: somehow we are inhibited from applying the rules of common sense to it even where we hardly recognize that it is symbolic action and can not possibly be plausible real life. The novel is also remarkable for having no wide divergences of prose style either, as even *Bleak House* has; almost the only rhetoric is the passage where Pip tries to explain to Estella his feelings for her, where the effect of weak egotism is required and deliberately obtained through rhetorical language. There is a consistent sobriety of language without losing idiomatic identity for the characters, who range widely nevertheless, as from Jaggers to Joe, from Wemmick to Herbert, from Miss Havisham to Mrs. Joe, and this personal idiom is even what distinguishes Magwitch from Orlick. While Dickens works here, as in his [short story] 'George Silverman's Explanation' (1868), with the minimum in word, setting and characterization, he does not sacrifice in *Great Expectations* scope, range, richness or imaginative complexity. This is the Dickens novel the mature and exigent are now likely to re-read most often and to find more and more in each time, perhaps because it seems to have more relevance outside its own age than any other of Dickens's creative work . . . . . .

One of the principal reasons for the homogeneous tone of the novel is that it is told to us by a narrator who is firmly kept before us as remote from the self who is the subject, a self that is seen in growth from childhood to adult status. Unlike David Copperfield the narrator Pip is not identified in sympathy with that child, boy or youth; far from it, the wry glance he directs at his follies and shortcomings and mistakes warns us off any easy sympathy with the youthful Pip. The frequent humour or amusement in the narrator's tone – which is not inconsistent with the narration's being painful, pathetic and at times even terrible – guarantees the narrator's detachment for us and under-plays (very notably if we think of David's) the exposed self's sufferings, so that there is no bitterness about others' treatment of him, only a clear insight into the causes of his mistakes. We thus grasp, without being told, that the narrator is now truly a free man, freed from the compulsions of childhood guilt and from shame imposed by the class distinctions that closed round him in his boyhood, and from the unreal aspirations imposed on him by his society – a society from which when he grasps its true nature he is finally seen to recoil. Yet we have also seen that the guilt and shame were necessary to produce the complex sensibility of an adult who can free himself by renuncia-tion, contrition and publicly manifested repentance.[30] □

Clearly, this reading constructs *Great Expectations* as a novel that conforms to the then-dominant criteria of literary quality such as unity and maturity (criteria that the Leavises had helped to promote). In this respect it is very much, as Worth suggests, in the critical mainstream. A more innov-ative and invigorating approach to *Great Expectations* emerged in Peter Wolfe's 1974 essay 'The Fictional Crux and the Double Structure of *Great Expectations*'. Like Q. D. Leavis, Wolfe registers in the novel what she calls 'the non-rational life' and what he sums up as 'those forces which, gain-saying causality, deal with unrevealed or barely revealed experience'.[31] But whereas Q. D. Leavis contends, in the extract above, that in *Great Expectations* 'we move without protest, or uneasiness even, from the "real" world of everyday experience into the non-rational life' and are *'somehow* . . . inhibited from applying the rules of common sense' [*Editor's italics*], Wolfe, in the extract below, locates the 'non-rational life' in what he calls the 'understructure' of *Great Expectations*, and sees a dis-junction between this 'design based on the novel's pattern' and 'its story'. Wolfe also shares with Q.D. Leavis a sense of the novel's irony; but for him the irony is not, as it is for Q.D. Leavis, a comfortable confirm-ation of the reader's security and superiority; the irony Wolfe finds in Dickens's novel jars and shakes, turns the world upside down. And whereas Q.D. Leavis sees Pip's story as one of moral growth and of progress towards freedom, Wolfe finds neither freedom nor growth. In presenting Pip as '[u]nredeemed', he becomes one of the few critics at this time to attach any significance, even if it is a negative one, to his life in the colonies, making a thought-provoking comparison between the Mr. Pirrip in Cairo and 'Graham Greene's seedy expatriates'. Like Philip L. Marcus, Wolfe is interested in plot, but he offers a more extended def-inition of plot as the 'logic' of '[n]arrative form, or design, or rhythm', which 'bridges event and theme, that is, empirical and non-empirical reality' and 'brings together a fiction's naturalistic and poetic data'.[32]

This extract begins at the point when Wolfe develops his idea of the novel's double structure:

■ *Great Expectations* has two overlapping structures; each obeys its own logic, follows its own curve, and creates its own time scheme. To the three-part organization marked by the formal endings at Chapters 19 (1:19) and 39 (2:20) belong the playful satire on social climbing con-nected with the Pocket family and the Finches of the Grove, and also the melodramatic piling-up of event towards the end. The Magwitch escape plot, the scheme to murder Pip, and the melodramatic death of Miss Havisham bring in more sensationalism than Part 3 can comfort-ably house.

Such crowding and colouring typify melodrama. Melodrama needs plenty of lurid touches to hide its superficiality and escapism, for melodrama ignores complexity and subtlety. It simplifies reality into ready categories of good and evil, and it aims at evoking a simple response – like horror, sympathy, or loathing. It engrosses the reader when he does not feel bullied or cheated. Stressing the masculine virtues of physical courage and decisiveness, it features threats of sudden death (the fire at Satis), hair-breadth escapes (Orlick's murder plot against Pip), coincidences (the reunion of Estella and Pip), and sur-prises (Magwitch's return to England). Speed is important: besides getting off to a fast start, the narrative must move ahead so quickly that we never catch our breath and disbelieve. Melodrama parts from real-istic art in attempting to be larger than life. It fails when it calls attention to its purpose. Thus the florid phrase, the event thrown into too sharp relief, the over-simplified moral stance, and the sentimental plea to gain sympathy for the hero can turn melodrama sour.

The understructure of *Great Expectations* – the design based on the novel's pattern rather than its story – refreshes the melodrama. It works like an intercheck. Where melodrama calls for physical energy and decisiveness, Pip has little personal drive. Where melodrama builds suspense, Pip drifts into a life style barren of drama. Where melodrama's rapid tempo blocks depth of characterization, Dickens substitutes 'bounce' (E. M. Forster [*Aspects of the Novel*, 1927[33]]) and the dazzle of showmanship (Robert Garis, *The Dickens Theatre* [see pp. 104–108 of this Guide]). Whatever primitive depth gets into the plot comes from the book's understructure – Pip's role as avenger, Orlick's malice, the psychological suddenness that strikes so vividly because the academic psychology of the day had not yet formulated it. Obeying an acausal, dreamlike logic, these data combine to take on a life of their own. They ignore, resonate with, and even join with the melodrama.

The understructure of *Great Expectations*, like its formal design, has three divisions . . . Though releasing no meanings, it imparts its essence through the rhythmical oscillation of its three cruces. [*Editor's Note*: The first crux comes in the opening chapter 'with Magwitch upending Pip and then scaring him into bringing a file and food back out to the marshes'; the second crux is Pip's first visit to Miss Havisham and Estella (1:8), which 'launches his career as a false gentleman';[34] the third crux occurs in chapter 39 (2:20), with Magwitch's return; this 'form[s] the linchpin of the novel's understructure' and 'joins the novel's pattern to its plot'.[35] Magwitch's burning of the two pound notes that Pip tries to return to him (2:20, p. 315), showing that he is now '[a] rich man [who] has money to burn', 'marks Magwitch's second upending of Pip, who, at the time, is both in debt and without prospects'.[36]] . . . . . .

. . . *Great Expectations* is rich in irony, most of which, especially towards the start, takes the form of reversal and serves to jar our mental habits. That a major climax can take place in a novel's opening pages expresses boldly Dickens's desire to shake our usual notions about the way things work. Instead of building mood or filling in facts, the opening of *Great Expectations* shocks us. And the early chapters, with their sudden turns in both fortune and setting, work on us the same way – making our collective outlook on things seem askew, backward, upside down. There is no character a reader will sympathize more readily with than a child in danger. Pip's fears in Chapter 1 become ours and, by extension, so do his other responses. The raw December day that opens the book brings Pip his 'first most vivid and broad impression of the identity of things' (1:1, p. 3) through a chain of reversals. Turned upside down by the escaped convict, he changes a graveyard into a birthplace; the switch Mrs. Joe uses to whip him is improperly called Tickler; Mrs. Joe's tidy housekeeping routine produces a negative rather than a pleasing effect: 'Mrs. Joe was a very clean housekeeper, but had an exquisite art of making her cleanliness more uncomfortable and unacceptable than dirt itself' (1:4, p. 23).

Dickens even denies the Christmas setting its usual uplift. Mrs. Joe and her guests browbeat Pip at dinner; a search party of soldiers interrupts the meal, orders Joe to the smithy, drinks the Christmas wine, and then leads a manhunt through the marshes which ends with Compeyson and Magwitch fighting in a cold, damp ditch. Joyce's Christmas dinner in *A Portrait of the Artist as a Young Man* (1916) is not the first picture in British fiction of a people acting out its damnation by profaning Christ's mass.

This December day foreshadows the one that ends the book some twenty-five or thirty years later. By patterning the novel to the cycle of a year and by returning to the Kentish setting of Chapter 1, Dickens brings his action full circle. The overall effect is one of a dwarfed, derailed humanity. Literally, we have not crept far from the primeval ooze. Supporting the view that people can do little either to know or save themselves is the December time-setting of the two episodes. Although the reasons differ, neither the material Christmas of Chapter 1 nor the implied one of Chapter 59 (3:20) is celebrated. Unredeemed, Pip is still close to the marshes. Opposing the Victorian nostrum of progress is a death drift which money, government, and religion cannot check. As with Graham Greene's seedy expatriates, bachelor life in Cairo labels Pip a discard in a fast-changing world.[37] □

Wolfe's essay demonstrated the possibility of fresh perspectives on the plot and structure of *Great Expectations* and even hinted, as in the last sentence of the extract above, at a post-colonial approach to the novel that would only emerge more fully in 1993 in Edward W. Said's *Culture and Imperialism*, discussed in the final chapter of this Guide (see pp. 144–49). Another perspective that promised new insights gained greater prominence due to Harry Stone's rich and fascinating book, *Dickens and the Invisible World: Fairy Tales, Fantasy and Novel-Making* (1979). The fairy-tale and fantasy aspects of Dickens had aroused interest before; in 1962, in the *Kenyon Review*, Stone himself had published an account of their significance in *Great Expectations*, which he draws on and develops in his book.[38] Q. D. Leavis's essay on *Great Expectations* had attacked 'the critics who reduce the novel to a matter of fairy godmothers and princesses, to fairy-tale dimensions and remoteness from any actuality, or to some other-world of folk-tale elements and primitive symbolism'[39] and had targeted Harry Stone for claiming that – as she paraphrased Stone's argument – Biddy is 'married off arbitrarily by Dickens to show that Joe is the true gentleman who must marry the true princess to fulfil the fairy-tale story that the novel is'.[40] As Q. D. Leavis's essay was published nine years before Stone's book, she presumably had his *Kenyon Review* essay in her sights, though she gave no references.[41] But in *Dickens and the Invisible World* itself, Stone does not 'reduce' *Great Expectations* to a fairy-tale or remove it 'from any actuality'; he offers a detailed and fascinating account of how, in his view, reality and fairy-tale combine in *Great Expectations*. In fact, he shares Q. D. Leavis's concern with the relationship between what she calls 'everyday experience' and 'the non-rational life'; but he offers a much more detailed account than she does of 'the non-rational life' and of its relationship with 'everyday experience'.

Like Peter Wolfe, Stone locates the non-rational elements of the novel on the level of structure to some extent, but he is more specific than Wolfe about the kind of structures he tries to identify, which are those of fairy-tale and fantasy. In *Dickens and the Invisible World*, his two long chapters on *Great Expectations*, 'The Factual Matrix' and 'The Fairy-Tale Transformation', aim to trace 'the genesis, evolution, and fulfilment of one of Dickens's most beautiful designs – to demonstrate how Dickens translated ordinary encounters and everyday circumstances into rich fairy-tale fabling'.[42] Stone stresses that the novel 'is more than a fairy-tale grown big; it is a narrative that partakes of fairy-tale transformation, a narrative that fuses autobiographical, sociological, psychological, and mythological elements into a deeply resonant unity, a unity that is at once esoteric and realistic'.[43]

Stone's enthusiasm, and his delight in piling up examples, mean that he sometimes goes over the top; but there is a sense in which this is an appropriate response to the extravagance of Dickens. His avid accumulation creates an Aladdin's Cave for future readers and critics. Part of his argument is that '*Great Expectations* throngs with storybook signs', with '[m]agical covenants and hidden correspondences' that 'testify to cosmic affinities';[44] in the extracts below, Stone explores how these storybook signs work in what he calls 'the great recognition chapter which marks Magwitch's return' and goes on to consider two patterns of signs that pervade the novel, 'the magical motif of light and fire' and, above all, 'the continuing ritual of hands'. It is interesting to compare Stone's account of the 'ritual of hands' with the rather different interpretation of the role of hands offered by William A. Cohen in the last chapter of this Guide (see pp. 149–59).

The extracts from Stone's book begin as he develops his discussion of 'the great recognition chapter':[45]

■ . . . the chapter is filled with supernatural tokens which explicate and magnify [Magwitch's] return. Pip greets the convict from the top of a black staircase, and he listens as Magwitch's disembodied voice rises from the depths, from the 'darkness beneath'. Pip holds a lamp over the stair rail, but the lamp is 'shaded' and its 'circle of light' is 'very contracted'. The lamp and its circle of light embody the relationship of the two. Magwitch moves into that circle for an instant, then out – just as he had moved in and out of Pip's life. It is only when

Magwitch ascends the last two steps, foreshadowing the ascension and confrontation about to take place, that Pip finds that 'the light of my lamp included us both'. Within that circle of light Pip sees a man dressed 'like a voyager by sea', a man with 'long iron grey hair' – terms that vibrate with distant echoes of transportation and leg irons, and that subtly, almost subliminally, evoke Magwitch's past – Pip sees that iron-grey voyager holding out both hands to him (2:20, p.312). But the magic circle of light that unites Pip and Magwitch, and the out-stretched hands that give that unity human expression, are not understood by Pip. He finds his rough visitor abhorrent and rejects his offered hands. Yet the ritual bond is still at work, and the compact sealed on the marshes by looks and oaths is carried forward by other storybook signs – by a continuing ritual of hands. When Pip sees tears of gratitude and love in Magwitch's eyes, he repents his earlier rudeness, and, when Magwitch again stretches out his hand, he gives him his own.

Pip's actions reflect his confused state. He does not recognize 'his convict', much less does he recognize that he is a part of the creature. He wavers between snobbery and humanity. His desire to spurn Magwitch grows out of notions superimposed upon his true self, self-wounding notions of gentility and class-consciousness; his impulsive willingness to clasp hands with him is a reflection of his innate good-ness. In other words, Pip is as Magwitch left him: self-deluded, erring, but warm-hearted – capable of being saved. And now Magwitch helps Pip save himself. He does this by forcing Pip to confront his sources and thus his true self. Pip, the made gentleman, must see himself and his maker, Magwitch, as they really are, and he must acknowledge their mutual guilt and mutual responsibility . . . He must publicly confess his oneness with the 'loathesome' convict.

That acknowledgement does not come with the first glimmerings of recognition; Pip's initial reaction to his maker and true self is terror. When Magwitch identified himself, Pip 'shrank from him' as 'if he had been some terrible beast'. Pip is horrified by his rough counter-part; he regards Magwitch with 'abhorrence', 'repugnance', and 'dread'. But Magwitch forces the truth on Pip: '"Look'ee here, Pip"' he says, '"I'm your second father. You're my son"' (2:20, p.317). Pip nearly faints. In that state he allows Magwitch to draw the gold watch out of his pocket, turn the diamond and ruby ring on his finger, and kiss his hands – the latter gesture another incident in the secret ritual of hands. These ritualistic actions, which draw attention to Magwitch's fairy-tale gifts and fairy-tale consanguinity, are received by Pip with fairy-tale reactions. In his trancelike state, he 'recoiled' from Magwitch's touch 'as if he had been a snake', and when the con-vict kissed his hands, his 'blood ran cold' within him (2:20, pp.317, 318). Pip's terrified response to Magwitch, with its unconscious acknowledgements of shared taint and blood relationship (not yet understood by Pip), is accentuated by the continuing ceremony of hands. 'He laid his hand on my shoulder', writes the uncomprehending Pip. 'I shuddered at the thought', he goes on with ironic disassociation, 'that, for anything I knew, his hand might be stained with blood' (2:20, p. 319) ... ...

[Magwitch], [t]his unacknowledged ghost of Pip's secret self, this fairy-tale ghost, at once so fanciful and real – the selfsame ghost, terrible and fearsome, that had started up from the graves at Pip's first consciousness, that had now started up again in the noontide of his prosperity – this nightmare ghost, guilt-engendering and forever haunting, will ultimately be exorcised, but only after it has been acknowledged and embraced. The first hesitant step in that acknowledgement had occurred when Pip, candle in hand, had regarded Magwitch as 'my dreadful burden' (2:20, p. 321). That Pip was able to identify his burden, that he was able to feel that the burden was part of himself, was *his* burden, is the beginning of his (and the continuation of Magwitch's) *Beauty and the Beast* transformation. For Pip, that transformation is slow, laborious, and fablelike; it involves purgation by fire, a sojourn in hell, symbolic illness, death, and rebirth. But it also involves the completion of the compact made in the graveyard, a completion carried forward by the evolving pattern of storybook signs – by the continuing ritual of hands, among others.

That ritual is not confined to Pip and his convict. It enmeshes many other characters in a strange fairy-tale web of correspondences. And the ritual of hands is sometimes combined with other motifs, with the magically directive motif of light and fire, for example. The latter motif moves intricately and centrally through the entire novel. It involves candles, beacons, forges, hearths, sparks, flares of gas, stage fire, and sheets of cleansing flame. It also engages virtually all the characters of the book. The blazing Christmas-tree accident in the home of W. O. Bigg, Esq., has been transformed by art into a cosmic mystery of fire. [*Editor's Note*: The accident, in which Christmas-tree candles set fire to a young woman's dress, is described in the January 1850 *Household Narrative of Current Events*, Dickens's supplement to his magazine *Household Words*.[46]]

That mystery flickers and flares through scene after scene. In one crucial intersection it combines with hand imagery to provide the specific means by which Pip uncovers Estella's lineage and criminal taint, a lineage and taint that mirror his own. Through a fiery version of the occult stigmata that appear so often in legend and romance, through firelit glimpses of Estella's delicate ladylike hands, which at last recall the fierce firelit hands of her violent mother, Pip establishes Estella's identity. His yearned-for princess, dainty and exquisite, the dazzling princess who had caused him to long for a fastidious gentility far removed from Joe's awkward loyalty or Magwitch's sordid gratitude, that fair princess has a coarse criminal past even more devastating than his own. Estella's hands, soft and delicate, the epitome of refinement, incorporate the violent hands of a murderess.

After a while we grow accustomed to such directive signalling; we realize that hand imagery, to dwell for a moment longer on it, accompanies and predicts, not only Estella's parentage, but Pip's as well. Pip's painful acknowledgement of his '"second father"' (2:20, p. 317) is signalled and then confirmed by a long intricate pantomime of hands. But this masque of hands is not confined to Pip's discovery of his origins; it surrounds his every move. Slowly, secretly, bit by bit, the invisible world becomes visible. One sees its subtle signalling everywhere; one sees it clearly in the ritual of hands. The mute language of hands, ordinary and yet hermetic, comments silently on Pip's blind stumbling progress through life. Pip, after all, has been brought up by hand (as his sister never tires of reminding him), and he has also been carefully hand-fashioned over long years by Magwitch. Pip is truly the equivocal product of a profane, lifelong laying on of hands. These central metaphors and insistent repetitions ultimately combine with the intricate web of hand imagery that surrounds Pip to give his most ordinary handshakes, hand injuries, and hand gestures the symbolic force and potency of ritual. That ritual, in turn, is part of an elaborate network of hand imagery that links half the characters in *Great Expectations* in a secret freemasonry of hands. One is constantly astonished by this magical ceremony of hands, for though plain to view, it is virtually invisible; it merges with – one might almost say it loses itself in – the book's compelling realism. This method of uniting object and thesis by modulating reiterated images until the mysterious code locked in their arcane signalling reveals itself can be seen with great clarity in the Pip–Magwitch ritual of hands.

In the daily intercourse between Pip and his returned convict, that magical ritual becomes one gauge of Pip's progression. Magwitch frequently initiates the ritual, frequently goes 'through his favourite action of holding out both his hands for mine' (3:1, p. 329). But Pip has not yet come to terms with Magwitch or himself. Magwitch's offered hands only bewilder and dismay him; they remind him of his demeaning involvement with taint and imprisonment, an involvement he has largely forgotten or suppressed or rationalized away. The true implications of that involvement and of Pip's responsibility for it are suggested by the surrounding imagery, an imagery which is unobtrusive but powerfully directive. 'I released my hands as soon as I could', says Pip. And then he continues with words that recall but do not describe Magwitch's convict past, his chains and irons, and his alter-ego relationship to himself: 'What I was chained to, and how heavily, became intelligible to me, as I heard his hoarse voice, and sat looking up at his furrowed bald head with its iron grey hair at the sides' (3:1, p.329) . . . . . .

. . . Herbert's nickname for Pip . . . is Handel. Like so many of the names in *Great Expectations*, and like the shamanistic names in ancient myths and tribal legends, the name that Herbert so cavalierly bestows on Pip has strange hidden potencies that gradually reveal themselves. The name Handel ('hand-el' also means 'handle') draws attention to Pip's early history (he was brought up by hand), to his blacksmith origins (he was christened Handel because of Handel's *Harmonious Blacksmith*), to his subsequent destiny (he was manhandled by Magwitch and then turned into a handmade gentleman by him), to his searing encounter with sin (he was burned and scorched on the hands in that encounter), and to his long spell-like involvement in the crucial ritual of hands . . . . . .

By the time Magwitch stands in the prisoners' dock on trial for his life, Pip has completed his *Beauty and the Beast* transformation. This is made clear by his action when Magwitch enters the prisoners' dock. 'No objection was made to my getting close to the dock, on the outside of it, and holding the hand that he stretched forth to me' (3:17, p.452). Through this gesture, Pip publicly acknowledges his oneness with his rough counterpart . . . During and after the sentencing, Magwitch clings to Pip's freely offered hand. '[H]e held my hand while all the others were removed, and while the audience got up' (3:17, p.454).[47] □

While Stone's focus upon the fairy-tale elements of *Great Expectations* is distinctive and fertile, we can see that his account of the novel remains, in significant respects, within the mainstream of mid-twentieth-century criticism. He continues to see Pip's story in terms of an individual's progress towards a heightened state of moral, and perhaps spiritual, awareness, and he affirms the overall unity of the apparently multifarious elements that he identifies. In these respects, he is close to Q.D. Leavis, despite their differing attitudes to the fairy tale. But as has been seen earlier in this Guide, Robert Garis had already suggested in 1965 (see pp.104–108), and Peter Wolfe in 1974 (see pp.111–14), that Pip might be unfulfilled or unredeemed, and that idea will be developed, in different terms, in the 1980s, for example in the accounts of Steven Connor and Jeremy Tambling in the next chapter of this Guide (pp.130–36, 136–41).

By the end of the 1970s, the accounts of *Great Expectations* by critics such as Dorothy Van Ghent, G. Robert Stange, J. Hillis Miller, Julian Moynahan, Barbara Hardy, Robert Garis, Peter Wolfe and Harry Stone constituted a rich resource base. But although much useful work on Dickens still went on, a sense of stagnation was spreading in the UK and the USA, not only across Dickens studies, but also over literary criticism in general. In this respect, Q.D. Leavis's attempt to arrest interpretation of *Great Expectations* by prescribing how the novel *must* be read was symptomatic. Her essay sought to become the critical counterpart of Satis House, a place where enough is enough, where time has stopped and readers are doomed to endless reiteration. Critics in the 1980s would have to break into the desolate house and set the clocks a-going; but paradoxically they would do so, not by trying to reanimate the story of Pip's progress to moral freedom, but by emphasising his entrapment in systems of repetition, language, society and patriarchy. The next chapter explores this assault on established critical expectations.

CHAPTER FIVE

Upsetting Expectations: The 1980s

G*REAT EXPECTATIONS* generated a rich crop of criticism in the 1980s. Dickens studies gained a new lease of life in a decade that saw large changes in literary study in the UK and the USA. Post-structuralism and deconstruction, which had first developed in France in the 1960s, crossed the Channel and the Atlantic and sometimes sparked bitter conflict. Almost exorcised spectres, such as Marxism and psychoanalysis, returned to stalk the corridors of criticism in strange and powerful forms. Critical missiles from the USSR, especially those launched by Mikhail Bakhtin, began to strike home on American campuses. It might seem strange that all this should benefit Dickens. After all, the new-minted critics of the eighties were often aggressively anti-bourgeois; their mission was to shatter commonsense views of reality and upset conventional expectations. Wasn't Dickens, for all his flashes of rebel-lion, the epitome of all that they abhorred, the very model of a modern bourgeois novelist, a soul swathed in the chintz of convention and cushioned by cosy commonsense? Partly, no doubt; but there was another side to the picture. Dickens's work had never quite fitted com-fortably into liberal-humanist critical categories such as 'maturity' and 'organic unity'. Indeed, a significant feature of the mid-twentieth-century criticism of *Great Expectations*, which has been looked at in this Guide, has been its *difficulty* in dealing with Dickens, its sense of a 'Dickens problem' that could result in almost complete dismissal (as with Q.D. Leavis in 1932 and F.R. Leavis in 1948), in carefully qualified endorsement (as in Q.D. and F.R. Leavis in 1970), in interpretations that played down or ignored the ways in which Dickens challenged the liberal-humanist ethos (as with Barbara Hardy and, again, the Leavises), or in occasional departures that drew on perspectives outside, and possibly alien to, that ethos (as with J. Hillis Miller's use of phenomenology and existentialism, Julian Moynahan's 'swoop beneath the literal level' (see p. 100), or Robert Garis's notion of 'the Dickens theatre'). The death of liberal-humanist criticism dissolved one kind of 'Dickens problem' and freed critics from the constraints of trying to turn him into George Eliot or Henry James.

It is thus not surprising that in the 1980s new and vigorous readings of *Great Expectations* began to emerge. The first of these, in the Spring 1980 issue of the North American journal *New Literary History*, was Peter Brooks's powerful, illuminating and influential essay 'Repetition, Repression and Return: *Great Expectations* and the Study of Plot'. Brooks begins by arguing that the concept of plot has been largely ignored in modern criticism because it seems 'to belong to the popular, even the commercial side of literature'. '"Reading for the plot"' is regarded as 'a low form of activity'. Brooks acknowledges that recent French narratology, following on from and developing Russian Formalism, has drawn attention to the way in which action, sequence, transformation, and narrative codes function, but he contends that the notion of plot suggests a more specific focus: plot is less 'a structure than . . . a structuring operation, used, or made necessary, by those meanings that develop only through sequence and succession'. A plot 'is not only the outline of a narrative, demarcating its boundaries, it also suggests its intention of meaning, the direction of its scheme or machination for accomplishing a purpose. Plots have not only design, but intentionality as well'.[1]

Moreover, Brooks suggests that plot is not merely a literary device but ultimately, perhaps, a human need, which he explains partly in terms of Sartrean existentialism but primarily in terms of Freudian psychoanalysis. For Jean-Paul Sartre, telling a story functions to shape and partly conceal the meaninglessness of experience, giving necessity to contingency;[2] similarly, Brooks argues that we seek a sense of plot in order to give significance to the flux of passing time and to make it possible to tell stories about our own lives. Brooks's major point of reference, however, is not Sartre, but Freud; and while Robert Garis, as was seen in the previous chapter of this Guide, took Freud's *Civilization and its Discontents* as the key to what he saw as the real meaning of *Great Expectations* (see pp.105, 106–108), Brooks turns to Freud's *Beyond the Pleasure Principle* to analyse the novel's plot.

In *Beyond the Pleasure Principle*, Freud postulates that the death drive – the desire to return eventually to a state of inorganic quiescence – is, in the last analysis, more powerful than the libidinal drive for gratification, the pleasure principle. The conflict of these two drives creates a self-regulating system, where, as Brooks paraphrases it, 'the organism lives in order to die, but to die its proper death, which means that it follows a detour and a vacillating rhythm, with new beginnings in resistance to the impending end, in its movement to the end'. Brooks likens this to the way in which 'narrative both seeks and delays its end'.[3] In *Beyond the Pleasure Principle*, Freud also explores the notion of what he calls the 'compulsion to repeat', which – whether in children's games, in literature, or in dreams – constitutes, in Brooks's words, 'an effort to "bind" mobile energy, to master the flood of stimuli that have breached the shield of the psychic apparatus at the moment of trauma'. This 'binding' produces a state of quiescence that makes it possible for the pleasure principle to operate and to produce an 'orderly and efficient discharge' of energy.[4] Thus repetition, in a sense, replicates the overall workings of the death and life drives in the organism. It works to produce a quiescence that can only be achieved fully and permanently in death; but in achieving that quiescence in a temporary and provisional way it makes it possible for the pleasure principle to function. Brooks contends that Freud's concept of repetition 'seems fully pertinent' to a discussion of plot, because 'repetition of all sorts is the very stuff of literary meanings'.[5]

Great Expectations is a text much concerned with repetition and return (Pip's returns to Satis House and the forge, the return of Magwitch). It is a text, Brooks affirms, 'that gives in the highest degree the sense of plottedness and the impression that its central meanings depend on the working-out of the plot . . . The novel will indeed be concerned with finding a plot and losing it, with the precipitation of the sense of plottedness around its hero, and his eventual "cure" from plot. The novel images in its structure the kind of structuring operation that plot is'.[6] The extract below joins his analysis as he considers the start of the novel, and then moves on to identify its plotlines: this text is from the revised version of the essay in Brooks's *Reading for the Plot: Design and Intention in Narrative* (1984):

■ *Great Expectations* is exemplary for a discourse on plot in many respects, not least of all for its beginning. For what the novel chooses to present at its outset is precisely the search for a beginning. As in so many nineteenth-century novels, the hero is an orphan, thus undetermined by any visible inheritance, apparently unauthored . . . There may be sociological and sentimental reasons to account for the high incidence of orphans in the nineteenth-century novel, but clearly the parentless protagonist frees an author from struggle with preexisting authorities, allowing him to create afresh all the determinants of plot within his text. He thus profits from what Gide called the 'lawlessness' of the novel[7] by starting with an undefined, rule-free character and then bringing the law to bear upon him – creating the rules – as the text proceeds. With Pip, Dickens begins as it were with a life that is for the moment precedent to plot, and indeed necessarily in search of plot. Pip when we first see him is himself in search of the 'authority' – the word stands in the second paragraph of the novel (1:1, p.3) – that would define and justify – authorize – the plot of his ensuing life . . . .

Schematically, we can identify four lines of plot that begin to crystallize around the young Pip, the Pip of Part I, before the arrival of his 'Expectations':

(1) Communion with the convict/criminal deviance.
(2) Naterally wicious/bringing up by hand.
(3) The dream of Satis House/the fairy tale.
(4) The nightmare of Satis House/the witch tale.

These plots . . . are paired as follows: 2/1 = 3/4. That is, there is in each case an 'official' and censoring plot standing over a 'repressed' plot. In terms of Pip's own choices, we could rewrite the formula: 3/4/2/1, to show (in accordance with one of Freud's favourite models) the archaeological layering of strata of repressed material.[8] When the Expectations are announced by Jaggers at the end of Part I, they will apparently coincide with Pip's choices ('My dream was out; my wild fancy was surpassed by sober reality' (1:18, p.137)), and will thus appear to take care of the question of plot. But this will be so only on the level of official plots; the Expectations will in fact only mask further the problem of the repressed plots . . . . . . We have, then, a quadripartite scheme of plots, organized into two pairs, each with an 'official' plot, or interpretation of plot, standing over a repressed plot . . . . . .

Taking our terminology from the scene where Pip is bound as apprentice, we may consider that education and repression operate in the novel as one form of 'binding': official ways of channelling and tying up the mobile energies of life. It is notable that after he has become apprenticed to Joe, Pip goes through a stage of purely iterative existence – presented in Chapter 14 – where the direction and movement of plot appear to be finished, where all life's 'interest and romance' appear shut out as by a 'thick curtain' (1:14, p.107), time reduced to repetitive duration. Conversely, when the Expectations have arrived, Miss Havisham is apparently identified as the fairy-tale donor, and the Satis House plot appears securely bound, Pip need only wait for the next stage of the plot to become manifest. Yet it is clear that for the reader, neither binding as an apprentice (the first accomplishment of an upbringing by hand) nor the tying up of Satis House as a fairy-tale plot constitutes valid and adequate means of dealing with and disposing of the communion with the convict and the nightmare of Satis House. The energy released in the text by its liminary [introductory, preparatory] 'primal scene' – in the graveyard – and by the early visits to Satis House, creating that 'smart without a name' (1:8, p.63), simply is not and cannot be bound by the bindings of the official, repressive plots. As readers we know that there has been created in the text an intensive level of energy that cannot be discharged through these official plots.

In fact, the text has been working simultaneously to bind these disavowed energies in other ways, ways over which Pip's ego, and the societal superego, have no control, and of which they have no knowledge, through repetitions that, for the reader, prepare an inevitable return of the repressed. Most striking are the periodic fragmentary returns of the convict-communion material: the leg iron used to bludgeon Mrs. Joe, guns firing from the hulks to signal further escapes, and especially the reappearance of Joe's file, the dramatic stage property used by Magwitch's emissary in a 'proceeding in dumb-show . . . pointedly addressed to me'. His stirring and tasting his rum and water 'pointedly . . . to' Pip suggests the establishment of an aim (Pip calls his proceeding 'a shot' (1:10. p.78)), a direction, an intention in Pip's life: the first covert announcement of another plot which will come to govern Pip's life, but of course misinterpreted as to its true aim. With the nightmare energies of Satis House, binding is at work in those repetitive journeys [in which Pip pushes Miss Havisham in her wheelchair] around the rotting bride cake, suggestive of the reproduction or working through of the traumatic neurotic whose affects remain fixed on the past, on the traumatic moment that never can be mastered. For Miss Havisham herself, these energies can never be plotted to effective discharge; and we will have occasion to doubt whether they are ever fully bound for Pip as well. The compulsive reproductive repetition that characterizes every detail of Satis House lets us perceive how the returns of the convict-communion suggest a more significant working through of an unmastered past, a repetition that can alter the form of the repeated. In both instances – but ultimately with different results – the progressive, educative plots, the plots of repression and advancement, are threatened by a repetitive process obscurely going on underneath and beyond them. We sense that forward progress will have to recover markings from the beginning, through a dialectic of return . . . .

The novelistic middle, which is perhaps the most difficult of Aristotle's 'parts' of a plot to talk about, is in this case notably characterized by the return.[9] Quite literally: it is Pip's repeated returns from London to his home town that constitute the organizing device of the whole of the London period, the time of the Expectations and their aftermath. Pip's returns are always ostensibly undertaken to make reparation to the neglected Joe, an intention never realized; and always implicitly an attempt to discover the intentions of the putative donor in Satis House, to bring her plot to completion. Yet the returns also always bring his regression, in Satis House, to the status of the 'coarse and common boy' (2:10, p.235) whose social ascension is hallucinatorily denied, his return to the nightmare of unprogressive repetition; and, too, a revival of the repressed convict association, the return of the childhood spell. Each return suggests that Pip's official plots, which seem to speak of progress, ascent, and the satisfaction of desire, are in fact subject to a process of repetition of the yet unmastered past, the true determinant of his life's direction . . . . . .

. . . [In] the novel's great 'recognition scene', the moment at which the latent becomes manifest, the repressed convict plot is forcibly brought to consciousness . . . [The] scene . . . decisively reenacts both a return of the repressed and a return to the primal moment of child-hood. The recognition comes in Chapter 39 (2:20), and it is preceded by two curious paragraphs at the end of Chapter 38 (2:19) in which Pip as narrator suggests that the pages he has just written, concerning his frustrated courtship of Estella, constitute, on the plane of narration itself, a last binding of that plot in its overt version, as a plot of romance, and that now he must move on to a deeper level of plot – reaching further back – which subsumes as it subverts all the other plots of the novel: 'all the work, near and afar, that tended to the end had been accomplished' (2:20, p.310). That this long-range plot is presented as analogous to 'the Eastern story' in which a heavy slab of stone is carved out and fitted into the roof in order that it may fall on 'the bed of state in the flush of conquest' (2:19, p.309) seems in coded fashion to suggest punishment for erotic transgression, which we may want to read as return of the nightmare plot of Satis House, forcing its way through the fairy tale, speaking of the perverse, sadistic eroticism that Pip has covered over with his erotic object choice – Estella, who in fact represents the wrong choice of plot and another danger of short-circuit. To anticipate later revelations, we should note that Estella will turn out to be approximately Pip's sister – natural daughter of Magwitch as he is Magwitch's adoptive son – which lends force to the idea that she, like so many Romantic maidens, is marked by the inter-dict, as well as the seduction, of incest, which, as the perfect androgynous coupling, is precisely the short-circuit of desire.[10]

The scene of Magwitch's return operates for Pip as a painful forcing through of layers of repression, an analogue of analytic work, com-pelling Pip to recognize that what he calls '"that chance intercourse . . . of long ago"' (2:20, p.314) is no chance and cannot be assigned to the buried past, but must be repeated, reenacted, worked through in the present. The scene replays numerous details of their earlier encounter, and the central moment of recognition comes as a reenactment and revival of the novel's primal scene, played in dumb show, a mute text which the more effectively stages recognition as a process of return to the inescapable past:

> Even yet, I could not recall a single feature, but I knew him! If the wind and the rain had driven away the intervening years, had scattered all the intervening objects, had swept us to the church-yard where we first stood face to face on such different levels, I

could not have known my convict more distinctly than I knew him now, as he sat in the chair before the fire. No need to take a file from his pocket and show it to me; no need to take the hand-kerchief from his neck and twist it round his head; no need to hug himself with both his arms, and take a shivering turn across the room, looking back at me for recognition. I knew him before he gave me one of those aids, though, a moment before, I had not been conscious of remotely suspecting his identity. (2:20, p. 313)

The praeterition [omission, disregard] on which the passage is con-structed – 'no need . . . no need' – marks the gradual retrieval of the past as its involuntary repetition within the present. The repetition takes place – as Magwitch's effective use of indicative signs may sug-gest – in the mode of the symbolic, offering a persuasive instance of Freud's conception of repetition as a form of recollection brought into action by repression and resistance to its removal.[11] It becomes clear that the necessity for Pip to repeat and work through everything asso-ciated with his original communion with Magwitch is a factor of his 'forgetting' this communion: a forgetting that is merely conscious. The reader has undergone a similar process through textual repetition and return, one that in his case has had the function of not permitting him to forget.

The scene of Magwitch's return is an important one for any study of plot since it demonstrates so well how such a novelist as Dickens can make plotting the central vehicle and armature [framework and/or motor] of meaning in the narrative text. All the issues raised in the novel – social, ethical, interpretive – are here simultaneously brought to climax through the peripety of the plot [*Editor's Note:* 'peripety', meaning 'sudden change, reversal', is another form of the term 'perepeteia', used by Q.D. Leavis in the previous chapter of this Guide (see p. 110).]. Exposure of the 'true' plot of Pip's life brings with it instantaneous consequences for all the other 'codes' of the novel, as he recognizes with the statement, 'All the truth of my position came *flash-ing* on me; and its disappointments, dangers, disgraces, consequences of all kinds' (2:20, p. 316 [Brooks's italics]). The return of the repressed – the repressed as knowledge of the self's other story, the true history of its misapprehended desire – forces a total revision of the subject's relation to the orders within which it constitutes meaning.

Magwitch poses unanswerable questions about the origins of Pip's property and the means of his social ascent, which force home to Pip that he has covered over a radical lack of original authority. Like Oedipus – who cannot answer Tiresias's final challenge: who are your parents? – Pip does not know where he stands. The result has been the intrusion of an aberrant, contingent authorship – Magwitch's – in the story of the self. That it should be the criminally deviant, transgressive plot that is shown to have priority over all the others stands within the logic of the model derived from *Beyond the Pleasure Principle*, since it is precisely this plot that most markedly constitutes the detour from inorganic quiescence: the arabesque of the narratable. One could almost derive a narratological law here: the true plot will be the most deviant. We might be tempted to see this deviant arabesque as gratuitous, the figure of pure narration. Yet we are obliged to remotivate it, for the return of the repressed shows that the story Pip would tell about himself has all along been undermined and rewritten by the more complex history of unconscious desire, unavailable to the conscious subject but at work in the text. Pip has in fact misread the plot of his life . . . .

. . . Whereas the model of the *Bildungsroman* [German for 'formation-novel' or 'education-novel', a kind of novel which shows its central character's development from childhood or youth to adulthood] seems to imply progress, a leading forth and developmental change, Pip's story – and this may be true of other nineteenth-century educative plots as well – becomes more and more as it nears its end the working through of past history, an attempted return to the origin as the motivation of all the rest, the clue to what must else appear, as Pip puts it to Miss Havisham, a '"blind and thankless"' life (3:10, p.395). The past needs to be incorporated *as past* within the present, mastered through the play of repetition in order for there to be an escape from repetition: in order for there to be difference, change, progress. In the failure ever to recover his own origin, Pip comes to concern himself with the question of Estella's origin, searching for her patronymics [the name(s) of her father or ancestor] where knowledge of his own is ever foreclosed. Estella's story in fact eventually links all the plots of the novel: Satis House, the aspiration to gentility, the convict identity, '"[n]aterally wicious"' (1:4, p.26) (the status from which Jaggers rescued her), bringing up by hand, the law. Pip's investigation of her origins as substitute for knowledge of his own has a certain validity in that, we discover, he appeared originally to Magwitch as a substitute for the lost Estella, his great expectations a compensation for the impossibility of hers: a chiasmus [reversal] of the true situation. Yet when Pip has proved himself to be the successful detective in this quest, when he has uncovered the convergence of lines of plot that previously appeared distinct and indeed proved himself more penetrating even than Jaggers, he discovers the knowledge he has gained to be radically unusable. When he has imparted his knowledge to Jaggers and Wemmick, he reaches a kind of standoff, between what he has called his 'poor dreams' (3:12, p.408) and the deep plot he has now exposed. As Jaggers puts it to him, there is no gain to be had from knowledge. We are in the heart of darkness, and the articulation of its meaning must simply be repressed. In this novel full of mysteries and hidden connections, detective work turns out to be both necessary and useless. It can offer no comfort and no true illumination to the detective himself. Like deciphering the letters on the tombstone, it produces no authority for the plot of life.

The novel in fact towards its end records a generalized breakdown of plots: none of the schemes machinated by the characters appears to accomplish its aims. The proof *a contrario* may be the 'oversuccessful' result of Miss Havisham's plot, which has turned Estella into so heart-less a creature that she cannot even experience emotional recognition of her benefactress. Miss Havisham's plotting has been a mechanical success but an intentional failure . . . . . .

We confront the paradox that in this most highly plotted of novels, where Dickens performs all his thematic demonstrations through the manipulation of plot, we witness an evident subversion and futiliza-tion of the very concept of plot. If the chosen plots turn out to be erroneous, unauthorized, self-delusive, the deep plots when brought to light turn out to be criminally tainted, deviant, and thus unusable. Plot as direction and intention in existence appears ultimately to be as evanescent as Magwitch's money, the product of immense labour, deprivation, and planning, which is in the end forfeit to the Crown. Like money in its role as universal modern (capitalist) signifier as described by Roland Barthes in *S/Z* (1970), tied to no referent (such as land), defined only by its exchange value, capable of unlimited metonymic circulation, the expectations of fortune, as both plot and its aim or intention, as vehicle and object of representation, circulate through inflation to devaluation[12] . . . . . .

As at the start of the novel we had the impression of a life not yet subject to plot – a life in search of the sense of plot that would only gradually begin to precipitate around it – so at the end we have the impression of a life that has outlived plot, renounced plot, been cured of it: life that is left over. What follows the recognition of Magwitch is left over, and any renewal of expectation and plotting – such as a revived romance with Estella – would have to belong to another story. It is with the image of a life bereft of plot, of movement and desire, that the novel most appropriately leaves us. Indeed, we have at the end what could appropriately be called a 'cure' from plot, in Pip's recognition of the general forfeiture of plotting, his renunciation of any attempt to direct his life.[13] □

Brooks's essay was an impressive demonstration of how a revived psychoanalysis, an interest in the apparently debased, 'popular' matter of plot, and a new narratological awareness, which itself drew partly on older rhetorical and formalist modes of analysis, could combine to produce a fresh and persuasive reading of *Great Expectations*. It showed the potential of approaches to criticism that broke away from the liberal-humanist and symbolist modes that had continued to dominate in the UK and the USA for much of the 1970s. The study that brought such approaches most fully to bear on Dickens in the 1980s appeared halfway through the decade: Steven Connor's *Charles Dickens* (1985). In his assault upon established Dickens studies, Connor marshals a formidable array of weapons. *The Pickwick Papers* and *Dombey and Son* are subjected to a structuralist reading, *Bleak House* and *Hard Times* undergo a post-structuralist or deconstructive analysis, and 'a blend of Marxist and psychoanalytic approaches' is applied to *Great Expectations* and *Our Mutual Friend*.[14] The results are provocative and illuminating.

In his account of *Great Expectations*, Connor draws upon the distinction between the 'Imaginary' and the 'Symbolic' orders proposed by the French psychoanalyst Jacques Lacan, whose complex writings were a major influence upon post-structuralist literary criticism. The 'Imaginary' order is that which the child enters through what Lacan calls 'the mirror stage' – the stage in which the child narcissistically identifies itself with its own image (as seen in a mirror, for example) and, in an attempt to capture that image, 'misrecognises' itself as an imaginary unity. In the Imaginary order, the child, as Connor puts it, 'repeats its narcissistic identification with its image in its relationship with things and people in the world'. In this process, it 'imaginatively envelop[s] pleasurable things and aggressively repuls[es] anything causing pain or displeasure'. Thus the Imaginary order involves 'a tendency to form strict binary oppositions'[15] (good/bad, black/white etc.). But two parallel developments then complicate this binary world. One is the passage through the Oedipus complex, in which, for the male child, the intervention of the father constitutes a third term, prohibiting the possession of the mother, but offering the compensation that the child 'may one day symbolically occupy the place of his father in the system of authority and family relationships'.[16] The other complicating development is the acquisition of language, a process that enforces the acceptance of the arbitrariness of language, the lack of any 'fixed and necessary bond between words and things'. It is through these two developments that the child enters the Symbolic order. Entry into the Symbolic order makes social life possible but it also entails, in Connor's words, 'the repression of unsociable desires and the cutting off of the jubilant unity of the Imaginary order with the acceptance of deferred gratification of various kinds. From now on the self is something diffused in the systems of language, condemned always to know and speak of itself as a sign which can only be itself because of its differences from other signs'.[17] Connor argues that 'Lacan's distinction between the Imaginary and Symbolic and his account of the passage from one to the other' can offer 'a new and profitable' perspective on the 'prime theme' of *Great Expectations*, which it shares with 'all *Bildungs-roman*[e] or novels of education'. This theme 'is the attempt to find some integration of an individual self into social life'.[18] The extract below begins as Connor starts to apply Lacan's notions to this theme:

■ . . . Pip systematically but wrongly recognizes his relationship to social life in a way that suggests a fixation upon Imaginary relationships. Throughout most of the narrative Pip mistakes 'otherness' for himself, remoulding people and events in order to have them conform to his private fantasy. This egotism involves the continual rejection of all antipathetic elements. So, in order to become a gentleman, Pip must always repress the memory of the association with Magwitch. He also rejects others, of course, including his bogus benefactor Pumblechook and the frightening Orlick, not to mention Joe and Biddy and the life of the forge. Pip therefore achieves totality and unity of self only at the cost of excluding fundamental parts of himself.

And so *Great Expectations* displays progressively Pip's alienation from himself. The two revelations of the book, that Magwitch is the real provider of his fortunes and that Miss Havisham only wishes to have Estella break his heart, are revelations of Pip's marginality in his own life. He therefore finds himself separated even from his own desires. He believes in each case that he has an Imaginary relationship with the object of desire, that, in other words, the two associated objects of his desire, Estella and gentility, exist outside himself, that his desire comes from himself and that by his own exertions he may hope or expect one day to attain or be united to those objects. Pip is forced to recognize that not only are the objects of his desire unattainable, but also that his desires are not even really his own. Rather, he is acting out the desires of others, or their desires are acting through him. It is Magwitch's desire that Pip should become a gentleman, and Miss Havisham's desire that he should love and be abandoned by Estella. Pip is in fact in a Symbolic relationship to the objects of his desire, because of the 'desire of the Other'[19] which is deflected through him. This creates a structure of displacement which . . . depends not on individual subjects but on patterns of interpersonal relationships.

Indeed, neither Magwitch nor Miss Havisham are the originators of their own desires any more than Pip is of his own. Magwitch's desire is the adoption of a generalized social ambition which it would make no sense for him to fulfil in person; his vengeful project requires him to see his wealth and legitimacy conferred on a surrogate at a distance from him. Similarly, Miss Havisham's desire is a deflected one which comes from 'somewhere else'; she desires to see inflicted on another man the pain which she has suffered, but this is in itself an identification with Arthur [her half-brother] and a reenactment of his desire to hurt and swindle her. Once caught in these trajectories of desire, Pip finds himself unconsciously repeating them – most strikingly in the fact that he starts to provide secretly for Herbert in a way very similar to Magwitch's anonymous provision for him.

Given these patterns of interpersonal transference, it is perhaps unlikely that *Great Expectations* is going to be able to offer anything very substantial in the way of a reconciliation of the individual and society. Even as he becomes aware of his narcissistic illusions, Pip recoils from the apprehension of the loss or envelopment of the self in systems of signs; during his illness he encounters images of the decentred self which . . . are terrifying in their implications:

> I confounded impossible existences with my own identity . . . I was a brick in the house-wall, and yet entreating to be released from the giddy place where the builders had set me . . . I was a steel beam of a vast engine, clashing and whirling over a gulf, and yet . . . I implored in my own person to have the engine stopped, and my part of it hammered off. (3:18, p. 458)

When Pip lies uneasily in his bed at the Hummums, thinking of the injunction 'Don't go home', which he has received, it is the system of language which suggests itself as a metaphor for the decentring of the self by shifting and unmotivated signs:

> When at last I dozed, in sheer exhaustion of mind and body, it became a vast shadowy verb which I had to conjugate. Imperative mood, present tense: Do not thou go home, let him not go home, let us not go home, do not ye or you go home, let not them go home. Then, potentially: I may not and I cannot go home; and I might not, could not, would not, and should not go home; until I felt that I was going distracted, and rolled over on the pillow, and looked at the staring rounds upon the wall again. (3:6, p. 365–66)

In fact Pip's alienation from himself is brought about because of a number of different sorts of sign systems which, though separate, interweave in various complex ways. Among these are the systems of language and of family relationships, but the most important of them is the system of money.

Money in *Great Expectations*, as in many of Dickens's novels, is the principal system whereby relations between the individual self and society are established. In Dickens's work . . . money is very often conceived and presented as a sort of language; and this equation is not too surprising. Money, like language, is a system of signification in which the meaning (value) of individual units (words or items of currency) can exist only by virtue of the whole economic system which lies behind them. For the *parole* [speech] of every transaction, we can say, there must be the *langue* [language system] of a general economy.

Although, like language, it is strictly speaking part of the Symbolic order, money can be apprehended in Imaginary and Symbolic ways. The bond between Magwitch and Pip is at first an Imaginary one, immediate and direct, cutting out all relationships of a more indirect social kind. Magwitch acknowledges this in his 'return' to Pip of the two one-pound notes, and Pip himself recognizes the reciprocal bond which this establishes; it can be seen as a financial recognition of the mirror stage in that it combines recognition with possessive hostility. Pip sees the 'two fat sweltering one-pound notes that seemed to have been on terms of the warmest intimacy with all the cattle markets in the county' (1:10, p. 79), not as abstract signs, but as belonging to Magwitch and full of his unpleasant, bestial 'presence' (even though, of course, it is Magwitch's surrogate who has brought them). What is more frightening for Pip is the fact that they are not spent but left in a tea pot to torment him, and this represents very nicely the Imaginary removal of signs from movement and exchange.

The Imaginary fixation on the nature and origins of money continues throughout *Great Expectations*. Pip, assuming, of course, that his money is coming from Miss Havisham, comes to believe that he deserves it, that it is, in a sense, already his; Magwitch spends his money in order to purchase and possess the image of a gentleman in an act of Imaginary aggression towards Pip.

Of course, there is no immediate relationship between Pip and Magwitch, any more than there is between any two people. Magwitch is forced to make his purchase through Jaggers and Wemmick (they themselves standing for the larger abstraction of the Law). Right up to the end, Magwitch seems to remain unaware of the fact that his money is not innocent, and not even his own in one sense; though he carries it round in his pocket-book and takes care to hand it over to Pip, this act of physical exchange can be and is negated by the structure of law which intervenes between them (and actually gives the money value in the first place). At the end of the narrative the money passes out of Pip's hands and into the possession of the Crown.

By the end of the novel Pip begins to have some apprehension of the alienation of the self from itself that social life involves. Wemmick, for all the benign comedy attaching to him, is a prime example of this alienation, with his oscillation between his official and unofficial existences, and it is he who reminds Pip, as his official self, of the splitting that money itself brings, remarking that, where Magwitch could not conceivably have been saved, the money could have –

'"That's the difference between the property and the owner, don't you see?"' (3:16, p.448). After having for so long identified money with its apparent owner . . . (the one-pound notes perhaps with Magwitch)[,] Pip himself seems to be coming to recognize this distinction. It has consequences for the conception of the self. Earlier on, Pip has expressed the absence within himself by a financial metaphor, that of swindling:

> All other swindlers upon earth are nothing to the self-swindlers, and with such pretences did I cheat myself. Surely a curious thing. That I should innocently take a bad half-crown of somebody else's manufacture, is reasonable enough; but that I should knowingly reckon the spurious coin of my own make, as good money! An obliging stranger, under pretence of compactly folding up my bank-notes for security's sake, abstracts the notes and gives me nutshells; but what is his sleight of hand to mine, when I fold up my own nutshells and pass them on myself as notes! (2:9, pp.225–26)

For the self conceived of as an Imaginary unity, this sort of self-swindling is indeed absurd. But if the self is taken to be dispersed and decentred by the structures of knowledge and repression then this self-swindling begins to look more reasonable and maybe, in the sort of society in which Pip is growing, even necessary. In fact, the metaphor seems to go beyond its particular purpose here, because it associates Pip with Magwitch, who tells him that his last criminal charge was that of '"putting stolen notes in circulation"' (3:3, p.348), along with Compeyson, whose business is '"swindling, handwriting forging, stolen bank-note passing, and such-like"' (3:3, p.346). In fact, criminality has from early on been associated specifically with swindling, for Pip is told by Mrs. Joe that '"People are put in the Hulks because they murder, and because they rob, and forge, and do all sorts of bad"' (2:2, p.15). Here, it is the crucial word 'forge' which reestablishes the unconscious link between Pip and Magwitch and between legitimacy and criminality. Pip rejects the secure and comfortable world of the 'forge' for a 'forged' narrative which he passes on to himself, as he acts out the desire of the Other in the chain of associations 'forged' through the narrative. (This uncomfortable association between the honest world of the blacksmith and falsity is perhaps also to be seen in the claim that Pumblechook makes to be the '"founder"' of Pip's fortunes (3:19, p.471).) The running together of respectability and criminality goes against the way that they are officially represented in *Great Expectations*, of course, and it's striking that the identification is made in a pun, as though the unconscious of the text were speaking here. Nevertheless, the world of the criminal and of the respectable citizen are part of the same thing, in that both are encompassed by a system in which real relationships are hidden or deferred. Wemmick and Jaggers operate a system of bullying exploitation which is really just as reprehensible as the swindling of Magwitch, but the 'Imaginary' binary opposition of the Law and the criminal prevents that association from being articulated.

Pip, then, reaches an impasse at the end of the novel. The world of the forge must be seen as inadequate because it is an instance of the Imaginary. But having once entered the Symbolic order a kind of uncertainty hovers over everything for Pip. The economic world in which Pip eventually finds respectability is of course a capitalist one, even though it is the indirect and differentiated human relationships typical of capitalism which *Great Expectations* has been concerned to explore and officially to reject. The capitalist world is a world of fluctuating value and unattached signifiers, a world in which authenticity, unity and honesty are systematically made impossible. This world is suggested by Herbert's feckless fantasies of being an insurer of ships (2:3, pp. 181–82), but is also present in Magwitch's investment in Pip and Pip's own investment in Herbert.

So the book seems to offer only two possible models for life in society. The first involves retreat into narcissistic domesticity, in which the individual forgets or misrecognizes the complexity of the relationships which constitute his being; however attractive they may be, the worlds of the forge and of Wemmick's castle represent this kind of untenable illusion. The second is the acceptance of the inevitability of the split self, and of the fact that the self cannot exist at all without this split. But *Great Expectations* seems unable to generate any options other than the consolations of narcissism or the surrender to alienation.

Pip attempts to accommodate himself to this by a compromise. He does not withdraw from social and economic relations altogether, but nor does he seek to exploit them. As a modestly successful partner in Clarriker and Co., he can occupy an optimal position between being a financial victim and a financial aggressor. But this compromise is an uneasy one, and the inability to imagine any other resolution of the individual and the systematic views of life reflects the historical limitations of *Great Expectations*.[20] □

Connor's reading draws heavily on Lacan but returns implicitly to Marx at the end. Lacan's model of the male child's passage from the Imaginary to the Symbolic and of the alienation that it necessarily entails is, in effect, a universal one: the implication is that it always happens like this. But Connor seems to want to retain a Marxist sense of historical specificity and possibility: that is, while he accepts that some degree of alienation is inevitable in the passage to social identity, he implies that there are degrees of alienation that vary in differing historical circumstances, and that it may be possible to imagine or construct a historical situation in which the gap between 'individual' and 'system' can be narrowed.

The relationship between system and self was a concern of another influential French post-structuralist thinker, Michel Foucault, and some of his ideas were to be applied to *Great Expectations* in an essay by Jeremy Tambling, 'Prison-Bound: Dickens and Foucault', which first appeared in *Essays in Criticism* in January 1986 and later became, in expanded form, the first chapter of his book *Dickens, Violence and the Modern State: Dreams of the Scaffold* (1995).[21] Like Lacan, Foucault rejected the notion of an individual self that is prior to and independent of social construction; but he saw the self not as emerging through a passage from the Imaginary to the Symbolic but as constructed through discourse. In other words, selves are created through the differing ways of talking and writing about selves that are active in different historical circumstances. These ways of talking and writing produce knowledges, which purport to explain what people are like and, for instance, why they behave as they do, and these knowledges are modes of power: they offer ways of keeping people in order, or ways in which people keep themselves in order – as in the religious practice of confession, which offers a knowledge of the soul and of sin, and a means of self-discipline. Given this knowledge/power function, these discourses are often embodied in institutions, such as the church, the prison, the mental hospital, or the army.

Foucault's book *Surveiller et Punir* (1975) (*Discipline and Punish* (1976)) explores what its subtitle calls 'the birth of the prison' in western society. Towards the end of the eighteenth century, forms of discourse develop – penal codes, for example – that construct a notion of the 'criminal' as a psychological type, or a set of psychological types, and the prison develops as a way of disciplining and controlling these psychological types. It does so at the same time as other 'disciplinary technologies' like that of the school and the factory. In this perspective, school, prison and factory are all ways of controlling a potentially unruly population at a time of massive social change, not primarily by coercion (although the element of physical force and constraint is clearly present) but by aiming to construct them as docile subjects. Foucault's most notable image of this disciplinary technology in *Discipline and Punish* is drawn from the British Utilitarian thinker Jeremy Bentham (1748–1832), who outlined the idea of what he called a Panopticon: a prison built so that all the prisoners' cells, on several storeys, would be observable from a central tower into which the prisoners would not themselves be able to see. Thus the prisoners would always, potentially, be under surveillance, but would never know at any given moment whether they were or not. No Panopticon was ever actually built, but it could be seen to constitute an ideal model for institutions such as the prison, the factory and the school.

Prison, factory and school were all institutions with which Dickens was concerned at one time or another, and if school and factory dominate *Hard Times*, it is the prison that is a potent presence in *Great Expectations*. To read *Great Expectations* in the light of Foucault is, Tambling contends, to discover how far a nineteenth-century text anticipates Foucault's ideas about power/knowledge, about the construction of selves in discourse for disciplinary purposes. The extract below, taken from the revised version of the essay in Tambling's book, begins as he focuses on the issue of the 'creation of identities':

■ *Great Expectations* is certainly about the creation of identities, imposed from higher to lower, from oppressor to oppressed. From the first page there is the 'first most vivid and broad impression of the identity of things', where a considerable amount of naming goes on – 'I called myself Pip and came to be called Pip'; where the seven-year old child names 'this bleak place overgrown with nettles' as 'the churchyard' (1:1, p.3); and similarly characterizes the marshes, the river, the sea, and himself as 'that . . . small bundle of shivers growing afraid of it all and beginning to cry' who 'was Pip' (1:1, p.4) . . . The self is misnamed from the beginning, minimized; and gross acts of naming take place thenceforth, from Mrs. Hubble's belief that the young are never grateful, not to say '"[n]aterally wicious"' (1:4, p.26) to Jaggers saying that boys are '"a bad set of fellows"' (1:11, p.83). Wopsle and company identify an accused with the criminal (1:18, pp.132–34), Pip sees himself as George Barnwell and receives a number of descriptions and names – Pip, Handel, '"the prowling boy"' (2:3, p.174), '"[y]ou young dog"' (1:1, p.5), '"my boy"' (1:3, p.19); '"you boy"' (1:8, p.63), '"you visionary boy"' (3:5, p.362). Anonymity, though not the absence of naming, hangs over Mrs. Joe (defined through the husband), Orlick, whose name Dolge is 'a clear impossibility' (1:15, p.111), Magwitch – Provis at all times to Jaggers, Trabb's boy, Drummle – the Spider, the Aged P. and Mr. Waldengarver. The power of naming confers identity: Q.D. Leavis's analysis sees the power as one that implants guilt[22] [see pp.109–11]. That guilt-fixing belongs to Foucault's Panopticon society, and indeed the sense of being looked at is pervasive [in *Great Expectations*]. Pip expects a constable to be waiting for him on his return from taking food to the convict, has the sensation of being watched by relatives at Satis House, has his house watched on the night of Magwitch's return, has Compeyson sit behind him in the theatre (where he himself is watching), and is watched by the coastguard and the river police in the attempt to take off Magwitch (none of the friendship here with the police implied in the 1853 article 'Down with the Tide':[23] the Dickensian hero is shown here as in flight from the agents of law). Where such spying is an integral part of the book, the sense of being someone constituted as having a secret to hide is not far away. Pip feels himself a criminal early and late, and Orlick tells him he is: '"[i]t was you as did for your shrew sister"' (3:14, p. 423) – this coming from the man who has tracked Pip constantly, and shadowed Biddy. Reflecting the first chapter's growth of self-awareness – where the child is crying over his parents' grave, as though not just feeling himself inadequate, but as already guilty, already needing to make some form of reparation – Magwitch says that he '"first become aware of [him]self, down in Essex, a thieving turnips for [his] living"' (3:3, p.344). Jaggers identifies Drummle as criminal – '"the true sort"' – and encourages him in his boorishness and readiness to brain Startop. His method of cross-examination is to criminalize everyone, himself resisting classification, no language being appropriate for one as '"[d]eep"' (2:5, p. 199) as he. '"You know what I am, don't you?"' is the last comment he makes after the dinner party where he has hinted that Molly (whom he owns) is a criminal type (2:7, p. 217). The question is to be answered negatively, for he is like the unseen watcher in the central tower of the Panopticon, naming others, but not named himself. (His centrality is implied in the address of his office [Little Britain] while that he leaves his doors unlocked when he leaves his house makes him like the Panopticon warder who may or may not be on duty: no one can be sure.) He is in the position, as criminal lawyer, of power, conferring identities, controlling destinies. Not for nothing are those criminals in Newgate compared to plants in the greenhouse, and regarded with the scientific detachment that for Foucault is part of the 'discourse of truth' of nineteenth-century positivism.

Identities become a matter of social control and naming: Estella might have turned out one way as one of the '"fish"' to come to Jaggers's net (3:12, p.410), yet she is constituted differently (though almost as nihilistically) by the identity she receives from Miss Havisham's hands. Pip remains the passive victim whose reaction is to blame himself for every action he is in: his willingness to see himself as his sister's murderer (1:16, p. 119) is of a piece with seeing himself characteristically unjust to Joe. Q. D. Leavis's account works against those who see the book as 'a snob's progress' [Humphry House's phrase – see p. 66 of this Guide]; her emphases are useful in suggesting that it is *Pip* who sees himself thus; and that now he is 'telling us dispassionately how he became the man who can now write thus about his former self'.[24] But the 'us', by eliding the 1860s readers of the text with these who come a century later, implies that there is a central, ahistorical way of taking the text: a liberal-humanist ideology under-writes this assumption which also implies that there is some decent norm Pip could approximate to which would untie all his problems. It thus assimilates all historical differences, at the least, to the notion of the free subject, who is at all times accessible to decent human feelings – and capable of reaching a central normality. If what Q.D. Leavis said were the case, Pip would have reached some degree of 'normality' by the end of what has happened to him, before he starts narrating. He is not a central human presence, but a writer whose text needs inspec-tion for its weakness of self-analysis, for he never dissociates himself from the accusations he piles on himself at the time of the events happening and afterwards. In Wemmick's and Jaggers's character-formulations of people as either '"beat[er]s or cringe[r]s"' (3:9, p. 387) he remains a cringer, and unable to recognize [himself in] Herbert's genial view – '"a good fellow, with impetuosity and hesitation, boldness and diffidence, action and dreaming, curiously mixed in him"' (2:11, p. 248). That positive evaluation is beyond him: his self-perception makes him oppressor, while, more accurately, he is victim. Foucault stresses how the healthy individual is defined in relation to that which has been labelled as delinquent, degenerate or perverse; and his studies of madness, of the birth of the clinic and of the prison all meet in this: 'when one wishes to individualize the healthy, normal and law-abiding adult, it is always by asking him how much of the child he has in him, what secret madness lies within him, what fundamen-tal crime he has dreamed of committing'.[25] On this basis, Pip might be said to be the creation of three intersecting discourses: he remains something of the child – his name, a diminutive, establishes that; he is never in a position, he feels, of equality with anyone else; his dreams of the file, of Miss Havisham hanging from the beam, of playing Hamlet without knowing more than five words of the play, his night-marish sense of phantasmagoric shapes perceived in the rushlight in the Hummums, and his sense of being a brick in a house-wall, or part of a machine, wanting 'to have the engine stopped, and my part in it hammered off' (3:18, p. 458) – all proclaim [what Foucault calls] his 'secret madness'. His sense of criminality is fed by virtually each act and its consequences that he undertakes.

A victim of the language system, only on one or two occasions does he reverse the role and become implicitly the accuser; one is where he prays over the head of the dead Magwitch: '"'Lord be merci-ful to him a sinner'"' (3:17, p. 457) . . . The odd thing is not that he fails to see himself as the sinner, as in the parable (Luke, ch. 18, verses 10–14), but that he should want to name Magwitch as such. But that act of naming is a reflection of the way the dominated have no choice but to take over the language of their domination – to continue to beat, as they have been beaten, to continue to name disparagingly, as they have been named . . .

A second time when the language of Pip's oppression becomes one to oppress another is at the end of the book where he meets the younger Pip and suggests to Biddy that she should '"give Pip to [him], one of these days; or lend him, at all events"' (3:20, p. 477). To this Biddy responds 'gently' '"no"', but her answer might well have been a horrified one in the light of what surrogate parents do to their children in the book: Pip is offering to play Magwitch to Biddy's child . . . .

[Tambling also discusses how Wemmick with his 'Castle', Magwitch with his '"owner[ship]"' of Pip (2:20, p. 319), and Orlick, who moves from 'cringing' to 'beating', all attempt to compensate for their oppression by adopting the values by which they are oppressed.]

Thus the production, and reproduction, of oppression is what [*Great Expectations*] charts. Orlick attempts to move over to the other side in the Panopticon, and from the attempted assumption of that position, turns against Pip. Magwitch's acquisition of money is his attempt to move to the other side, to create a Pip, whom he surveys. In fact, he remains for ever the criminal. Nor can Orlick change, and though he is in the county jail at the end, the replication of the book's past events seems safe with him when he is released: he really has no alternative, and as such he remains an apt commentary on the course an oppressed class must follow. Pip, in terms of status, moves over to the other side, in Panopticon terms, but his social formation is already firm, and basically he cannot change either: the events in the second part of his 'expectations' are an aberration from what he is in the first and third parts. Ironically, since he is cast there as guilty, what he is at those points is preferable to what he becomes in the second part.

As the recidivist [the former offender who relapses into crime], he wishes to be given Biddy's child, which would start again the whole cycle of oppression; and self-oppressive to the end, he writes out his autobiography – one that remains remarkably terse as to its intentions and its status as writing and which, while beautifully written, rolls out as though automatically[,] the product of a consciousness that remains fixed. There is, in *Great Expectations*, implicit commentary about the mode of autobiography. Autobiography defines the subject confessionally; it puts upon it the onus of 'explanation', makes it prison-bound: a state that proves naturally acceptable to so much Romantic writing, where the tragic intensity of those who have to inhabit alienating spaces or constrictions can be defined as the source and inspiration of their reality. 'We think of the key, each in his prison' – [T. S.] Eliot's reading of [the philosopher] F. H. Bradley in *The Waste Land* (1922) suggests that the essence of humanity is that it is confined, this is its common condition. In contrast, Foucault's analysis stresses the prison as the mode that gives the person the sense of uniqueness, the sense of difference from the others. In that sense, autobiography becomes a mode that helps reproduce the discourse that the Panopticon society promotes . . . *Great Expectations* comes close to suggesting that in an understanding of a society, the concept of the individual is unhelpful, that what is important are the total manipulations of power and language by whatever group has the power of definition and control. Autobiography provides an inadequate paradigm . . . . . . The final irony of *Great Expectations* is that it displays the bankruptcy of Pip's efforts to understand what has happened to him . . . . . .

. . . Whatever liberalism affects the book – as in the '"poor dreams"' that nearly save Mr. Jaggers in spite of himself (3:12, p. 411), or in the way that Pip seems to enjoy a reasonable bourgeois existence in the Eastern Branch of Herbert's firm – is not central[,] nor does interest in character sanction belief in the individual as ultimately irrepressible. Rather, the idea of the Panopticon as the chief model for the formation of any individuality in nineteenth-century Britain makes for something much more complex and gives rise to the sense that the formation of individuality is itself delusory as a hope. It is itself the problem it seeks to solve – through its way of dividing a society and separating it. To that diagnosis, which demands a consideration of power structures in society such as Foucault gives, and which draws attention to language as a way of making the person prison-bound, the autobiographical mode of *Great Expectations* bears witness, keeping the narrator in the prison. Just as Wemmick's father and his pleasant and playful ways, and the possibility that Jaggers himself might one day want a pleasant home, ensure that the prison's durability is not in question: these individual escapes, by staying within the limits of the individual idea, address, effectively, no problem at all.[26] □

Tambling's final emphasis, like that of Steven Connor's, is characteristic of the new criticism of the 1980s in its rejection of the 'individualist' solutions of liberal humanism. And the very mode that for Q. D. Leavis signified Pip's attainment of maturity – his 'homogeneous' first-person narrative – is for Tambling both the sign and means of his oppression. There is another potentially oppressive aspect of such a narrative, however, which, in the 1986 version of his analysis, Tambling does not mention: the fact that it excludes, or at least controls, other voices, that it is, to use Mikhail Bakhtin's terminology, 'monologic', comprising one dominant voice, rather than 'heteroglossic', made up of many contesting voices. For example, the 'homogeneous' first-person narrative denies an inner voice to Estella: what are her expectations? As Kate Flint remarked in her lively, well-informed and concise study of Dickens that came out in the same year as Tambling's essay:

■ Estella, throughout *Great Expectations*, is both manipulated and manipulator: the means through which Miss Havisham hopes to revenge *her* betrayal by a man, and a taunter of Pip on both class and emotional grounds. That she makes, initially, an unhappy marriage is clear, as is the fact, in the original ending of the novel, that there is little hint of her expiating her faults through this: she is left riding away in her carriage conveying the fact that she has passed through a period of sombre suffering [see Appendix A of this Guide]. In the revised version, her destiny is as uncertain as that of Pip, seeing 'the shadow of no parting' (3:20, p. 480). If that shadow is one last example of Pip's lack of foresight and self-knowledge, it can become, for the reader, a premonition of one further capricious act on Estella's part. The effect on the reader is to make Estella, at the end, as unpredictable to us as she has been to Pip throughout the book. For we have continually been denied access to her own voice, her own point of view. The first-person narrative has . . . ensured this.[27] □

For Flint, however, the denial of access to Estella's voice seems, paradoxically, to endow her with a certain autonomy, making her 'unpredictable'. For Carolyn Brown, in her 1987 essay '*Great Expectations*: Masculinity and Modernity', Estella, who is 'constructed as a reflection of "normal" masculine narcissism', is 'denied any autonomy'.[28] Brown interprets *Great Expectations* as 'an account of development of identity' in a world that is '"modern"' but also 'extraordinarily masculine'.[29] The world of *Great Expectations* is 'modern' because it is 'in a process of rapid social and textual transformation',[30] in which 'traditional narratives' are being 'review[ed]'[31] and perhaps revised; it is 'a transitional world' in which 'Pip moves between the small local scale of organization in the village in Kent, and the vast global system which radiates from London'[32] – though 'the village almost as much as the city' is very violent and 'abounds in orphans, in non-existent or inadequate parenting'.[33] This modernising world is 'masculine' because of its denial of female 'power[s] of transformation'.[34] The maternal function is taken over by a man, Joe Gargery; the unmaternal Mrs. Joe is violently silenced; Miss Havisham's apparent power only reproduces, in Estella, a mirror of male narcissism that is shattered by masculine brutality. Brown draws attention, not only to what the novel says, but also to what it does not say, to its 'exclusions, and prohibitions',[35] especially of female narrative and power.

The interpretations of Brooks, Connor, Tambling, Flint and Brown helped to effect a major reorientation of *Great Expectations* studies in the 1980s. All of these readings moved away from the liberal-humanist view that the novel shows the development of a unified individual subject who is, or comes to be, in possession of his experience. Brooks, with his argument that Pip ends up 'cured of plot', comes closest to the more traditional view that the novel traces a passage from illusion to maturity; but his psychoanalytic perspective posits, not a unified, self-conscious individual, but an existence that is interesting only when it is in the grip of unconscious drives and compulsive repetitions: Pip's life is merely residual once he is 'cured'. Connor allows Pip some progress from the narcissistic, binary world of Lacan's Imaginary to the necessary renunciations and complexities of the Symbolic; but he finally springs the dual traps of self and system, catching Pip between the two in ways from which the novel cannot release him. Tambling seals Pip into the Foucault–Bentham Panopticon, imprisoning him in a network of surveillance and control that permits no possibility of freedom. The autobiographical mode that, in other critical perspectives, might seem to enact and represent the achievement of an autonomous selfhood is, for Tambling, a final turn of the key; it confirms Pip in a solitary confinement that is not the last refuge of romantic or existentialist independence, but the ultimate site of subjection, the space in which the technology of control operates most intimately and completely. Flint implies that Pip's autonomy is dependent on the denial of a voice to Estella but that, paradoxically, this denial means that Estella remains unpredictable, forever outside Pip's control and always liable to thwart his desires. Brown regards Pip as achieving identity within the terms of a masculine world conditioned by inequalities of class, money and gender.

Each of these readings, in its different way, emphasises the determining elements – psychological, social, cultural, economic – that constrict the freedom of the individual subject to make his or her own life: each decentres Pip within what is ostensibly his own narrative, stressing the pressure of those forces and discourses within which, through which and against which his individuality, such as it is, is constructed.

After such readings, *Great Expectations* looks rather different: and critics and readers at the end of the 1980s might well have wondered what would come next. As shall be seen in the final chapter, the last decade of the twentieth century had more surprises in store.

CHAPTER SIX

Exceeding Expectations: The 1990s

BY THE start of the 1990s, the revolution in literary criticism that had begun in Paris in the 1960s had been accomplished. In the academies of the UK and the USA, once bizarre movements and names – post-structuralism and deconstruction, the Imaginary and the Symbolic, Lacan and Foucault – had grown familiar as household words. This did not mean, of course, that the consequences of that revolution were universally acknowledged; there were many varieties of resistance, from reasoned argument to a refusal to believe that things had really changed; but the liberal-humanist criticism that had dominated literary studies from the 1950s to the 1970s could no longer command widespread assent, although it continued to produce useful work. Liberal-humanist criticism was not, however, replaced by another dominant approach: the post-revolutionary state of criticism was characterised by a proliferation of difference, by a kind of continuous self-interrogation and innovation, as new ideas and approaches were themselves questioned and transcended, and as new categories of critics, from previously marginalised groups – women, gays, lesbians, ethnic minorities, post-colonial peoples – began to enter the scene and adapt and challenge the theory and criticism that emerged from the old white male heterosexual metropolitan centres.

A striking example of this is Edward W. Said's discussion of *Great Expectations* in his important book *Culture and Imperialism* (1993). In this book Said argues, persuasively and provocatively, for what he calls a 'contrapuntal' reading of cultural forms that brings them constantly into conjunction with imperialism and its aftermath. He eschews, however, what he calls a 'rhetoric of blame'[1] that 'attacks [writers and artists], retrospectively, for being white, privileged, insensitive, complicit'[2] and which can fall into 'a kind of retrospective vindictiveness'.[3] Moreover, he unrepentantly retains a notion of literary and artistic value: thus, in the Introduction to *Culture and Imperialism*, he tells us his first reason for analysing the specific 'works of art and learning' he has chosen is because he finds them 'estimable and admirable' and because they offer the reader 'pleasure and profit'. His second reason, however, is that he wants to take up 'the challenge . . . to connect them not only with that pleasure and profit but also with the imperial process of which they were manifestly and unconcealedly a part'; to explore 'this hitherto ignored aspect' of such works does not belittle them, but 'actually and truly *enhances* our reading and understanding of them'. He then moves on immediately to discuss the first book he has chosen, which he calls, along with Conrad's *Nostromo* (1904), a 'well-known and very great' novel – *Great Expectations*.[4]

The 'imperialist' and 'colonialist' dimension of *Great Expectations* had not been wholly ignored in previous decades. In 1965, in the leading article in a symposium on 'Commonwealth Literature' in the *New Statesman*, the South African novelist Dan Jacobson had raised the general question of 'why the whole colonial and imperial adventure – which did, after all, in one way or another actively involve over a long period so many millions of Englishmen and so large a part of British military and commercial power – should have left so small a mark on English literature'. He points out that for most eighteenth- and nineteenth-century writers, 'the colonies were merely places to which people went or from which they dramatically returned, altogether unaltered except for having made, lost or consolidated their fortunes in the meantime'. *Great Expectations* may provide 'a partial exception to the rule', but 'it isn't because Dickens is at all interested in Magwitch's Australian adventure'; it is, rather, 'because one of the things he is showing in the novel is so closely related to what [Jacobson is saying in his article]: that, like young Pip, the gentlemen of England preferred for the most part not to know the truth about just where, and how, and by whom, their fortunes were being made'.[5] It is interesting that Jacobson makes no reference here to Pip's own career in the colonies after the death of Magwitch. This is perhaps because that career is passed over quickly in the novel. In an essay of 1972, '*Great Expectations*: The Three Endings', Milton Millhauser observes that this 'should have been . . . an important period'[6] but becomes merely 'a plot expedient', possibly because Dickens 'felt no particular interest in it'. Millhauser goes on: '[w]hen one considers both what might have been done with these new characters and scenes, and how easily Dickens might have availed himself of less exotic alternatives had he chosen, had the locale mattered, it becomes apparent that Cairo was for him precisely an expedient and nothing more'.[7] The fact that Pip's colonial experience was nothing more than an expedient for Dickens is itself significant, of course, of the way in which the empire was occluded in nineteenth-century British fiction. Peter Wolfe's comparison, which was noted in chapter five of this Guide (pp. 112, 114), between Pip abroad and 'Graham Greene's seedy expatriates' highlights some of the things that might have been done – or might still be done – with this period of Pip's life. Has anyone yet written a novel about Pip in the colonies?

Despite references such as those of Jacobson, Millhauser and Wolfe, and the remarks on *Great Expectations*, cited by Said, in Robert Hughes's *The Fatal Shore* (1987), it is the case that most criticism of *Great Expectations* has either ignored the colonialist and imperialist dimensions of the novel or referred to them in a very marginal way that sometimes displays an unawareness of their possible importance. There are a number of examples from critics discussed in previous chapters of this Guide. Dorothy Van Ghent's 1953 account, which was considered in chapter three, attributes the 'full-scale demolition of traditional values' and 'the uprooting and dehumanization' of millions of men, women and children in Dickens's time to 'a process brought about by industrialization, colonial imperialism, and the exploitation of the human being as a "thing" or an engine or a part of an engine capable of being used for profit'.[8] She does not develop the point about 'colonial imperialism', however. In 1960, Julian Moynahan says of Pip: '[l]iving abroad as the partner of a small, unambitious firm, he is to devote his remaining life to doing the least possible harm to the smallest number of people'.[9] There is no sense here of Pip's possible role in a system of imperial exploitation and oppression, and of the 'harm' that this might do. Steven Connor, in 1985, states firmly that '[t]he economic world in which Pip eventually finds respectability is of course a capitalist one'[10] (see p. 135), but he makes no mention of the fact that it is also an imperialist one, and that its imperialism and capitalism are inextricably intertwined. In her 1987 essay, Carolyn Brown, alert both to the masculinist and capitalist aspects of *Great Expectations*, implies the existence of imperialism, for example when she refers to 'the vast global system which radiates from London'[11] in a 'period of British ascendancy over the globe';[12] but she offers no developed discussion of the topic. So it opens up an important new road in *Great Expectations* studies when, in 1993, a critic of Edward W. Said's standing focuses on the imperialist and colonialist dimensions of Dickens's novel near the start of a major book. This is what he has to say:

■ Dickens's *Great Expectations* is primarily a novel about self-delusion, about Pip's vain attempts to become a gentleman with neither the hard work nor the aristocratic source of income required for such a role. Early in life he helps a condemned convict, Abel Magwitch, who, after being transported to Australia, pays back his young benefactor with large sums of money; because the lawyer involved says nothing as he disburses the money, Pip persuades himself that an elderly gentlewoman, Miss Havisham, has been his patron. Magwitch then reappears illegally in London, unwelcomed by Pip because everything about the man reeks of delinquency and unpleasantness. In the end, though, Pip is reconciled to Magwitch and to his reality: he finally acknowledges Magwitch – hunted, apprehended, and fatally ill – as his surrogate father, not as someone to be denied or rejected, though Magwitch is in fact unacceptable, being from Australia, a penal colony designed for the rehabilitation but not the repatriation of transported English criminals.

Most, if not all, readings of this remarkable work situate it squarely within the metropolitan history of British fiction, whereas I believe that it belongs in a history both more inclusive and more dynamic than such interpretations allow. It has been left to two more recent books than Dickens's – Robert Hughes's magisterial *The Fatal Shore* and Paul Carter's brilliantly speculative *The Road to Botany Bay* (1988) – to reveal a vast history of speculation about and experience of Australia, a 'white' colony like Ireland, in which we can locate Magwitch and Dickens not as mere coincidental references in that history, but as participants in it, through the novel and through a much older and wider experience between England and its overseas territories.

Australia was established as a penal colony in the late eighteenth century mainly so that England could transport an irredeemable, unwanted excess population of felons to a place, originally charted by Captain Cook, that would also function as a colony replacing those lost in America. The pursuit of profit, the building of empire, and what Hughes calls social *apartheid* together produced modern Australia, which by the times [*sic*] Dickens first took an interest in it during the 1840s (in *David Copperfield* Wilkins Micawber happily immigrates [*sic*] there) had progressed somewhat into profitability and a sort of 'free system' where labourers could do well on their own if allowed to do so. Yet in Magwitch

> Dickens knotted several strands in the English perception of convicts in Australia at the end of transportation. They could succeed, but they could hardly, in the real sense, return. They could expiate their crimes in a technical, legal sense, but what they suffered there warped them into permanent outsiders. And yet they were capable of redemption – as long as they stayed in Australia.[13]

Carter's exploration of what he calls Australia's spatial history offers us another version of that same experience. Here explorers, convicts, ethnographers, profiteers, soldiers chart the vast and relatively empty continent each in a discourse that jostles, displaces, or incorporates the others. *Botany Bay* is therefore first of all an Enlightenment discourse of travel and discovery, then a set of travelling narrators (including Cook) whose words, charts, and intentions accumulate the strange territories and gradually turn them into 'home'. The adjacence between the Benthamite organization of space (which produced the city of Melbourne) and the apparent disorder of the Australian bush is shown by Carter to have become an optimistic transformation of social space, which produced an Elysium for gentlemen, an Eden for labourers in the 1840s.[14] What Dickens envisions for Pip, being Magwitch's "'London gentleman'" (2:20, p.319), is roughly equivalent to what was envisioned by English benevolence for Australia, one social space authorizing another.

But *Great Expectations* was not written with anything like the concern for native Australian accounts that Hughes or Carter has, nor did it presume or forecast a tradition of Australian writing, which in fact came later to include the literary works of David Malouf, Peter Carey, and Patrick White. The prohibition placed on Magwitch's return is not only penal but imperial: subjects can be taken to places like Australia, but they cannot be allowed a 'return' to metropolitan space, which, as all Dickens's fiction testifies, is meticulously charted, spoken for, inhabited by a hierarchy of metropolitan personages. So on the one hand, interpreters like Hughes and Carter expand on the relatively attenuated presence of Australia in nineteenth-century British writing, expressing the fullness and earned integrity of an Australian history that became independent from Britain's in the twentieth century; yet, on the other, an accurate reading of *Great Expectations* must note that after Magwitch's delinquency is expiated, so to speak, after Pip redemptively acknowledges his debt to the old, bitterly energized, and vengeful convict, Pip himself collapses and is revived in two explicitly positive ways. A new Pip appears, less laden than the old Pip with the chains of the past – he is glimpsed in the form of a child, also called Pip; and the old Pip takes on a new career with his boyhood friend Herbert Pocket, this time not as an idle gentleman but as a hard-working trader in the East, where Britain's other colonies offer a sort of normality that Australia never could.

Thus even as Dickens settles the difficulty with Australia, another structure of attitude and reference emerges to suggest Britain's imperial intercourse through trade and travel with the Orient. In his new career as colonial businessman, Pip is hardly an exceptional figure, since nearly all of Dickens's businessmen, wayward relatives, and frightening outsiders have a fairly normal and secure connection with the empire. But it is only in recent years that these connections have taken on interpretative importance. [Later in *Culture and Imperialism,* Said contends that '[t]o lose sight of or ignore the national and international context of, say, Dickens's representations of Victorian businessmen, and to focus only on the internal coherence of their roles in his novels is to miss an essential connection between his fiction and its historical world'.[15]] A new generation of scholars and critics – the children of decolonization in some instances, the beneficiaries (like sexual, religious, and racial minorities) of advances in human freedom at home – have seen in such great texts of Western literature a standing interest in what was considered a lesser world, populated with lesser people of colour, portrayed as open to the intervention of so many Robinson Crusoes.[16] □

Said opens up one important set of issues for critics of *Great Expectations* in the 1990s. Another set of issues is opened up by William A. Cohen in his essay 'Manual Conduct in *Great Expectations*'. As George H. Ford had pointed out back in 1955, one of the recurrent general objections to Dickens's work had been 'that his novels fail to deal with sexual relations'.[17] Twenty years later George Steiner was still reiterating this objection, though recasting it as a 'problem'. In his essay 'Eros and Idiom', originally published in 1975, Steiner suggests that of the 'many problems' posed by '[t]he complicated energies released in Dickens's work', '[n]one is more arresting than the fact that no other writer of comparable stature, of even related imaginative multiplicity in any modern literature, has ever been so innocent of stated adult sexuality'. He goes on to propose that 'Dickens's refusal of adult sexuality left clear marks. The symbolic vehemence and scarcely mastered crudity of melodrama in *Bleak House* and *Great Expectations* suggest a subterranean pressure of erotic recognition'.[18] Cohen does not adopt the normative terms of Steiner with their assumption of an 'adult sexuality'; but his playful, provocative and penetrating essay does seek to uncover something like Steiner's 'subterranean pressure of erotic recognition'. He does so by focusing on an aspect of the novel that had long been noticed and discussed by other critics – as was seen in one example, by Harry Stone, in the fourth chapter of this Guide (see pp. 115–19). This is the matter of hands. In Dickens, Cohen suggests, the hand is a metonymy for masturbation. As the only bodily member apart from the head publicly visible to the Victorians, it could stand for the unspeakable. 'In a genre that forbids direct observation of genitals in action, this manual code gives voice to what otherwise cannot be spoken.'[19] Cohen contends that '[i]n the masturbator's guide to the English novel, at least under the heading "men's bodies", Charles Dickens would doubtless merit a good deal of attention',[20] and that 'all his *Bildungsromane* . . . trace not only their heroes' social, emotional, and intellectual development, but their sexual maturation as well'. In contrast to an earlier *Bildungsroman*, *Oliver Twist*, *Great Expectations* 'relegates sexual sensations to parts of the body different from those in which they are usually imagined to originate; *Great Expectations* . . . manages to anatomize whole species of erotic dispositions without ever mentioning sex'.[21]

In developing his argument, Cohen points to a passage that is, indeed, difficult to read today without feeling that there is a sexual reference. This is the passage in 1:2 in which Pip, having concealed the slice of bread-and-butter for Magwitch in his trousers, says: 'Conscience is a dreadful thing when it accuses man or boy; but when, in the case of a boy, that secret burden co-operates with another secret burden down the leg of his trousers, it is (as I can testify) a great punishment' (1:2, p. 13). Cohen goes on to point out the autoerotic implications of the phrase: 'Happily, I slipped away, and deposited that part of my conscience in my garret bedroom' (1: 2, p. 14). Cohen suggests that the imagery of this whole section implies a set of analogies between masturbation, theft and wastefulness. 'Whether through the profligacy of moneyed leisure or the degeneracy of desperate theft, autoeroticism is figured as wasteful sexual energy.'[22] A further analogy is suggested when Pip first visits Satis House and Estella calls attention to his '"coarse hands"' (1:8, p. 61); here the hand – which is the metonymy for masturbation – also becomes the metonymy for what Cohen calls 'that other subject routinely repressed – work'.[23] Thus Cohen proposes a complex set of links between sexuality, manual labour, moneyed leisure and theft, all of which contribute to Pip's shame.

Cohen also points to other features of the novel that may figure masturbation – for example, Jaggers's large hands and 'his trademark "bit[ing] the side of [his] great forefinger"'[24] (1:18, p. 132) (a trademark that was noticed by some early reviewers, though of course without any mention of masturbation! (see pp. 18, 28)). But as well as these solitary hands in the novel, which 'are marked, via a metonymic connection, for male masturbation', '[t]he novel's erotic investment in hands is so general . . . as to allow for metaphoric links as well, so that sexual practices less directly managed by the hand may nonetheless be imagined as manual'.[25] Cohen moves on to look at the amount of manhandling that goes on in the novel, focusing especially on handshakes and fistfighting. As was seen in the previous chapter, Carolyn Brown saw Pip's world as a remarkably masculine, homosocial one (p. 142); Cohen considers the erotic aspect of this masculine world, the ways in which what he sees as homoerotic contacts between men are managed in the novel. The extract begins as he starts to explore this matter:

■ We now shift our attention from singular hands to redoubled ones in order to read sexuality: the moments at which two men's hands are engaged arise first, in the most highly socialized form of male hand-holding – the handshake – and then, in the other shape they principally assume in the novel, pugilism . . . While [Jaggers] is frequently 'throwing his finger at [one] sideways' (1:18, p. 137), and is quick to lay a hand on Pip's shoulder or arm (1:18, p. 135; 2:1, p. 165; 3:12, p. 409), he rarely takes the young man in hand. Indeed, Jaggers is all but unwilling to extend his hand – and the largeness of his endowment makes the fact of his withholding all the more disappointing:

> It was November, and my guardian was standing before his fire leaning his back against the chimney-piece, with his hands under his coat-tails.
> 'Well, Pip,' said he, 'I must call you Mr. Pip today. Congratulations, Mr. Pip.'
> We shook hands – he was always a remarkably short shaker – and I thanked him. (2:2, p.285)

A man who has so noticeably large a hand and yet is such a 'remarkably short shaker' will always fail to satisfy.[26] As Pip comes to learn, however, handshaking in the world of this novel has a curiously negative valence in any case.

The handshake is the one social ritual by which men – most especially those who are strangers – routinely touch each other. It functions to draw people together by holding them apart; it interposes hands between other body parts as a safe form of contact. Why, then, this shortness on the part of Jaggers's shaker? Why, even more pertinently, the castigation of this ritual in the form of Pumblechook's unctuous insistence on it? One recalls how the seedsman, after learning that Pip has come into his expectations, clings to the boy with an obsequiousness as oppressive as the proverbial cheap suit that Pip has just come from being fitted for by Trabb.

> 'But do I,' said Mr. Pumblechook, getting up again the moment after he had sat down, 'see afore me, him as I ever sported with in his times of happy infancy? And may I – *may* I – ?'
> This May I, meant might he shake hands? I consented, and he was fervent, and then sat down again.
> 'Here is wine,' said Mr. Pumblechook. 'Let us drink, Thanks to Fortúne, and may she ever pick out her favourites with equal judgement! And yet I cannot,' said Mr. Pumblechook, getting up again, 'see afore me One – and likeways drink to One – without again expressing – May I – *may* I – ?' (1:19, p.151–52)

Pumblechook's sycophancy is insatiable, at least so long as Pip stays in the money; once Pip is 'brought low', however, the hand is extended 'with a magnificently forgiving air' and Pip notes 'the wonderful difference between the servile manner in which he had offered his hand to me in my new prosperity, saying "May I?" and the ostentatious clemency with which he had just now exhibited the same fat five fingers' (3:19, p.470). Here is the novel's signal instance of a hand freighted with meaning, yet what it bespeaks is not the efficacy of gestural communication. Instead, at the moment it raises the possibility that in the most familiar code of manual conduct – the handshake – something might supervene upon the literal, the narrative can be nothing but derisive (as if to confirm that hands are evocative only where they are not, in the novel's conscious terms, meant to be so). At the point where connotations of the manual – including but not limited to the erotic – seem most likely to proliferate, the mode of parodic excess preempts all meanings but the most repugnant hypocrisy.[27]

Though Pip's hand may remain insufficiently chafed by Pumblechook's grip, in the progressive tale of his body's schooling it receives a final chastening lesson. Jaggers's second, Wemmick, is noted for parodically representing the schizophrenic divide between the office persona of the bureaucratic modern man and his home life ('"the office is one thing, and private life is another"' (2:6, p.208)). While on the job, Wemmick faithfully emulates the withholding posture of his employer: 'something of the state of Mr. Jaggers hung about him too, forbidding approach beyond certain limits' (2:13, p.260). And like Jaggers, Wemmick finds distasteful Pip's provincial penchant for handshaking:

> 'As I keep the cash,' Mr. Wemmick observed, 'we shall most likely meet pretty often. Good day.'
> 'Good day.'
> I put out my hand, and Mr. Wemmick at first looked at it as if he thought I wanted something. Then he looked at me, and said, correcting himself,
> 'To be sure! Yes. You're in the habit of shaking hands?'
> I was rather confused, thinking it must be out of the London fashion, but said yes.
> 'I have got so out of it!' said Mr. Wemmick – 'except at last. Very glad, I'm sure, to make your acquaintance. Good day!' (2:2, p.172)

The perplexity that Wemmick evinces at Pip's quaint amiability here is only elucidated later. For the man of business, handshaking is shown to have practical purposes: besides the exhibition of the '"portable property"' (2:5, p.201) he has acquired from condemned prisoners ('he wore at least four mourning rings' (2:2, p.169)), he reserves demonstrative use of his hands for its utility *as* a sign. As he leads Pip on a tour of Newgate prison, the narrator notes: 'He turned to me and said, "Notice the man I shall shake hands with." I should have done so, without the preparation, as he had shaken hands with no one yet'. After the brief conversation between Wemmick and the designated man, 'They shook hands again, and as we walked away

Wemmick said to me, "A Coiner, a very good workman. The Recorder's report is made to-day, and he is sure to be executed on Monday"' (2:13, pp. 260–61, 262). Wemmick hopes to land a bit of portable property from the condemned man, and reserves his embrace to satisfy this materialistic impulse. His handshake, like Pumblechook's, foregrounds its own function as coded behaviour; divested of any erotic significance, Wemmick's secret handshake holds no secret (except so far as the unwitting Coiner is concerned) because its code is transparent. No wonder he is so reluctant to take up Pip's hand when they first meet: to do so would, in Wemmick's bodily lexicon, be tantamount to marking him for the gallows.

While the handshake routinizes and sublates [destroys and preserves] manual contact among characters, the other context in which hands regularly meet – fisticuffs – tends in a rather different direction. Unlike the ostentatious signification with which the text loads handshaking (a system of meaning, I have argued, so manifest that it paradoxically empties itself out), the novel's most fully embodied moments of physical violence are either so curiously undermotivated or so thoroughly overdetermined as to proliferate the meanings available to a manual semiotics. Although in the logic of the novel's plot, fights interpose at junctures of fierce romantic rivalry, the *narration* of the battles consistently provides the occasion for the playing out of erotic contact, both homo- and heterosexual, between combatants.[28] . . .

At Pip's first encounter with Herbert Pocket, for instance, the relationship is one of immediate and unmediated physical aggression: '"Come and fight," said the pale young gentleman'. As Herbert's provocation appears wholly unmotivated, he soon supplies the incitement it is felt to require: '"I ought to give you a reason for fighting, too. There it is!" In a most irritating manner he instantly slapped his hands against one another, daintily flung one of his legs up behind him, pulled my hair, slapped his hands again, dipped his head, and butted it into my stomach' (1:11, p. 91). To such ungentlemanly conduct the gentleman's reaction – that is, the bellicosity Herbert desires – itself must be reconfigured, albeit in hindsight, as a form of chivalrous combat for feminine affections. Thus, Pip's payoff for sparring with Herbert is the opportunity to kiss Estella, the scene's unseen observer. Yet even if this putative erotic aim were capable of sustaining a state of arousal, it would nonetheless function only retrospectively and defensively as the alibi for the more provoking touches elaborated in the battle with Herbert. In fact, Pip feels as a result that he has prostituted himself, 'that the kiss was given to the coarse common boy as a piece of money might have been, and that it was worth nothing' (1:11, p. 93). In compensation for the tussle's lack of motivation, then, the text supplies a series of rationales – ranging from insult to romance to monetary recompense – whose insufficiency is demonstrated by the very rapidity of their deployment.

However persuasive the pretext for pugnacity in the novel may be (in this case, hardly at all), it thus functions primarily as the occasion for physical contact between adversaries – contact whose cathexes evince a logic quite different from the plot's [a 'cathexis' is a 'concentration of mental energy in one channel' (*Concise Oxford Dictionary*)]. And while the sensory modality of the novel's eroticism is primarily tactile, there is a peculiarly embodied form of the visual – an assaultive kind of looking – which also partakes of these haptic significations ['haptic' means 'pertaining to the sense of touch' (*Concise Oxford Dictionary*)]. In the present scene, the bout between Herbert and Pip is preceded by both narrator-Pip's account of Herbert's awkward frame (he later discreetly terms it 'a little ungainly' (2:3, p. 176)) and Herbert's somewhat more suspect examination of Pip's physique. In a remarkable description of his adversary's seminudity, Pip recounts:

> [Herbert] fell to pulling off, not only his jacket and waistcoat, but his shirt too, in a manner at once light-hearted, businesslike, and bloodthirsty.
>
> Although he did not look very healthy – having pimples on his face, and a breaking out at his mouth – these dreadful preparations quite appalled me . . . He was a young gentleman in a grey suit (when not denuded for battle), with his elbows, knees, wrists, and heels, considerably in advance of the rest of him as to development.
>
> My heart failed me when I saw him squaring at me with every demonstration of mechanical nicety, and eyeing my anatomy as if he were minutely choosing his bone. (1:11, pp. 91–92)

The investment of Pip's narration in looking at and rendering the repulsive particulars of his antagonist's body is strangely at odds with the character's professed distaste for the figure that Herbert cuts.[29] And at the moment that Pip, almost despite himself, catalogues the corners of the pale young gentleman's frame, Herbert returns the gaze. The fight then proceeds from this curiously cruising scrutiny; from sizing up to feeling up, we will see, the novel's pattern is here established.

The striptease that Pip witnesses at his introduction to Herbert enacts a form of male-to-male perusal not uncommon in Dickens's work . . . . . . The point at which one man can no longer anatomize another's body . . . is always telling. But as if to rectify Herbert's enticing literalization of that familiar gaze ('he undressed me with his eyes'), the revelation moves in the opposite direction when the two meet again, now grown up. As Pip first espies the mature Herbert mounting the stairs, he reverses the striptease both by clothing his friend and by moving this time from the head downward: 'Gradually there arose before me the hat, head, neckcloth, waistcoat, trousers, boots, of a member of society of about my own standing' (2:2, p. 172). Here the progressive dressing (of a nude ascending a staircase) ensures their rivalry is at an end; proleptically [in anticipation] asserting a Freudian developmental mythology, it insists that a more happily socialized and sublimated relation will ensue[30] . . . . . .

Through the shift from denuding to redressing . . . Herbert's youthful belligerence is rehabilitated as properly sublimated, adult male homosociality. Following his adolescent ineptitude in the boxing ring, moreover, Herbert's mastery of the hand correspondingly matures as well. Although we learn surprisingly little about his grown-up appendages, this lack is more than compensated by the peculiar knack he develops for tending to Pip's hands – a taste initiated, perhaps, in those first moments of 'eyeing [Pip's] anatomy as if he were minutely choosing his bone' (1:11, p. 92). Indeed, Herbert's proclivity is confirmed both by his impulse, almost immediately upon becoming reacquainted with Pip, to christen him '"Handel"' (2:3, p. 177) and by his own surname, Pocket, the usual receptacle for hands in the novel. At their first dinner in town, Herbert interlards his conversa-tion with a course in table manners for the newly arrived Pip, instructing him in the proper handling of utensils and other matters of the body's polite disposition at table ('"the spoon is not generally used over-hand, but under,"' etc (2:3, pp. 177–78)). Herbert interjaculates this manual conduct lesson (as if to literalize a parody of the silver fork novel [a 'silver-fork novel' was a satirical term for a kind of novel, popular in England from the 1820s to the 1840s, which focused on fashionable society]) through his recounting of Miss Havisham's history. In the second instalment of this tale – when Pip realizes that Magwitch is Estella's father – Herbert is again preoccupied with the condition of his friend's hands, this time changing the bandages that cover Pip's burns ('"Lay your arm out upon the back of the sofa, my dear boy, and I'll sit down here, and get the bandage off so gradually that you shall not know when it comes"' (3:12, p. 402)). Through both stories, then, the narrative interpolates information about Pip's hands, as though, at these crucial moments of the protagonist's overt erotic interest, the novel's encrypted sign of that desire need literally be close at hand.

The story that Herbert tells in the midst of his bodywork on Pip is not merely incidental: significantly, this narrative concerns the conspiracy of Miss Havisham's half-brother, Arthur, with her fiancé, Compeyson, to defraud her:

'It has been supposed that the man to whom she gave her misplaced confidence, acted throughout in concert with her half-brother; that it was a conspiracy between them; and that they shared the profits.'

'I wonder he didn't marry her and get all the property,' said I.

'He may have been married already, and her cruel mortification may have been a part of her half-brother's scheme,' said Herbert. 'Mind! I don't know that.'

'What became of the two men?' I asked, after again considering the subject.

'They fell into deeper shame and degradation – if there can be deeper – and ruin.' (2:3, pp. 180–81)

The implication of a debased, presumably homosexual criminality in this last line derives its force from contrast with the scene of its narration. Compeyson's story functions as a cautionary tale about the dangers of excessive intimacy between two young men; conversely, Pip's and Herbert's is the comfortably homosocialized relation, where eros is sublimated as pugilism, camaraderie, bachelor-marriage, and eventually marriage brokering. While in the boys' earlier encounter (the adolescent sparring match) eroticism was registered only as a 'supposititious case' (1:17, p. 130), their newfound intimacy (the now far gentler touching) can be more frankly denoted. In forming the frame of an interpolated tale (which itself has an antithetical disciplinary moral) the hand-holding dispersed throughout the present scenes is rendered explicitly – it *is* the scene of narration – by virtue of being more highly socialized.

For Magwitch, the other figure given to excessive handling of Pip, socialization again requires a transposition of eros from narrative discourse to plot, though in his case the change is accomplished through more radical means. From the first, Magwitch embodies a certain paedophilia: the novel's opening, showing his combined aggression and affection for Pip, suggests a species of man-boy love, and it is primarily through his man-handling of Pip that we come to register such pederastic impulses. At their initial encounter, '[t]he man, after looking at me for a moment, turned me upside down and emptied my pockets' (1:1, p. 4); and, '[a]fter darkly looking at his leg and at me several times, he came closer . . . took me by both arms, and tilted me back as far as he could hold me' (1:1, p. 5). The recognition scene between patron and protégé stages the climax of the touching here initiated, in the form of an erotic ballet performed by the hands:

I saw, with a stupid kind of amazement, that he was holding out both his hands to me (2:20, p. 312) . . . He came back to where I stood, and again held out both his hands. Not knowing what to do

– for in my astonishment I had lost my self-possession – I reluctantly gave him my hands. He grasped them heartily, raised them to his lips, kissed them, and still held them (2:20, p.313) . . . At a change in his manner as if he were even going to embrace me, I laid a hand upon his breast and put him away (2:20, p.313) . . . I stood, with a hand on the chair-back and a hand on my breast, where I seemed to be suffocating – I stood so, looking wildly at him, until I grasped at the chair, when the room began to surge and turn. He caught me, drew me to the sofa, put me up against the cushions, and bent on one knee before me: bringing the face that I now well remembered, and that I shuddered at, very near to mine (2:20, p.316) . . . The abhorrence in which I held the man, the dread I had of him, the repugnance with which I shrank from him, could not have been exceeded if he had been some terrible beast . . . I recoiled from his touch as if he had been a snake (2:20, p.317) . . . Again he took both my hands and put them to his lips, while my blood ran cold within me (2:20, p.318) . . . He laid his hand on my shoulder. I shuddered at the thought that for anything I knew, his hand might be stained with blood. (2:20, p.319)

This narration has a perilously overt sexual charge: one need hardly cite the bended knee, the kissing of hands, the prostration on the couch, the insistent caresses, to locate the courtship conventions of which it partakes. Pip's gag reflex serves to bolster, not to diminish the eroticism of the episode, for it demonstrates his revulsion to be as highly cathected as the convict's attraction ['cathected' means concentrated in one channel, in this case the erotic channel – it is the adjective derived from the noun 'cathexis', defined earlier in this chapter – see p.154]. The narrative attention to Magwitch's manipulation, in its root sense, empowers his cataclysmic revelation even as it threatens to run out of control through a homoeroticism we are made to feel and, through Pip, to feel repulsed by.[31] But like his former partner, Molly, this 'terrible beast' must be tamed as well.

How does the novel recuperate Magwitch's erotic palpation and Pip's corresponding palpitation? For Pip, the immediate antidote to the fearsome caress of the grizzled convict's ''large brown veinous hands' (2:20, p.313) arrives in the form of his companion's reassuring embrace: 'Herbert received me with open arms . . . got up, and linked his arm in mine' (3:2, pp.340, 342). Through the developments of the plot, moreover, Pip is capable of turning Magwitch's lecherous pawing back upon him, lending it a normalized, moralized signification. On his deathbed, Magwitch again feels Pip's hands, now silently communicating through a sentimentalized hand-holding. 'He had spoken his last words. He smiled, and I understood his touch to mean that he wished to lift my hand, and lay it on his breast. I laid it there, and he smiled again, and put both his hands upon it.' (3:17, p. 456) Then, as if to repay Magwitch for the earlier episode, Pip makes his own revelation:

> 'You had a child once, whom you loved and lost . . . . She is living now. She is a lady and very beautiful. And I love her!'
> With a last faint effort, which would have been powerless but for my yielding to it and assisting it, he raised my hand to his lips. Then, he gently let it sink upon his breast again, with his own hands lying on it. (3:17, p. 456)

Pip is at last able to translate his benefactor's uncomfortable stroking into heterosexual terms, now giving that touch a proper meaning in the plot: he transposes it onto the heterosexual economy by lending it the valence of the 'consent of a beloved's father to a suitor's entreaty'. Much as he has had to endure Magwitch's caress, that is to say, the hand he now can own to wanting is Estella's, in marriage. Those earlier, less fully accountable hand-squeezings are now available to him reworked retrospectively as the beneficence of a future father-in-law. Pip can afford to be 'yielding' and 'assisting' to the old man's supplications by virtue of his knowledge that whatever homoerotic force they might once have had has been defused and rewritten – written into the story proper – as straight desire.[32] □

Cohen goes on to suggest that the novel's strategies for regulating auto-eroticism and homoeroticism are so effective that in the end they even inhibit the expression of heterosexual desire in marriage – hence Dickens's difficulty in concluding the novel with a straightforward affirmation of the union of Pip and Estella. But this overly strenuous policing of sexuality does not wholly eliminate erotic possibilities: 'the very irresolution of the ending offers an alternative to erotic abjuration, one that animates the oscillation between the hegemony of the marriage plot and the violence of its refusal. Rather than resolving all the previous travails of hands through the story, the novel's ultimate ambivalence may instead reinscribe the mode of sexual deferral by which it has operated from the first: in the manner of an imaginary object held perpetually at bay by autoerotic reverie, its eroticism can persist precisely by being suspended as undecidable'.[33] The uncertainty as to whether Pip gets what he wants reopens the possibility that he may be left alone again: this reopens the question of masturbation and, more generally, the potential for erotic pleasures beyond the bounds of heterosexual marriage.

While Cohen does pay some attention to the female figures in the novel – other parts of his essay discuss Miss Skiffins, Biddy, Molly and Estella – his primary focus is on male-to-male encounters, on the erotic implications of what Carolyn Brown, in the previous chapter of this Guide, identified as Pip's 'masculine world' (see p. 142). Another approach to that 'masculine world', which relates it to representations both of the family and of women, can be found in Catherine Waters's important book *Dickens and the Politics of the Family* (1997). Like Brown, Waters locates Pip in a time of rapid transition: '[d]espite being set earlier in the century, his story is a record of mid-Victorian anxieties about male identity in a period of rapid industrial change and rampant individualism'. As the phrase 'male identity' suggests, Waters also makes Pip's anxieties gender-specific: '*Great Expectations* is distinguished by a pervading pessimism about the bourgeois male plot of aspiration and upward mobility'. Waters suggests that Peter Brooks and Steven Connor (see pp. 122–30 and 130–36), along with Anny Sadrin in her study *Parentage and Inheritance in the Novels of Charles Dickens* (1994), all 'tend to assume that the individual, the self, is gender-neutral, or to ignore the historical specificity of the family's form and cultural meaning'. But to consider, as her book does, 'the role of the family'[34] in *Great Expectations* 'immediately raises the issue of sexual difference and its historical definition in the formation of sub-jectivity'. In the novel, 'the question of Pip's identity is necessarily bound up with his masculinity, his shifting class position and their determina-tion by the system of family relationships in which he is caught'.[35] The extract below begins as Waters challenges the notion that Pip's self-naming on the first page of the novel implies his autonomy, his freedom from the determining influences of the family. She goes on to explore the representations of women and of the family in *Great Expectations*, and to consider the links the novel establishes between gender and class:

■ Despite the assertion of autonomy implied in Pip's self-naming on the novel's opening page, the determination of his identity by a familial context and the difference made by gender in these arrangements are made apparent in his contemplation of the family tombstones. The tombstones represent the members of an absent family, and his engagement in speculation about what they were like is combined with a reconstruction of the relationships between them. The authority of the father is confirmed by the way in which the inscriptions upon the tombstones of his wife and children refer back to his own, depending upon it as an origin of meaning: while Philip Pirrip is described as 'late of this parish', Georgiana is identified as 'wife of the above' and Alexander, Bartholomew, Abraham, Tobias and Roger are also identified as 'infant children of the aforesaid' (1:1, p. 4). Philip is both the source of meaning here – the named subject needed to make sense of the terms 'above' and 'aforesaid' – and the mediator between his family and the parish, between the private and the public spheres ... The tombstone text inscribes divisions of power within the family which are registered in Pip's reading, and indicate that the process of identity-formation expressed here is not conducted in some neutral linguistic medium. The language Pip works with is already gendered.

Indeed, Pip's interpretation of the appearance of his lost parents from the shape of the letters in their epitaphs curiously accords with Victorian stereotypes of masculinity and femininity. He derives contrasting impressions of his father and mother, giving ironic expression to Victorian middle-class assumptions about gender complementarity. He has an 'odd idea' that his father 'was a square, stout, dark man, with curly black hair', while he concludes that his mother 'was freckled and sickly' (1:1, p. 3). The terms of the contrast suggest the stereotypical oppositions between vigour and debility, hardness and softness, strength and weakness, darkness and fairness, that characterized middle-class ideals of manhood and womanhood, and the determining effects of sexual difference shown here continue to pervade the narrative of Pip's childhood.

In a novel that is filled with defective parents and dysfunctional families, Mrs. Joe stands forth in Pip's account of his upbringing as the first in a series of inadequate mothers. The satire of the older Pip, who records the injustices suffered by his younger self, complicates the representation of the family . . . the novel's comedy is often black – tinged with anxiety and unease – and its representation of the family is equally ambivalent, as the adult narrator is torn between self-justification and self-condemnation, between the impulses of desire and guilt, in the account of his childhood.

On the one hand, Pip's portrait of his sister invokes a missing familial ideal, an expectation of maternal devotion that she fails to embody. Her representation helps to define a norm of motherhood and domesticity that was an important part of the affirmation of middle-class values in the nineteenth century. Pip's narrative is dominated by families showing a deviation from the domestic ideal, and by mothers who fail to fulfil their proper duty. The representations of the Gargery and Pocket families, and of the perverse parenting provided by Miss Havisham, are three crucial sources for the production of the ideology of domesticity in the novel. On the other hand, however, Dickens seems to challenge and subvert the middle-class ideal of the family through the comic violence and black humour of Pip's satire. The narrator exacts a kind of revenge for the cruel treatment he is shown to have received from Mrs. Joe, deriving a retributive satisfaction from the satire used to portray her. The amusing naivety of the child's point of view is often used to license the highly unflattering portrait of his sister, as in the young Pip's speculation about her 'prevailing redness of skin' and whether 'she washed herself with a nutmeg-grater instead of soap' (1:2, p. 8). However, while the revenge enjoyed by the adult narrator is hidden behind the 'innocent' perspective of the child here, it has the potential to undermine the moral analysis that justifies his satiric attack. Pip's account of his sister shows something of the very savagery he complains about. As an exemplary 'bad mother', Mrs. Joe is exposed with a salutary purpose; but the critique of motherhood and family is presented with a bad conscience, like so much of Pip's story. The imaginative relish with which Mrs. Joe's atrocities are recorded, and the comic delight with which her pretensions are displayed for ridicule, have the effect of throwing the moral discourse of the adult narrator into question[36] . . . . . .

. . . the most bizarre example of maternal deviance in the novel is provided by the figure of Miss Havisham. As the emblem of faded virginity, Miss Havisham forms the focus for a cluster of ideas associated with sterility, solitude, decay and death in the novel. She has reached the third biological stage of womanhood defined in Victorian medical discourse, the 'climacteric' or menopause, without ever having experienced the stage most crucial in the formation of female subjectivity: pregnancy. Her ageing female body, like the 'wilderness of empty casks' (1:1, p.64) scattered in the disused brewery-yard surrounding the house, suggests barrenness and senescence. Given the importance of reproductive activity in defining the 'nature' of women in the dominant discourses of the period, the surcease of menstruation in effect meant that womanhood itself was at an end.[37] Miss Havisham is represented as a decaying woman in white, a woman who has apparently failed to undergo the 'proper' female development from bride to mother. Pip's description of her ironically named home, Satis House, lays great emphasis upon the exclusion of 'nature' from the ghostly building. The rooms are lit by candles which burn 'with the steady dulness [sic] of artificial light in air that is seldom renewed' (2:19, p.301), the fire kindled in the grate is 'more disposed to go out than to burn up' (1:11, p.84), and Miss Havisham herself looks 'as if the admission of the natural light of day would have struck her to dust' (1:8, p.61). This weird, artificial atmosphere provides the context for her 'unnatural' mothering of Estella, the child '"brought up in that strange house from a mere baby"' (2:14, p.266).

Miss Havisham is Estella's mother by adoption. However, it is not the absence of a blood-tie that accounts for the abnormality perceived by Pip in their relationship, but rather the quality of Miss Havisham's affection and the deformation of Estella's female 'nature' as a result of her peculiar upbringing. In Pip's narrative, the fading white garments of Miss Havisham act as a reminder of her arrested development from bride to mother, a sign of female 'insufficiency' in the frozen anticipation of an ever-imminent wedding. Devoid of the prospect of motherhood, she adopts a daughter to rear upon her cold hearth, where she gives forth "'a burning love, inseparable from jealousy at all times, and from sharp pain'" (2:19, p.302). The perversity of this mother-daughter bond is continually suggested in the references to the rapacity of Miss Havisham's affection for Estella; she has a 'miserly relish of Estella's moods' (1:12, p.95), she kisses her hand to the departing Estella 'with a ravenous intensity that was of its kind quite dreadful' (2:10, p.239), and as Estella grows older, Pip notes that 'there was something positively dreadful in the energy of [Miss Havisham's] looks and embraces. She hung upon Estella's beauty, hung upon her words, hung upon her gestures, and sat mumbling her own trembling fingers while she looked at her, as though she were devouring the beautiful creature she had reared' (2:19, p.300).

The ferocious affection evident in Miss Havisham's mothering has its inevitable effect upon Estella's 'nature'. Estella calmly warns Pip (2:10, p.237) that she has no heart, and [later] points out the unreasonableness of Miss Havisham's demand for love from her adopted daughter, likening it to the situation of a child kept in darkness and taught to abhor the light who is then, "'for a purpose'", expected "'to take naturally to the daylight'" (2:19, pp.303, 304). Estella's lack of feeling is held to be a product of her 'unnatural' upbringing: "'I am what you have made me'" (2:19, p.302), she tells Miss Havisham, and "'I must be taken as I have been made'" (2:19, p.304). Herbert Pocket explains to Pip that Estella "'has been brought up by Miss Havisham to wreak revenge on all the male sex'" (2:3, p.175), her vindictive purpose forming a parallel with Magwitch's determination to make Pip a gentleman so as to revenge himself upon the moneyed social class he holds responsible for his victimization. Unlike Magwitch, Miss Havisham is eventually brought to the realization of her error by the example of Pip's sorrow, and admits the destructive effects of her teaching: "'I stole her heart away and put ice in its place'". "'Better,'" says Pip, "'to have left her a natural heart, even to be bruised or broken'" (3:10, p.397). However, the very notion of female 'nature' involved in this account is put into question by the insistence upon the constructedness of identity in Pip's narrative, by the suggestion that women like Estella are not born but made. The distance between the moral discourse of the adult narrator, and the illusions associated with his younger self, is measured by the persistence with which Pip attempts to understand Estella in the light of Victorian middle-class assumptions about female 'nature'.

Pip's account of Miss Havisham, like his accounts of Mrs. Joe and Mrs. Pocket, implicitly invokes an absent ideal of motherhood, and situates the narrator within the discourse of domesticity. Through the depiction of female deviance, Pip assumes a shared image of maternity that is not only constitutive of his own identity, but of his readership as well. In articulating the values and assumptions of domestic ideology, Pip positions his readers as middle-class individuals and draws them together by basing his account upon a concept of family and female identity supposedly held in common. This construction of the universality of middle-class norms is also part of the narrative of personal development. These representations of female deviance function to produce the effect of Pip's moral growth and maturity, as he moves from the selfish pursuit of wealth and gentility to the fellowship and familial love of the 'true' gentleman in the course of the novel. They help to suggest his destination as a man who has come to perceive the value of home and family, one who appreciates the virtues of kindness, gentleness and loyalty, and who has no more illusions about the lures of wealth and social pretension. But the progress implied in this movement towards understanding and the eschewal of romance is by no means straightforward. Pip's autobiographical narrative rests upon a conception of the self as an autonomous subject that is gradually undermined by the very means used to chart his development. This radical self-questioning emerges in his representation of the two women he contemplates marrying – Estella and Biddy – as well as inhering in the confessional form of his first-person narrative.

The star imagery of Estella's name situates her as a glittering goal, an unattainable prize for the young Pip. She is the object of his desire, awakening in him that sense of a lack which motivates his narrative. She has no 'self'; she has only a role. She is not constructed as a psychologized, classed, developmental individual in the way that Pip is, notwithstanding the destabilization of identity he is forced to undergo; and she therefore helps to sharpen the focus on the role of gender and autobiographical narrative in the construction of the 'self' in the novel. For Pip, she functions as a sign of the restless pursuit of gentility that characterizes his unreformed self (and she is contrasted with Biddy for this purpose). He returns from his first visit to Satis House with a new view of himself as a 'common labouring-boy' (1:8, p.66) obtained from Estella. The two words she uses to condemn him – 'coarse' and 'common' – are repeated in the narrative as a kind of mnemonic formula [a device intended to aid the memory] designed to connect Pip's discontent with its origin in her disdain. In Chapter 10, after meeting the stranger with the file at the Three Jolly Bargemen, Pip thinks of what a 'guiltily coarse and common thing it was, to be on secret terms of conspiracy with convicts' (1:10, p.79); in Chapter 14, he rejects his earlier perception of the forge 'as the glowing road to manhood and independence' with the admission '[n]ow, it was all coarse and common, and I would not have had Miss Havisham and Estella see it on any account' (1:14, p.106); and in Chapter 18, he declines showing his new clothes to the patrons of the Three Jolly

Bargemen because they would make '"such a coarse and common business"' of the exhibition (1:18, p. 143) . . . . . .

Biddy is made to stand for home and the forge, to represent the values of domesticity, in Pip's narrative. Christened with the generic name for an Irish servant-maid, she represents the antithesis of Pip's aristocratic aspirations. Her role in the narrative is most clearly delineated in Chapter 17, which opens with Pip's comment upon the 'regular routine of apprenticeship life' and his loathing for it under the influence of Satis House. With the admission that he 'continued at heart to hate [his] trade and to be ashamed of home' (1:17, p. 124), Pip proceeds to examine his relationship with Biddy – the conspicuous shift in his focus, from work to woman, pointing to her narrative function: 'Imperceptibly I became conscious of a change in Biddy, however. Her shoes came up at the heel, her hair grew bright and neat, her hands were always clean. She was not beautiful – she was common, and could not be like Estella – but she was pleasant and wholesome and sweet-tempered' (1:17, p. 124). Pip draws a distinction here between the charms of Biddy and Estella that is based upon a difference of class. 'Beauty' is made an attribute of gentility. Biddy's designation as 'common' refers at once to her rank and her physiognomy – the ambiguity marking a slippage from the social to the 'natural' in Pip's thinking. He notes that 'she had curiously thoughtful and attentive eyes; eyes that were very pretty and very good'. But while noting that her eyes are 'pretty', most of his appreciation is devoted to the moral virtues they seem to signify: her 'thoughtfulness' and 'attentiveness'. Her eyes suggest a capacity for kindness and self-sacrifice stereotypically associated with the middle-class feminine ideal. Watching her busily engaged in her needlework, Pip marvels at Biddy's ability to keep pace with him in his learning. His wonder draws attention to the invisibility of women's work, since Biddy's self-education is apparently pursued with the same quietness and undemonstrativeness that characterize her housekeeping. But while the young Pip acknowledges the domestic virtues of Biddy, he nevertheless discounts their value. Her 'wholesomeness' is no match for Estella's promise of glamour and exclusivity.

In analyzing his feelings and motives, Pip constantly compares the two women, and his vacillation between them creates the effect of his self-division and psychological development. That Pip's dissatisfaction with his own lot should be registered in the form of a choice between two contrasting images of womanhood highlights the link between the family and female identity in middle-class ideology. The family played a vital role as an imaginary construct in mitigating the effects of the alienation of market relations under capitalism in the nineteenth century. The representation of gender as an apparently fixed system of differences between female and male 'nature' was used to determine social roles and to provide a grounding for the separation of the spheres in which the home could be ideologically preserved as a space where no one was alienated. This special sanctity of the home of course depended upon the conceptualization of the woman who superintended it. Thus the domestic woman – 'naturally' self-sacrificing, pure and loving – occupied a vital place in the symbolic economy as the guarantor of, among other things, male identity. It comes as no surprise, then, that Pip's identity should depend upon his mobilization of two contrasting images of womanhood. The adult narrator charts the young Pip's moral and psychological development by analyzing his shifting relationships with, and attitudes towards, these two women. They signify his wavering between the worlds of gentility and domesticity. The narrative opposition between Biddy and Estella displays the shift in meaning associated with the idea of 'the gentleman' in the novel, as merit comes to dominate birth in the definition of the term . . . . . .

Pip's rebirth into a new and better self after his illness is marked by his decision to return to the forge and marry Biddy. He casts himself as a prodigal son in describing his homecoming . . . : '[M]y heart was softened by my return, and such a change had come to pass, that I felt like one who was toiling home barefoot from distant travel, and whose wanderings had lasted many years' (3:19, p.473). Pip imagines 'the change for the better that would come over my character when I had a guiding spirit at my side whose simple faith and clear home-wisdom I had proved' (3:19, p.473). In finally choosing Biddy to be his 'guiding spirit', Pip would appear to demonstrate his moral growth. Abandoning the hopeless pursuit of gentility that has been signified by his desire for Estella, he seems to acknowledge the true value of domesticity. But . . . this looked-for union . . . does not eventuate. Biddy is discovered to be already married to Joe, and Pip is forced to attach himself as an adjunct to the family of Herbert and Clara. Pip's inability to marry Biddy disrupts the conventional closure towards which his narrative seemed to be moving. It destabilizes the identity he has been desperately attempting to construct and transforms the remaining pages of his autobiography into a kind of postscript. Coming back to the forge after his sojourn in the East, he looks into the old kitchen 'unseen': 'There, smoking his pipe in the old place by the kitchen firelight, as hale and as strong as ever though a little grey, sat Joe; and there, fenced into the corner with Joe's leg, and sitting on my own little stool and looking at the fire, was – I again!' (3:20, p.476). Pip finds himself displaced from the family fireside by his namesake, just as he has been displaced from the centre of his own narrative. He is not part of this cosy family unit, and his marginality is further emphasized by his status as voyeur, gazing in upon the hearth-side scene of domestic life . . . .

As an autobiographical narrative apparently devoted to the faithful record of Pip's quest to establish his own identity, *Great Expectations* ultimately questions the assumptions about selfhood which underlie its form. Not surprisingly, the ideology of domesticity figures significantly in Pip's attempt to write the self, but the novel offers a profoundly ambiguous representation of the family. On the one hand, it invests heavily in the domestic ideal, for Pip's portraits of Mrs. Joe, Mrs. Pocket, and Miss Havisham invoke a norm of maternal behaviour that would appear to situate him securely within the discourse of the middle-class family. Allied to this is his belated choice of Biddy as a proper partner for marriage. His eventual recognition of Biddy's true worth is meant to indicate his moral and emotional development, and to mark his adherence to the values of domesticity. On the other hand, however, these efforts to situate himself at the centre of things by appealing to the norms of the middle-class family prove to be mistaken. He is shown to have deluded himself about the plot of his own life, which turns out to be quite different from the tale of 'great expectations' he had imagined. The autonomy conventionally associated with autobiographical narration is gradually revealed to be an illusion. The very process by which conceptualizations of the family and female identity are used to write the narrative of Pip's development is undermined by its exposure as a symbolic operation that is fraught with contradiction. The representation of Estella unsettles the illusion of autobiographical achievement, making visible her imaginary function within the novel. Instead of closing securely with the formation of a new family, *Great Expectations* ends in indeterminacy, with a narrator who remains vulnerable and radically displaced.[38] □

In chapter one of this Guide, H. F. Chorley's review of *Great Expectations* in July 1861 registered a certain indeterminacy in the ending with regard to the question of whether Pip married Estella (see pp. 13, 15). In 1997, 136 years later, Catherine Waters also registers an indeterminacy located not in the ending alone but spreading throughout the novel to disrupt its attempts at coherence. Waters's reading, like those of Said and Cohen, demonstrates the continued fertility and variety of *Great Expectations* studies in the 1990s, their capacity to exceed expectations. Readers of the novel can entertain, without fear of disappointment, great expectations of further readings of Dickens's novel which will relate it to colonialism, to sexuality, and to gender, and which will strike out in other as yet unsuspected directions. In 1972, William F. Axton began an essay called '*Great Expectations* Yet Again' with the remark that '[i]t hardly seems possible, or at least permissible to add to the store of commentary on *Great*

Expectations';[39] in 1998, his observation seems rather premature. The last three decades have shown that adding to the store of commentary on *Great Expectations* is possible, permissible, and perhaps irresistible, that there shall never be a lack of critics compelled to pursue this astonishing story from its first, dizzying encounter in a bleak churchyard, through its shattering shock of recognition in the dark heart of London, to its last ambiguous handclasp in evening mists.

APPENDIX A

The proof version of the original ending, as printed in the Clarendon Dickens edition of *Great Expectations* (pp. 481–82), is given below. It was intended to follow Pip's statement to Biddy in the last chapter: '"My dear Biddy, I have forgotten nothing in my life that ever had a foremost place there, and little that ever had any place there. But that poor dream, as I once used to call it, has all gone by, Biddy, all gone by!"' (3:20, p. 477).

The original ending then read:

■ It was four years more, before I saw herself. I had heard of her as leading a most unhappy life, and as being separated from her husband who had used her with great cruelty, and who had become quite renowned as a compound of pride, brutality, and meanness. I had heard of the death of her husband (from an accident consequent on ill-treating a horse), and of her being married again to a Shropshire doctor, who, against his interest, had once very manfully interposed, on an occasion when he was in professional attendance on Mr. Drummle, and had witnessed some outrageous treatment of her. I had heard that the Shropshire doctor was not rich, and that they lived on her own personal fortune.

I was in England again – in London, and walking along Piccadilly with little Pip – when a servant came running after me to ask would I step back to a lady in a carriage who wished to speak to me. It was a little pony carriage, which the lady was driving; and the lady and I looked sadly enough on one another.

'I am greatly changed, I know; but I thought you would like to shake hands with Estella too, Pip. Lift up that pretty child and let me kiss it!' (She supposed the child, I think, to be my child.)

I was very glad afterwards to have had the interview; for, in her face and in her voice, and in her touch, she gave me the assurance, that suffering had been stronger than Miss Havisham's teaching, and had given her a heart to understand what my heart used to be. □

APPENDIX B

As mentioned in the 'Note on References', the authoritative Clarendon Dickens edition of *Great Expectations* retains, in one volume, the original volume divisions and chapter numbers of the novel. Many modern editions, however, leave out the volume divisions and number the chapters consecutively straight through the novel. To facilitate references between this Guide, the Clarendon edition, and other editions, the table below gives, on the left, the volume and chapter numbers of the Clarendon edition and, on the right, the equivalent chapter numbers in editions without volume divisions.

Clarendon edition: Editions without volume divisions:

Volume and chapter numbers	Chapter numbers
1:1	1
1:2	2
1:3	3
1:4	4
1:5	5
1:6	6
1:7	7
1:8	8
1:9	9
1:10	10
1:11	11
1:12	12
1:13	13
1:14	14
1:15	15
1:16	16
1:17	17
1:18	18
1:19	19
2:1	20
2:2	21
2:3	22
2:4	23
2:5	24
2:6	25
2:7	26

Volume and chapter numbers	Chapter numbers
2:8	27
2:9	28
2:10	29
2:11	30
2:12	31
2:13	32
2:14	33
2:15	34
2:16	35
2:17	36
2:18	37
2:19	38
2:20	39
3:1	40
3:2	41
3:3	42
3:4	43
3:5	44
3:6	45
3:7	46
3:8	47
3:9	48
3:10	49
3:11	50
3:12	51
3:13	52
3:14	53
3:15	54
3:16	55
3:17	56
3:18	57
3:19	58
3:20	59

NOTES

INTRODUCTION

1 For a fascinating study of the 'afterlife' of *Great Expectations* in contemporary 'high' and 'popular' culture, especially in the USA, see Jay Clayton, 'Is Pip Postmodern? Or, Dickens at the End of the Twentieth Century' in Janice Carlisle, ed., *Charles Dickens: 'Great Expectations': Complete, Authoritative Text with Biographical and Historical Contexts, Critical History, and Essays from Five Contemporary Critical Perspectives* (Boston: Bedford Books of St Martin's Press, 1996), pp. 606–24.

2 John Forster, *The Life of Charles Dickens*, vol. 3: *1852–1870.* (London: Chapman and Hall, 1874), p. 328.

3 Forster (1874), p. 329.

4 See Robert L. Patten, *Dickens and His Publishers* (Oxford: Clarendon Press, 1978), pp. 288–93.

5 The front page of *Household Words* for 12 June 1858 is reproduced in Allan Grant, *A Preface to Dickens*, Preface Books series (London: Longman, 1984), p. 187.

CHAPTER ONE

1 Walter Dexter, ed., *The Letters of Charles Dickens*, vol. 3 (London: Nonesuch Press, 1938), p. 228. Quoted in Carlisle (1996), p. 19.

2 The 'From Whom We Have Great Expectations' caricature is reproduced in a number of biographies, for example, Peter Ackroyd, *Dickens* (London: Sinclair-Stevenson, 1990), following p. 816, illustration no. 15; Edgar Johnson, *Charles Dickens: His Tragedy and Triumph*, vol. 2 (London: Gollancz, 1953), following p. viii, illustration no. 70; abridged and revised edition (London: Allen Lane, 1977), following p. 382, illustration no. 70; J.B. Priestley, *Charles Dickens and His World* (London: Thames and Hudson, 1961), p. 107. The caricature is also reproduced in Carlisle, p. 18, which

quotes, on p. 19, Dickens's remark that the caricature was 'much more like me than the grave portrait done in earnest'.

3 G.H. Lewes, 'Dickens in Relation to Criticism', *Fortnightly Review*, 17 (1872), pp. 143–51. Extracts in Alice R. Kaminsky, ed., *Literary Criticism of George Henry Lewes*, Regents Critics series (Lincoln, Nebraska: University of Nebraska Press, 1964), pp. 94–105; Stephen Wall, ed., *Charles Dickens: A Critical Anthology*, Penguin Critical Anthologies series (Harmondsworth: Penguin, 1970), pp. 191–202. Reprinted in George H. Ford and Lauriat Lane, Jr., eds, *The Dickens Critics* (Ithaca, New York: Cornell University Press, 1961), pp. 54–74. Future Lewes page references to Ford and Lane (1961). This quotation, Ford and Lane (1961), p. 64.

4 George J. Worth, *Great Expectations: An Annotated Bibliography*, Garland Dickens Bibliographies series (New York: Garland Publishing, Inc., 1986), p. 51.

5 See Edgar J. Rosenberg, 'Last Words on *Great Expectations*: A Textual Brief on the Six Endings', *Dickens Studies Annual*, 9 (1981), p. 87–115, especially p. 93; Walter Dexter, 'The End of *Great Expectations*', *The Dickensian*, 34 (Spring 1938), p. 82; Angus Calder, ed., *Great Expectations*, Penguin English Library series (Harmondsworth: Penguin, 1965), Appendix A, 'The End of the Novel', pp. 494–96. On p. 496, Calder suggests that, in changing 'I saw the shadow of no parting from her' to 'I saw no shadow of another parting from her', 'Dickens perhaps intended to make the last phrase less definite, and even ambiguous. For the later version hints at the buried meaning: '". . . at this happy moment, I did not see the shadow of our subsequent parting looming over us"'. See also Margaret Cardwell's 'Introduction' to her Clarendon Dickens edition of *Great Expectations* (Oxford: Clarendon Press, 1993), especially p. xliii, where she points out that 'the alteration [of the final clause] has provided material for critical speculation ever since'.

6 See Daniel Defoe, *The Life and*

Adventures of Robinson Crusoe, Penguin Classics series (London: Penguin, 1985), p.162. 'It happened one day about noon going towards my boat, I was exceedingly surprized [*sic*] with the print of a man's naked foot on the shore, which was very plain to be seen in the sand. I stood like one thunder-struck, or as if I had seen an apparition. . .'.

7 In relation to H.F. Chorley's playful mention of the 'works of art' on Wemmick's Walworth 'estate', it is interesting to consider Lawrence Jay Dessner's comparison of Wemmick and the great Victorian art critic and cultural analyst, John Ruskin. See Dessner, '*Great Expectations*: The Tragic Comedy of John Wemmick', *Ariel: A Review of International English*, 6:2 (April 1975), pp.65–80, especially pp.66–68.

8 [H.F. Chorley], '*Great Expectations*', *Athenaeum*, 159 (2319) (13 July 1861), pp.43–5. Extracts in Norman Page, ed., *Charles Dickens: 'Hard Times', 'Great Expectations', and 'Our Mutual Friend': A Casebook*, Casebook series (London: Macmillan, 1979), pp.94–6.

9 See Worth (1986), p.51.

10 Anon., '*Great Expectations*', *The Literary Gazette*, 7: 159 (13 July 1861), p.32. Hereafter referenced as *LG*.

11 *LG*, p.32.

12 *LG*, p.33.

13 *LG*, p.32.

14 *LG*, p.33.

15 Worth (1986), pp.51–52.

16 [Forster, John or Morley, Henry?], '*Great Expectations*', *The Examiner*, (20 July 1861), p.453. Hereafter referenced as *E*.

17 *E*, p.452.

18 *E*, p.453.

19 See Worth (1986), p.52.

20 [Meredith Townsend?], '*Great Expectations*', *The Spectator*, 34 (20 July 1861), p.784. Hereafter referenced as *S*.

21 *S*, p.784.

22 *S*, p.785.

23 See Worth (1986), p.52.

24 Anon., '*Great Expectations*', *The Saturday Review*, 12 (20 July 1861), p.69. Hereafter referenced as *SR*.

25 *SR*, p.70.

26 *SR*, p.69.

27 *SR*, p.69.

28 *SR*, p.70.

29 *SR*, p.69.

30 Worth (1986), p.53.

31 William Shakespeare, *The Complete Works*, Stanley Wells, Gary Taylor, John Jowett, William Montgomery, eds. (Oxford: Oxford University Press, 1988), p.584.

32 [Edwin P. Whipple], '*Great Expectations*', *Atlantic Monthly*, 8 (September 1861), pp.380–82. Extracts in Philip Collins, ed., *Dickens: The Critical Heritage* (London: Routledge and Kegan Paul, 1971), pp.428–30; Page (1979), p.98. The extracts in this Guide are from *Atlantic Monthly*, pp.380–81, 382.

33 See Worth (1986), pp.53–54. Collins (1971), p.430, says that 'Dallas (1828–79) [was] the author of *The Gay Science* (1866), and other notable critical books and reviews [including *Poetics: An Essay on Poetry* (1852)].

34 [E.S. Dallas], '*Great Expectations*', *The Times* (17 October 1861), p.6. Extracts in Collins (1971), pp.430–34; Page (1979), p.99. Hereafter referenced as *Times* (1861).

35 J. Hillis Miller, *Charles Dickens: The World of His Novels* (Cambridge, Massachusetts: Harvard University Press, 1958), p.255. Miller makes a similar point in his 'Introduction' to Charles Dickens, *Oliver Twist* (New York: Holt, Rinehart and Winston, 1962), reprinted in J. Hillis Miller, *Victorian Subjects* (Hemel Hempstead: Harvester Wheatsheaf, 1990), pp.31–48. Comparing Oliver and Pip, he says: 'But all Pip's expectations are exploded. The actual source of his wealth and status as a gentleman turns out to be a strange permutation of Mr. Brownlow [in *Oliver Twist*] – Magwitch, transported felon and "'hunted dunghill dog'" (ch. 39, p.337), a man more like Fagin or Sikes than like any of the good characters in *Oliver Twist*'(Miller (1990), pp.48–49.

36 *Times* (1861), p.6.

37 See Worth (1986), p. 53.

38 Anon., 'Charles Dickens'[s] *Great Expectations*', *The Eclectic Review*, 1 (October 1861), p. 460. Hereafter referenced as *ER*.

39 *ER*, p. 465.

40 *ER*, p. 458.

41 *ER*, p. 459.

42 *ER*, p. 458.

43 *ER*, p. 459.

44 *ER*, pp. 459–60.

45 *ER*, p. 474.

46 *ER*, p. 472.

47 *ER*, p. 471.

48 *ER*, p. 472.

49 *ER*, p. 471.

50 *ER*, p. 473.

51 *ER*, p. 463.

52 See Worth (1986), p. 54.

53 [L. J. Trotter], 'Mr. Dickens's Last Novel', *Dublin University Magazine*, 68 (December 1861), p. 685. Extracts in Collins (1971), pp. 434–36. Hereafter referenced as *DUM*.

54 *DUM*, p. 686.

55 *DUM*, p. 685.

56 *DUM*, p. 686.

57 *DUM*, p. 687.

58 *DUM*, p. 688.

59 *DUM*, p. 692.

60 *DUM*, pp. 692–93.

61 *DUM*, p. 693.

62 *DUM*, p. 690.

63 *DUM*, p. 692.

64 *DUM*, p. 693.

65 *DUM*, p. 692.

66 *DUM*, pp. 690–91.

67 See Worth (1986), p. 54.

68 J. A., '*Great Expectations*', *Ladies Companion and Monthly Magazine*, 20 (1861), p. 218. Hereafter referenced as *LCM*.

69 *LCM*, p. 219.

70 *LCM*, p. 218.

71 *LCM*, p. 219.

72 *LCM*, p. 218.

73 *LCM*, p. 219.

74 *LCM*, pp. 219–20.

75 *LCM*, p. 220.

76 *LCM*, p. 219.

77 Worth (1986), p. 55.

78 Anon., 'The Collected Works of Charles Dickens', *British Quarterly Review*, 35 (January 1862), p. 154.

79 *British Quarterly Review*, p. 155.

80 On the issue of women and violence in *Great Expectations*, see Lucy Frost, 'Taming to Improve: Dickens and the Women in *Great Expectations*', *Meridian*, 1 (1982), pp. 11–20; reprinted in Roger D. Sell, ed., *New Casebooks:* Great Expectations, New Casebooks series (London: Macmillan, 1994), pp. 60–78; Hilary Schor, '"If He Should Turn To and Beat Her": Violence, Desire, and the Woman's Story in *Great Expectations*' in Carlisle (1996), pp. 541–57.

81 See Worth (1968), p. 55. According to Collins (1971), p. 436, the review was originally written by John Moore Capes, the founder, former editor, and, in 1862, proprietor of *The Rambler*, and it incorporated remarks from Lord Acton's letters to *The Rambler*'s current editor, Richard Simpson – for example, that Dickens 'knows nothing of sin when it is not crime'.

82 [John Moore Capes and J. E. E. D. Acton], '*Great Expectations*', *The Rambler*, 6 (January 1862), p. 275. Extracts in Collins (1971), pp. 436–38.

83 *The Rambler*, p. 276.

84 See Worth (1986), p. 55 and Collins (1971), p. 439.

85 [Margaret Oliphant], 'Sensation Novels', *Blackwood's Edinburgh Magazine*, 91 (May 1862), p. 575. Extracts in Collins (1971), pp. 439–42. Hereafter referenced as *BM*.

86 *BM*, p. 577.

87 *BM*, p. 578.

88 *BM*, p. 577.

89 *BM*, p. 579.

90 *BM*, p. 580.

CHAPTER TWO

1 *The Empty Chair* is reproduced in Ackroyd (1990), following p. 816, illustration no. 18; Johnson (1953), following p. viii, illustration no. 84; Johnson (1977), following p. 382, illustration no.

84; in its embellished cartoon form, it is reproduced in Priestley (1961), p. 128; Angus Wilson, *The World of Charles Dickens* (London: Secker and Warburg, 1970; Harmondsworth: Penguin, 1972), p. 297.

2 Benjamin Jowett, 'Sermon at Dickens's Funeral Service', *The Times*, 20 June 1870, reprinted in Wall (1970), p. 176.

3 Quoted Wall (1970), p. 32.

4 [*Forster's Note, on Thomas Carlyle's response, at his Chelsea home, to the weekly episodes of* Great Expectations:] A dear friend now gone, used laughingly to relate what outcry there used to be, on the night of the week when a number was due, for 'that Pip nonsense!' and what roars of laughter followed, though at first it was entirely put aside, as not on any account to have time wasted over it.

5 Forster (1874), pp. 335–36.

6 Forster (1874), p. 335. Rosenberg (1981), p. 88, observed that '[t]he two endings of *Great Expectations* have generated enough talk in the last 30 years to call for some sort of moratorium' – but this remark is a prelude to his own discussion of the topic, indicating its ongoing fascination and the improbability of any such 'moratorium'! Worth (1986), p. xvi, observes that the Subject Index of his Bibliography of *Great Expectations* criticism contains 'nearly one hundred entries' on the topic. Most critics who write about *Great Expectations* mention the changed ending, and many take up a position for or against it. A number of critical essays focus on the topic, for example: Martin Meisel, 'The Ending of *Great Expectations*', *Essays in Criticism*, 15 (July 1965), pp. 326–31; reprinted under the heading 'The Problem of the Novel's Ending' in Page (1979), pp. 125–29; Marshall W. Gregory, 'Values and Meanings in *Great Expectations*: The Two Endings Revisited', *Essays in Criticism*, 19 (October 1969), pp. 402–09; Milton Millhauser, '*Great Expectations*: The Three Endings', *Dickens Studies Annual*, 2 (1972), pp. 267–77; John Kucich, 'Action in the Dickens

Ending: *Bleak House* and *Great Expectations*', *Nineteenth-Century Fiction*, 33 (June 1978), pp. 88–109, especially pp. 102–107; Rosenberg (1981); Jerome Meckier, 'Charles Dickens's *Great Expectations*: A Defence of the Second Ending', *Studies in the Novel*, 25 (1993), pp. 28–58.

7 George H. Ford, *Dickens and His Readers: Aspects of Novel-Criticism Since 1836* (Princeton, New Jersey: Princeton University Press for the University of Cincinnati, 1955), p. 159.

8 Ford and Lane (1961), p. 58.

9 Ford and Lane (1961), p. 59.

10 Ford and Lane (1961), p. 61.

11 Ford and Lane (1961), p. 63.

12 Ford and Lane (1961), p. 69.

13 Ford and Lane (1961), p. 58.

14 Q. D. Leavis, *Fiction and the Reading Public* (London: Chatto and Windus, 1932; Harmondsworth: Penguin, 1979), p. 130.

15 Ford and Lane (1961), p. 58.

16 Ford and Lane (1961), p. 59.

17 Ford and Lane (1961), p. 61.

18 Ford and Lane (1961), p. 65.

19 Andrew Lang, 'Charles Dickens', *Fortnightly Review*, 64 (December 1898), pp. 944–60. Also in Charles Dickens, *Reprinted Pieces: The Lamplighter, To be Read at Dusk, Sunday Under Three Heads*, Gadshill Edition of the Works of Charles Dickens (London: Chapman and Hall), vol. 34 (1899), pp. ix–xxxvi. References that follow are to *Fortnighly Review* and are referenced as Lang (1898a).

20 Lang (1898a), p. 948.

21 Lang (1898a), p. 951.

22 Lang (1898a), p. 956.

23 Lang (1898a), p. 957.

24 Andrew Lang, 'Introduction' to Charles Dickens, *Great Expectations*, Gadshill Edition of The Works of Charles Dickens, vol. 22 (London: Chapman and Hall, 1898), pp. v–xi. Hereafter referenced as Lang (1898b).

25 Lang (1898b), p. vii.

26 Lang (1898b), pp. viii, ix, x–xi.

27 Algernon Charles Swinburne, 'Charles Dickens', *The Quarterly Review*, 196 (July

1902), pp. 20–39. Incorporated in Swinburne, *Charles Dickens* (London: Chatto and Windus, 1913. Extract in Wall (1970), pp. 250–53; Cotsell (1990), pp. 22–4. This quotation, Swinburne (1902), p. 39.

28 George Gissing, *Charles Dickens: A Critical Study*. The Victorian Era series. (London: Blackie, 1898); The Imperial Edition of the Works of Charles Dickens (London: Gresham, 1902). Extracts in Wall (1970), pp. 222–39; Cotsell (1990), pp. 24–7.

29 Ford (1955), pp. 245–49.

30 Gissing (1902), p. 70.

31 Gissing (1902), p. 71.

32 Gissing (1902), p. 85.

33 Gissing (1902), p. 82.

34 Gissing (1902), p. 151.

35 Gissing (1902), p. 60.

36 Gissing (1902), p. 110.

37 Gissing (1902), p. 109.

38 Gissing (1902), p. 110.

39 Gissing (1902), p. 118.

40 Gissing (1902), p. 151.

41 Gissing (1902), p. 152.

42 George Gissing, *New Grub Street* (London: Smith Elder, 1891), 3 vols; Penguin Classics series (Harmondsworth: Penguin, 1985), p. 38.

43 Gissing (1902), p. 167.

44 Gissing (1902), p. 168.

45 Gissing (1902), p. 168–69.

46 John Halperin, *Gissing: A Life in Books* (Oxford: Oxford University Press, 1982; paperback edn, 1987), p. 265.

47 See, for example, Frost (1982) and Schor (1996), details at chapter one, note 78 and in Bibliography; and Albert D. Hutter, 'Crime and Fantasy in *Great Expectations*', Frederick Crews, ed., *Psychoanalysis and Literary Process* (Cambridge, Massachusetts: Winthrop, 1970), pp. 25–65. Reprinted Cotsell (1990), pp. 93–124. See also Moynahan and Garis in chapter four of this Guide.

48 Gissing (1902), p. 66.

49 Gissing (1902), p. 213.

50 Gissing (1902), p. 214.

51 Swinburne (1902), p. 39.

52 Worth (1986), p. 78.

53 Swinburne (1902), pp. 250–53.

54 Swinburne (1902), p. 32.

55 Swinburne (1902), p. 33.

56 Swinburne (1902), p. 34.

57 G. K. Chesterton, *Charles Dickens* (London: Methuen, 1906, 1946). The details of the number of editions are taken from the verso of the title page of the 1946 edition. Extracts in Wall (1970), pp. 244–50; Page (1979), p. 102; Cotsell (1990), pp. 27–28.

58 Chesterton (1946), p. 11.

59 Chesterton (1946), p. 10.

60 Chesterton (1946), p. 4.

61 Chesterton (1946), p. 5. It is the case that Gissing, in *Charles Dickens: A Critical Study*, stresses the harshness of the world in which Dickens grew up – 'it was a time by several degrees harsher, coarser, and uglier than our own [that is, the late nineteenth century]' (Gissing (1902), p. 8); but he does not, as Chesterton implies, wholly deny it some positive aspects – for example, he calls it '[a] time of suffering, of conflict, of expansion, of progress' (p. 3) and 'cruel, unlovely, but abounding in vital force' (p. 10).

62 Chesterton (1946), p. 11.

63 Chesterton (1946), p. 12.

64 Chesterton (1946), p. 14.

65 Chesterton (1946), p. 13.

66 Chesterton (1946), p. 14.

67 Chesterton (1946), p. 165.

68 Chesterton (1946), pp. 168–69.

69 G. K. Chesterton, *Appreciations and Criticisms of the Works of Charles Dickens* (London: J. M. Dent, 1911), pp. 197, 199–205, 206. Extracts in Cotsell (1990), pp. 28–33.

70 Chesterton (1911), pp. 197, 199–205, 206.

71 G. K. Chesterton, 'Foreword', Edwin Charles, *Some Dickens Women* (London: T. Werner Laurie, 1926), p. v.

72 See Sell (1994), pp. 31–32 for an interesting discussion of *The Dickensian*, where he says that the 'characteristic aim' of the magazine 'has been to winkle out all there is to know about the sources of Dickens's novels in his own life, about the "true" geographical location of his

fictional settings, about the real-life "models" for his characters, and about other socio-cultural minutiae as well' (pp. 31–32). Sell makes an intriguing suggestion about one possible development of Dickens criticism in the 1990s and beyond: 'now that "new historical" and "cultural materialist" critics are extending their Marxist or post-Marxist critique from Shakespeare to other writers, we can expect them to establish new and surprising connections between Dickens and society by using just the kind of miscellaneous socio-cultural detail which has always been *The Dickensian*'s forte' (p. 32).

73 Willoughby Matchett, 'The Strange Case of *Great Expectations*', *The Dickensian*, 9 (February 1913), p. 33.

74 Matchett (1913), p. 34.

75 See Ford (1955), pp. 172–73.

76 Leavis (1979), p. 129.

77 Leavis (1979), p. 130.

78 Leavis (1979), p. 131.

79 Stephen Leacock, *Charles Dickens: His Life and Work* (London: Peter Davies, 1933), p. 201.

80 Leacock (1933), pp. 201–02.

81 Leacock (1933), p. 202.

82 See K. J. Fielding, *Charles Dickens*, Bibliographical Series of Supplements to 'British Book News' (London: Longmans, Green for the British Council and the National Book League, 1953), pp. 27–28. Wright quote, p. 28.

83 See Fielding (1953), pp. 30–31.

84 George Bernard Shaw, 'Preface', Charles Dickens, *Great Expectations* (New York: Limited Editions Club, 1937), pp. v–xxii; 'Foreword', Charles Dickens, *Great Expectations*, The Novel Library series (London: Hamish Hamilton, 1947), pp. v–xx; this bears the heading 'Foreword' in the 1947 edition, although it is described on the title page as an 'Introduction', and Worth (1986), Rosenberg (1981) and House (1955) (see below) all refer to it by the latter term. Shaw restored Dickens's original ending for the 1937 edition but the revised ending was reinstated for the 1947 edition.

Shaw's 1947 'Foreword' is reprinted in Wall (1970), pp. 284–97; Cotsell (1990), pp. 33–44. In Wall's anthology (p. 284), the bibliographical note at the head of the Shaw piece claims that the 1947 version was 'reprinted' in 1937 and makes no mention of any difference between the two. See Worth (1986), pp. 76–77, for an account of the 1937 version and Worth (1986), pp. 126–27 for an account of the 1947 version and comments on the differences between the two versions. Worth cites Edgar J. Rosenberg's argument that the 1947 version was the one Shaw had intended to publish in 1937; Rosenberg says that '[o]n the available evidence, the Introduction published by Hamish Hamilton in 1947 had been intended by Shaw to supersede the 1937 Preface all along, and only the failure to get it to the printer in time prevented its appearance for Limited Editions ten years earlier . . . I conclude that Shaw himself looked on his 1947 Introduction as the final authority' (Rosenberg (1981), pp. 112–13, note 27). For a discussion of Shaw's 1947 'Foreword', see Humphry House, 'G. B. S. on *Great Expectations*', *The Dickensian* 44 (Spring 1948), pp. 63–70, and 44 (Autumn 1948), pp. 183–86, reprinted in House, *All in Due Time: The Collected Essays and Broadcast Talks* (London: Hart-Davis, 1955), pp. 201–20.

85 See Ford (1955) and Shaw himself in 'George Bernard Shaw Thinks All Dickens's Later Works Magnificent', *The Bookman*, 41 (February 1912), p. 247. Shaw states here: 'My works are all over Dickens; and nothing but the stupendous illiteracy of modern criticism could have missed this glaring feature of my methods – especially my continual exploitation of Dickens's demonstration that it is possible to combine a mirrorlike exactness of character drawing with the wildest extravagance of humorous expression and grotesque situation. I have actually transferred characters of Dickens to my plays – Jaggers in *Great Expectations*, to *You Never Can Tell* (1897), for example –

with complete success'.
86 Shaw (1947), p. viii.
87 Shaw (1947), p. ix.
88 Shaw (1947), p. xii.
89 Shaw (1947), p. vi.
90 Shaw (1947), p. xvi.
91 Shaw (1947), p. xvii.
92 Shaw (1947), p. xviii.
93 In the first paragraph of his 'Foreword', Shaw says 'we shall never know whether in that immensely broadened outlook and knowledge of the world which began with *Hard Times* and *Little Dorrit*, and left all his earlier works behind, he may not have come to see that making his living by sticking labels on blacking bottles and rubbing shoulders with boys who were not gentlemen, was as little shameful as being the genteel apprentice in the office of Mr. Spenlow [in *David Copperfield*], or the shorthand writer [Dickens himself, in his early career] recording the unending twaddle of the House of Commons and electioneering bunk on the hustings of all the Eatanswills in the country' (Shaw (1947), p. v).
94 Shaw (1947), pp. xviii–xx.
95 T.A. Jackson, *Charles Dickens: The Progress of A Radical* (London: Lawrence and Wishart, 1937; New York: Haskell House Publishers Ltd, 1971), pp. ix–x.
96 Jackson (1971), p. x.
97 Jackson (1971), pp. 197–98.
98 For two recent helpful and interesting accounts of *Great Expectations* in relation to the Victorian economy, see W.J. Lohman, Jr., 'The Economic Background of *Great Expectations*', *Victorians Institute Journal*, 14 (1986), pp. 53–66, and Susan Walsh, 'Bodies of Capital: *Great Expectations* and the Climacteric Economy', *Victorian Studies: A Journal of the Humanities, Arts and Sciences*, 37:1 (Fall 1993), pp. 73–98.
99 For citations of Jackson, see George Orwell, 'Charles Dickens', *Inside the Whale* (London: Gollancz, 1940). Reprinted in Sonia Orwell and Ian Angus, eds, *The Collected Essays, Journalism and Letters of George Orwell: Volume I: An Age Like This 1920–1940* (Harmondsworth: Penguin in association with Martin Secker and Warburg, 1968), pp. 454, 455; Edmund Wilson, 'Dickens: The Two Scrooges', *The Wound and the Bow: Seven Studies in Literature* (London: W.H. Allen, 1941; revised edition, 1942; Methuen, 1961), pp. 2, 24, 54; Humphry House, *The Dickens World*, 2nd edn (Oxford: Oxford University Press, 1942), pp. 11, 152, 157–58.
100 Jackson (1971), p. 198.
101 Jackson (1971), p. 199.
102 Jackson (1971), p. 200.
103 Orwell (1968), p. 504. Extracts from Orwell's 'Charles Dickens' in Wall (1970), pp. 297–313; Ford and Lane (1961), pp. 157–71.
104 Orwell (1968), p. 454.
105 Orwell (1968), p. 455.
106 Orwell (1968), p. 456.
107 Orwell (1968), p. 455.
108 Orwell (1968), p. 456.
109 Orwell (1968), p. 457.
110 Orwell (1968), p. 468.
111 Orwell (1968), p. 475.
112 Orwell (1968), p. 476.
113 Orwell (1968), pp. 476–77.
114 Orwell (1968), p. 465.
115 Orwell (1968), p. 493.
116 Orwell (1968), p. 496.
117 Orwell (1968), pp. 496–97.
118 Wilson (1961), p. 8.
119 Wilson (1961), p. 5.
120 Wilson (1961), pp. 57–58.
121 Wilson (1961), p. 22.
122 Wilson (1961), p. 24.
123 Wilson (1961), p. 13.
124 Wilson (1961), p. 26.
125 Wilson (1961), p. 3.
126 Wilson (1961), p. 32.
127 Wilson (1961), p. 31.
128 Wilson (1961), p. 46.
129 Wilson (1961), p. 55.
130 Wilson (1961), p. 59.
131 Wilson (1961), p. 53.
132 Wilson (1961), pp. 58–59.
133 Wilson (1961), p. 55.
134 House (1942), p. 15.
135 House (1942), p. 10.
136 House (1942), p. 14.

137 House (1942), p.156.
138 House (1942), pp.156–57, 159. As W.J. Lohman, Jr. pointed out in 1986, 'the assumption that England was uniformly prosperous from 1850–1873' has been challenged by economic data that have recently become available. He suggests that this period 'included both a time of unprecedented boom and one of the sharpest, longest and most painful depressions in the nineteenth century, an economic reversal which began in 1857 and lasted past the publication of *Great Expectations* in 1860–61' (Lohman (1986), p.53.
139 F.R. Leavis, *The Great Tradition: George Eliot; Henry James; Joseph Conrad* (London: Chatto and Windus, 1948; Penguin, 1972), p.9.
140 George Santayana, 'Dickens', *The Dial*, 71 (1921), pp.537–49; reprinted Ford and Lane (1961), pp.135–51; Norman Henfrey, ed., *Selected Critical Writings of George Santayana*, vol. 1 (Cambridge: Cambridge University Press, 1968); extract in Wall (1968), pp.258–69. This quotation, Santayana (1968), p.202. Leavis has 'would do well' for 'will do well'.
141 In the 1972 edition, Leavis inserts a footnote at this point that reads: 'Rather, childhood memory and the potent family-reading experience must be invoked to excuse what is absurd in this paragraph. Others will testify to the power of the "interference". I now think that, if any one writer can be said to have created the modern novel, it is Dickens' (Leavis (1972), p.30, n. 1). In F.R. and Q.D. Leavis's *Dickens the Novelist* (London: Chatto and Windus, 1970), their highly positive evaluation of Dickens is not accompanied by any direct explanation of their earlier dismissive judgements or their later change of mind; and the footnote added to *The Great Tradition* itself is, both by its nature as a footnote and by what it actually says, a reticent and partial retraction – to plead indulgence for 'what is absurd' in his earlier judgement of Dickens is to imply that there are ele-

ments of that judgement that are still valid, without committing himself to identifying those elements.
142 Leavis (1972), p.30.
143 Leavis (1972), p.30.
144 Reprinted in Wall (1970), pp.363–75.
145 Lionel Trilling, 'Manners, Morals, and the Novel', *Kenyon Review*, 10 (Winter 1948), pp.1–27; reprinted in Trilling, *The Liberal Imagination: Essays on Literature and Society* (New York: Viking, 1950; London: Secker and Warburg, 1955), pp.205–22.
146 Trilling (1955), p.211.
147 See Nicolas Tredell, ed., *The Great Gatsby*, Icon Critical Guides series (Cambridge: Icon, 1997), pp.51–56. Two essays that compare *Great Expectations* and *The Great Gatsby* are: Norman Friedman, 'Versions of Form in Fiction – *Great Expectations* and *The Great Gatsby*', *Accent*, 14 (Autumn 1954), pp.246–63; revised version appears as 'Pluralism Exemplified: *Great Expectations* and *The Great Gatsby*' in Friedman, *Form and Meaning in Fiction* (Athens: University of Georgia Press, 1975), pp.21–41; Edward Vasta, '*Great Expectations* and *The Great Gatsby*', *The Dickensian*, 60 (1964), pp.167–72.

CHAPTER THREE

1 Jack Lindsay, *Charles Dickens: A Biographical and Critical Study* (London: Andrew Dakers, 1950), p.5.
2 Lindsay (1950), pp.370–73.
3 Johnson (1953), pp.989, 992.
4 Dorothy Van Ghent, *The English Novel: Form and Function* (New York: Holt, Rinehart and Winston, 1953). In this book, essay 9, pp.125–38, is on *Great Expectations*. Reprinted in A.E. Dyson, ed., *Dickens: Modern Judgements*, Modern Judgements series (London: Macmillan, 1968), pp.244–57; extract in Wall (1970), pp.375–79. See pp.370–79 of Ghent's book for the 'Problems for Study and Discussion' on *Great Expectations*.
5 Van Ghent (1966), p.vii.
6 Van Ghent (1966), p.6.

7 Van Ghent (1966), p. 7.
8 Van Ghent (1966), p. 129.
9 Van Ghent (1966), p. 131.
10 Van Ghent (1966), p. 132.
11 Van Ghent (1966), p. 130.
12 Van Ghent (1966), p. 131.
13 Van Ghent (1966), p. 133.
14 Van Ghent (1966), pp. 134–38.
15 See Walter Benjamin's discussion of the *flâneur* in the nineteenth-century city in his essay 'On Some Motifs in Baudelaire' (1939), collected in Benjamin's *Illuminations*, Hannah Arendt, ed., translated by Harry Zohn (London: Fontana/Collins, 1973), especially pp. 174–76.
16 James Joyce, *Stephen Hero: Part of the First Draft of 'A Portrait of the Artist as a Young Man'* (London: Jonathan Cape, 1944; revised edn., 1956), pp. 216, 218.
17 G. Robert Stange, 'Expectations Well Lost: Dickens'[s] Fable for His Time', *College English*, 16 (1954–55), pp. 9–17. Reprinted in Ford and Lane (1961), pp. 294–368; Cotsell (1990), pp. 63–73. Extract above from Ford and Lane (1961), pp. 294–95, 296–306, 307.
18 Ford and Lane (1961), p. 308.
19 Miller (1958), p. ix.
20 Miller (1958), p. x.
21 Miller (1958), p. 249.
22 Miller (1958), p. 254.
23 Miller (1958), p. 258.
24 Miller (1958), pp. 261–62, 263–64, 268–69, 270–74, 276.

CHAPTER FOUR

1 See, for example, John H. Hagan, Jr., 'Structural Patterns in Charles Dickens's *Great Expectations*', *ELH: A Journal of English Literary History*, 21:1 (March 1954), pp. 54–66, and 'The Poor Labyrinth: The Theme of Social Injustice in Dickens's *Great Expectations*', *Nineteenth-Century Fiction*, 9 (December 1954), pp. 169–78; Monroe Engel, *The Maturity of Dickens* (Cambridge, Massachusetts: Harvard University Press, 1959), especially pp. 156–68.
2 Julian Moynahan, 'The Hero's Guilt: The Case of *Great Expectations*', *Essays in Criticism*, 10 (January 1960), pp. 60–79. Reprinted in Page (1979), pp. 103–18; Cotsell, pp. 73–87.
3 Moynahan (1960), p. 60.
4 Moynahan (1960), p. 64.
5 House (1955), p. 218. House's interpretation of Orlick is more political than Moynahan's; for House, 'Orlick represents the element in English society with which Dickens never came to terms . . . There was an underlying fear that "the people" in the mass might turn out to be Orlicks' (House (1955), p. 218).
6 T. S. Eliot, *'Hamlet'* (1919) in *Selected Essays*, 2nd edition (London: Faber and Faber, 1934), p. 145.
7 Moynahan (1960), pp. 64–67, 69–70, 77.
8 Barbara Hardy, 'Formal Analysis and Common Sense', *Essays in Criticism*, 11 (January 1961), p. 112. Hardy's article is also, in part, a reply to another response to Moynahan's essay, Donald W. Crompton's 'The New Criticism: A Caveat', *Essays in Criticism*, 10:3 (July 1960), pp. 359–64; Crompton judges Moynahan's essay to be ingenious but unconvincing, and challenges what he sees as the more widespread critical assumption that the essay exemplifies, 'that the presence of an underlying unifying theme is by itself a sufficient guarantee of a book's quality' (Crompton (1960), p. 360).
9 Barbara Hardy, 'Work in Progress IV; Food and Ceremony in *Great Expectations*', *Essays in Criticism*, 13 (October 1963), pp. 351–63. Reprinted with small changes in Hardy, *The Moral Art of Dickens: Essays* (London: Athlone Press, 1970), pp. 139–55. 1963 version in Wall (1970), pp. 478–90; 1970 version in Page (1979), pp. 130–40. References that follow to Hardy (1970).
10 Hardy (1970), p. 140–41.
11 Shakespeare (1988), p. 924. See p. 958 for same lines in the Folio Text, Act 2, Scene 2, lines 440–41.
12 Shakespeare (1988), p. 988.
13 Hardy (1970), pp. 141–47.

14 Robert Garis, *The Dickens Theatre: A Reassessment of the Novels* (Oxford: Oxford University Press, 1965). Extracts in Wall (1970), pp. 492–99; Cotsell (1990), pp. 87–93. This quotation, Garis (1965), p. 4.

15 Garis (1965), p. 5.

16 Garis (1965), p. 24.

17 Garis (1965), p. 15.

18 Garis (1965), p. 16.

19 Garis (1965), p. 18.

20 Robert B. Partlow, Jr., 'The Moving I: A Study of the Point of View in *Great Expectations*', *College English*, 23 (November 1961), pp. 122–26, 131. Extract in Page (1979), pp. 118–24. This quotation, Page (1979), p. 119.

21 Garis (1965), pp. 200–01, 204, 207–08, 211–12.

22 Philip L. Marcus, 'Theme and Suspense in the Plot of *Great Expectations*', *Dickens Studies Annual*, 2 (1966), pp. 57–73. This quotation, p. 57.

23 George Steiner, *Language and Silence: Essays 1958–1966* (London: Faber, 1967; abridged edition, Harmondsworth: Penguin, 1969), p. 244, note 1.

24 Leavis (1970), p. ix.

25 John Lucas, *Charles Dickens: The Major Novels*, Penguin Critical Studies series (London: Penguin, 1992), p. 124.

26 Worth (1986), p. 188.

27 Leavis (1970), p. 292, note 1. Q. D. Leavis's comparison between *Great Expectations* and *The Scarlet Letter* implicitly raises one interesting issue that she does not consider – though her silence is not surprising given her overall approach and her dismissal of psychoanalysis ('the antics of critics searching for Freudian explanations' (Leavis (1970), p. 321). A key theme of *The Scarlet Letter* is *sexual* transgression and guilt, and to compare it to *Great Expectations* could prompt the question as to whether there is also sexual transgression and guilt in Dickens's text. It is a matter that is taken up in William A. Cohen's provocative essay in the final chapter of this Guide. In relation to Cohen's teasing out of the homoerotic subtext of *Great Expectations*, it is worth noting Q. D. Leavis's observation that the scene of Magwitch's return 'carries the added power of a hidden *man-trap* that has been suddenly sprung under the studious young man just about to go peacefully to bed' (Leavis (1970), p. 314. Editor's italics.

28 Leavis (1970), p. 320. See John Bunyan, *The Pilgrim's Progress*, Penguin English Library series (Harmondsworth: Penguin, 1965), pp. 90–95.

29 'Perepeteia', or 'peripety' is 'classical' because it was the term used by the ancient Greek philosopher Aristotle (384–322 B.C.) in his *Poetics*. There, Aristotle defines 'peripeteia' or 'peripety' as 'the change from one state of affairs to its opposite', 'from misery to happiness or happiness to misery'. Aristotle also discusses 'discovery' or 'recognition' ('anagnorisis'): 'a change from ignorance to knowledge' that 'leads either to love or to hatred between persons destined for good and ill fortune'. He contends that a complex plot is 'one in which the change is accompanied by a discovery or a reversal, or both' and that the 'most effective form of discovery is that which is accompanied by reversals [peripeties]' (*Classical Literary Criticism: Aristotle*, On the Art of Poetry, *Horace*, On the Art of Poetry, *Longinus*, On the Sublime, translated by T. S. Dorsch, Penguin Classics series (Harmondsworth: Penguin, 1965), pp. 42, 46). In these terms, *Great Expectations* offers a complex plot in which the change in Pip's fortunes on Magwitch's return exemplifies 'the most effective form of discovery' since it is accompanied by reversal: Pip's change from ignorance to knowledge of his true benefactor is simultaneously the moment of an abrupt reversal of his fortunes from prosperity to prospective penury, and from happiness – of a kind – to misfortune. Peter Brooks employs the term 'peripety' in his analysis of *Great Expectations* in chapter five of this Guide (see p. 127).

30 Leavis (1970), pp. 288–89, 290. One later dissenting note from Q. D. Leavis's interpretation came from an interesting

source. An essay in 1987 concluded by quoting the final paragraph of the extract from Q.D. Leavis's essay included in this Guide, and then commenting: 'Great Expectations in fact reveals a tragic sadness that comes from the narrator not transcending his sense of shame, and . . . the path dramatized in his recoiling from his society does not set him freed [sic] in a liberating sense'. The author of the essay was L.R. Leavis, presumably Q.D. Leavis's younger son, who was clearly not wholly inclined to accept his mother's instructions as to how Great Expectations 'must' be read! See L.R. Leavis, 'The Dramatic Narrator in Great Expectations', English Studies: A Journal of English Language and Literature, 68:3 (June 1987), pp.236–48. Quotation in this note from p.248.

31 Peter Wolfe, 'The Fictional Crux and the Double Structure of Great Expectations', South Atlantic Quarterly, 73 (1974), pp.335–47. This quotation, p.336.

32 Wolfe (1974), p.339.

33 [Editor's Note:] See E.M. Forster, Aspects of the Novel (London: Edward Arnold, 1927; Oliver Stallybrass, ed., Harmondsworth: Penguin, 1976). Discussing Percy Lubbock's The Craft of Fiction (London: Cape, 1921), Forster says: 'for me the whole intricate question of method resolves itself not into formulae but into the power of the writer to bounce the reader into accepting what he says . . . I should put [this power] plumb in the centre [of the problem of method]. Look how Dickens bounces us in Bleak House . . . Logically, Bleak House is all to pieces, but Dickens bounces us, so that we do not mind the shiftings of the viewpoints' (pp.81–82). It is interesting to note that G.K. Chesterton, in the extracts from Appreciations and Criticisms of the Works of Charles Dickens quoted in chapter two of this Guide, also uses the word 'bounce', with regard to Dickens's power of characterisation, when he asserts that 'exactly what [Thackeray or George Eliot] could never have given, and exactly what Dickens does give, is the

bounce of Trabb's boy. It is the real unconquerable rush and energy in a character which was the supreme and quite indescribable greatness of Dickens' (Chesterton (1911), pp.202–203).

34 Wolfe (1974), p.344.
35 Wolfe (1974), p.338.
36 Wolfe (1974), p.345.
37 Wolfe (1974), pp.336–37, 338, 339–40.
38 Harry Stone, 'Fire, Hand, and Gate: Dickens's Great Expectations', Kenyon Review, 24 (Autumn 1962), pp.652–91.
39 Leavis (1970), p.278.
40 Leavis (1970), p.326.
41 Leavis is perhaps referring to the following remark in Stone's 1962 essay: 'though Pip fails to marry the true princess in the primary fairy tale, Joe, the true prince, does win her, and so fulfils a minor fairy-tale theme' (Stone (1962), p.678).
42 Harry Stone, Dickens and the Invisible World: Fairy Tales, Fantasy and Novel-Making (London: Macmillan, 1980), p.xii.
43 Stone (1980), p.337. This quotation, up to 'a deeply resonant unity', is identical to that in Stone's 1962 essay – see Stone (1962), p.690; this similarity demonstrates that, even in that essay, Stone was not, despite Q.D. Leavis's implication, concerned with the 'fairy-tale dimensions' of Great Expectations in a way that removed the novel 'from any actuality'; rather he was – and remained in Dickens and the Invisible World – concerned with the way in which the fairy-tale elements were fused with 'actuality' to enhance 'our apprehension of life' (Stone 1962), p.690.
44 Stone (1980), p.327.
45 Stone (1980), p.329.
46 See Stone (1980), p.285.
47 Stone (1980), pp.329, 330, 332–33, 334, 335, 336.

CHAPTER FIVE

1 Peter Brooks, 'Repetition, Repression, and Return: Great Expectations and the Study of Plot', New Literary History: A Journal of Theoretical Criticism, 11 (1980),

pp. 503–26. Reprinted with revisions in Brooks's *Reading for the Plot: Design and Intention in Narrative* (Cambridge, Massachusetts: Harvard University Press, 1984), pp. 113–42. Extracts in Cotsell (1990), pp. 124–46; Sell (1994), pp. 98–109; Carlisle (1996), pp. 477–501. These quotations, Brooks (1980), p. 503.

2 See Jean-Paul Sartre, *La Nausée* (1938), translated by Robert Baldick as *Nausea* (Harmondsworth: Penguin, 1965), pp. 61–63. 'When you are living, nothing happens. The settings change, people come in and go out, that's all. There are never any beginnings. Days are tacked on to days without rhyme or reason, it is an endless, monotonous addition . . . There isn't any end either . . . That's living. But when you tell about life, everything changes; only it's a change nobody notices: the proof of that is that people talk about true stories. As if there could possibly be such things as true stories; events take place one way and we recount them the opposite way. You appear to begin at the beginning . . . [a]nd in fact you have begun at the end. It is there, invisible and present, and it is the end which gives . . . the pomp and value of a beginning . . . And the story goes on in reverse: the moments have stopped piling up on one another in a happy-go-lucky manner, they are caught by the end of the story which attracts them and each of them in turn attracts the preceding moment . . . I wanted the moments of my life to follow one another in an orderly fashion like those of a life remembered. You might as well try to catch time by the tail' (Sartre (1965), pp. 61, 62, 63).

3 Brooks (1980), p. 512.

4 Brooks (1980), p. 511.

5 Brooks (1980), p. 512.

6 Brooks (1980), p. 504.

7 See André Gide, *Les Faux-Monnayeurs* (*The Counterfeiters*) in *Oeuvres Complètes* (*Complete Works*), 15 vols (Paris: Nouvelle Revue Française, 1932–39), 'de tous les genres littéraires . . . le roman reste le plus libre, le plus *lawless*' ('of all literary genres, the novel remains the freest, the most *lawless*' (vol. 12, p. 268).

8 [*Brooks's Note:*] On the archaeological model in Freud, see in particular the use he makes of Pompeii in 'Delusions and Dreams in Jensen's *Gradiva*' [*Der Wahn und die Träume in W. Jensens* Gradiva] (1907) in James Strachey, ed. and translated, Standard Edition of the *Complete Psychological Works of Sigmund Freud* (London: Hogarth Press, 1953–74), vol. 9: 1906–1908 (1959), pp. 1–95.

9 Aristotle wrote in his *Poetics* that a tragedy is a whole 'which has a beginning, a middle, and an end. A beginning is that which does not necessarily come after something else, although something else exists or comes about after it. An end, on the contrary, is that which naturally follows something else either as a necessary or as a usual consequence, and is not itself followed by anything. A middle is that which follows something else, and is itself followed by something'. Dorsch (1965) (see chapter four, note 29), p. 41.

10 [*Brooks's Note:*] The pattern of the incestuous couple, where the implication of the brother–sister relation serves as both attraction and prohibition, has been noted by several critics. See especially Harry Stone, 'The Love Pattern in Dickens'[s] Novels' in *Dickens the Craftsman: Strategies of Prešentation*, ed. Robert B. Partlow, Jr., (Carbondale and Edwardsville: Southern Illinois University Press, 1970), pp. 1–20, and Albert J. Guerard, *The Triumph of the Novel* (New York: Oxford University Press, 1976), p. 70. *Great Expectations* gives particular weight to the role of the Father as source of the Law: Magwitch, assuming in different registers the role of father both to Estella and to Pip, becomes, not a figure of authority, but a principle of pure interdiction.

11 In a section of the 1980 version of his essay, omitted from the 1984 version in *Reading for the Plot*, Brooks says, of the passage from *Great Expectations* beginning 'Even yet, I could not recall a single

feature . . .' and ending '. . . remotely suspecting his identity' (2:20, p. 313): 'The passage offers the most striking example of the fact, already encountered in Pip's "returns", that key moments of Pip's life bring back the past not simply as recollection, but as reproduction: as a living-through of the past as if it were present. This corresponds to Freud's discovery – recorded in the essay, "Remembering, Repeating and Working-Through" – that repetition and working through of material from the past as if it were an active force in the present come into play when recollection properly speaking is blocked by resistance' (Brooks (1980), p. 515). Brooks's endnote in his 1980 essay refers us to Freud's 'Remembering, Repeating and Working-Through' [*Erinnern, Wiederholen und Durcharbeiten*], Standard Edition, vol. 12: 1911–1913 (1958), pp. 145–56.

12 [*Brooks's Note, from 1980 version of his essay:*] See Roland Barthes, *S/Z* (Paris: Seuil, 1970), translated Richard Miller (Oxford: Blackwell, 1990), pp. 39–40.

13 Brooks (1984), pp. 115, 117, 120, 121–23, 125, 127–30, 134–35, 136, 138.

14 Steven Connor, *Charles Dickens*, ReReading Literature series (Oxford: Blackwell, 1985). Extract in Sell (1994), pp. 166–76. This quotation, Connor (1985), p. 1.

15 Connor (1985), p. 112.

16 Connor (1985), p. 113. [*Connor's Note:*] We are talking here about male children. There are notorious problems about the theory of the Oedipus complex when applied to female children. This issue is discussed in Juliet Mitchell, *Psychoanalysis and Feminism* (Harmondsworth: Penguin, 1975), pp. 5–120.

17 Connor (1985), p. 114.

18 Connor (1985), p. 137.

19 [*Connor's Note:*] This term ['the Other'], usually capitalized by Lacan, has a range of meanings, which go beyond the ordinary one of 'other people'. It often signifies the category of 'otherness' erected by consciousness to expel or exclude unwelcome areas of thought and feeling, but it can also signify the 'otherness' of the unconscious, or of language itself. See Anthony Wilden, 'Lacan and the discourse of the Other' in Jacques Lacan, *Speech and Language in Psychoanalysis* (Baltimore and London: Johns Hopkins University Press, 1981).

20 Connor (1985), pp. 137–144.

21 Jeremy Tambling, 'Prison-Bound: Dickens and Foucault', *Essays in Criticism*, 36:1 (January, 1986), pp. 11–30; reprinted in Cotsell (1990), pp. 182–97; Sell (1994), pp. 123–42. *Dickens, Violence and the Modern State: Dreams of the Scaffold* (London: Macmillan, 1995), pp. 17–47.

22 Leavis (1970), p. 288.

23 Charles Dickens, 'Down with the Tide' *Household Words*, vol. 4 (in original issue), vol. 6 (in current British Library reference), no. 150 (5 February 1853), pp. 481–85. Reprinted in Gadshill Edition of Dickens, vol. 34, pp. 190–201.

24 Leavis (1970), p. 291.

25 Michel Foucault, *Surveiller et Punir: Naissance de la Prison* (Paris: Gallimard, 1975), translated by Alan Sheridan as *Discipline and Punish: The Birth of the Prison* (London: Allen Lane, 1977; Harmondsworth: Penguin, 1979). This quotation, Foucault (1979), p. 193.

26 Tambling (1986), pp. 30–34, 36–37, 38, 46–47.

27 Kate Flint, *Dickens*, Harvester New Readings series (Brighton: Harvester Press, 1986), p. 130. Flint's own version of the final clause of *Great Expectations* reads 'no shadow of a future parting', which is perhaps her own variant!

28 Carolyn Brown, '*Great Expectations*: Masculinity and Modernity', *Essays and Studies*, 40 (1987), p. 71.

29 Brown (1987), p. 61.

30 Brown (1987), p. 63.

31 Brown (1987), p. 61.

32 Brown (1987), p. 64.

33 Brown (1987), p. 65.

34 Brown (1987), p. 70.

35 Brown (1987), p. 72.

CHAPTER SIX

1 Edward W. Said, *Culture and Imperialism* (London: Chatto and Windus, 1993), pp. 19, 115.

2 Said (1993), p. 115.

3 Said (1993), p. xxiv.

4 Said (1993), p. xv. Said had published two previous pieces on *Great Expectations*, though not directly on its colonialist and imperialist dimensions. These are: 'Molestation and Authority in Narrative Fiction' in J. Hillis Miller, ed., *Aspects of Narrative: Selected Papers from the* [1969–70] *English Institute* (New York: Columbia University Press, 1971), pp. 47–68; 'The Problem of Textuality: Two Exemplary Positions', *Critical Inquiry*, 4 (Summer 1978), pp. 673–714; reprinted with small changes in Said's *The World, the Text, and the Critic* (Cambridge, Massachusetts: Harvard University Press, 1983; London: Faber and Faber, 1984), pp. 196–200 and in Carlisle (1996), pp. 518–24.

5 Dan Jacobson, 'Out of Empire', *New Statesman*, 69:1768 (29 January 1965), p. 153.

6 Millhauser (1972), p. 272.

7 Millhauser (1972), p. 273.

8 Van Ghent (1966), p. 128.

9 Moynahan (1960), p. 79.

10 Connor (1985), p. 143.

11 Brown (1987), p. 64.

12 Brown (1987), p. 71.

13 Robert Hughes, *The Fatal Shore: A History of the Transportation of Convicts to Australia* (London: Collins Harvill, 1987), p. 586.

14 [*Said's Note*:] Paul Carter, *The Road to Botany Bay: An Exploration of Landscape and History* (New York: Knopf, 1988), pp. 202–60. As a supplement to Hughes and Carter, see Sneja Gunew, 'Denaturalizing Cultural Nationalisms: Multicultural Readings of "Australia"' in Homi K. Bhabha, ed., *Nation and Narration* (London: Routledge, 1990), pp. 99–120.

15 Said (1993), p. 13.

16 Said (1993), pp. xv–xviii. Reprinted in Carlisle (1996), pp. 524–26.

17 Ford (1955), p. 229.

18 George Steiner, *On Difficulty and Other Essays* (Oxford: Oxford University Press, 1978; paperback edn., 1979), p. 99.

19 William A. Cohen, 'Manual Conduct in *Great Expectations*', *ELH* [formerly subtitled *A Journal of English Literary History*], 60 (1993), pp. 217–59. Shortened version in Carlisle (1996), pp. 572–91. This quotation, Cohen (1993), pp. 221–22.

20 Cohen (1993), p. 217.

21 Cohen (1993), p. 219.

22 Cohen (1993), p. 220.

23 Cohen (1993), p. 224.

24 Cohen (1993), p. 228.

25 Cohen (1993), pp. 230–32.

26 [*Cohen's Note*:] Jaggers offers a hand in one other place (3:1, p. 335). When it fails to issue its olfactory warning [that is, of scented soap], this appendage is capable of inciting Pip's paranoiac delusions through an approach from the rear: 'I had strolled up into Cheapside, and was strolling along it, surely the most unsettled person in all the busy concourse, when a large hand was laid upon my shoulder, by some one overtaking me. It was Mr. Jaggers's hand, and he passed it through my arm' (3:9, p. 385). The 'large hand' that claps Pip on the shoulder gives fleshy form to the fantasies that so often 'unsettle' him.

27 [*Cohen's Note*:] Dickens exploits the handshake's erotic possibilities in, for instance, the following reunion in *The Mystery of Edwin Drood* (1870; Margaret Cardwell, ed. The Clarendon Dickens. Oxford: Oxford University Press, 1972): 'The two shook hands with the greatest heartiness, and then went the wonderful length – for Englishmen – of laying their hands each on the other's shoulders, and looking joyfully each into the other's face. "My old fag!" said Mr. Crisparkle. "My old master!" said Mr. Tartar' (p. 184). In 'The Pursuit of Homosexuality in the 18th Century: "Utterly Confused Category" and/or Rich Repository?' in Robert Purks Maccubbin, ed., *'Tis Nature's Fault: Unauthorized Sexuality*

During the Enlightenment (Cambridge: Cambridge University Press, 1987), pp. 132–68, G. S. Rousseau suggests that, at least in the mid-eighteenth century, handshaking was felt to provoke (rather than to sublimate) closer erotic encounters between men. He cites a 1749 tract: '"Tho' many Gentlemen of Worth, are oftentimes, out of pure good *Manners*, obliged to give into it [squeezing of the hand]; yet the Land [England] will never be purged of its *Abominations*, till this *Unmanly, Unnatural* Usage be totally abolish'd: For it is the first Inlet to the detestable Sin of *Sodomy*"' (p. 150).

28 [*Cohen's Note*:] Eve Kosofsky Sedgwick, in *Between Men: English Literature and Male Homosocial Desire* (New York: Columbia University Press, 1985), chs. 9–10, writes persuasively of the murderous anal erotics that pervade male–male combat – 'male rape' – in late Dickens novels. Even in its reliance on the minimal 'alibi' of heterosexual motives, however, Sedgwick's assessment of the Magwitch/Compeyson and Pip/Orlick violence may overstate the case.

29 [*Cohen's Note*:] This is not the only instance of Pip's noticing – and then blanching at having noticed – another man's all-too-visible body under the banner of revulsion. At the theatre one night he notes, 'I found a virtuous boatswain in his Majesty's service – a most excellent man, though I could have wished his trousers not quite so tight in some places and not quite so loose in others' (3:8, p. 381). When Pip meets with the 'secret-looking man . . . with an invisible gun', who seems inexplicably to be making a pass at him, he notes: '[t]he strange man, after glancing at Joe, and seeing that his attention was otherwise engaged, nodded to me again when I had taken my seat, and then rubbed his leg – in a very odd way, as it struck me' (1:10, p. 75). In each case, the euphemism is so startling as to beg decoding.

30 [*Cohen's Note*:] Other intermale relationships mediated by erotically charged

fights could be adduced here as well: the two scenes of Magwitch and Compeyson fighting, as well as Pip's confrontations with Drummle. Besides the arm-wrestling [Cohen refers here to what he calls in his essay 'the boys' dilettantish display of arm-wrestling aptitude' (Cohen (1993), p. 246) at Jaggers's house, where Drummle, Pip and Herbert, egged on by the barrister, 'all f[a]ll to baring and spanning [their] arms in a ridiculous manner' to show how muscular they are (2:7, p. 213) – an activity whose 'gleeful erotics' Cohen likens to 'the comparison of equipment usual in any high-school boys' locker room' (Cohen (1993), p. 229)], the following scene exemplifies the high-voltage wire that delineates hostile looking from tantalising touching: 'I had to put my hand behind [Drummle's] legs for the poker . . . Here Mr. Drummle looked at his boots, and I looked at mine, and then Mr. Drummle looked at my boots, and I looked at his . . . I felt here, through a tingling in my blood, that if Mr. Drummle's shoulder had claimed another hair's breadth of room, I should have jerked him into the window; equally, that if my own shoulder had urged a similar claim, Mr. Drummle would have jerked me into the nearest box' (3: 4, pp. 353, 354).

31 [*Cohen's Note*:] By comparison with Pip's relation to Miss Havisham, it might be argued that this eroticism has more to do with age than gender, but a careful examination of the touches between Pip and his 'fairy godmother' indicates a cathexis far less entailed upon physical contact than his relation with Magwitch. At his departure for London (when he believes Miss Havisham to be his benefactress), Pip reverses and naturalises the choreography of supplication that will later (with Magwitch) become so suggestive: 'She stretched out her hand, and I went down on my knee and put it to my lips. I had not considered how I should take leave of her; it came naturally to me at the moment, to do this' (1: 19, p. 156).

At his final interview with Miss Havisham, a series of touches fail their mark: '[s]he stretched out her tremulous right hand, as though she was going to touch me; but she recalled it again before I understood the action, or knew how to receive it' (3:10, p.393); 'her hand . . . trembled again, and it trembled more as she took off the chain to which the pencil was attached, and put it in mine. All this she did, without looking at me' (3:10, p.395). Finally she manages, like Magwitch, to go down on bended knee before Pip: 'She turned her face to me . . . and, to my amazement, I may even add to my terror, dropped on her knees at my feet; with her folded hands raised to me . . . I entreated her to rise, and got my arms about her to help her up; but she only pressed that hand of mine which was nearest to her grasp, and hung her head over it and wept' (3: 10, p.395). No revulsion and retreat here, only an embrace in return for the one she offers.

32 Cohen (1993), pp.231–35, 241–44.

33 Cohen (1993), p.252.

34 Catherine Waters, *Dickens and the Politics of the Family* (Cambridge: Cambridge University Press, 1997), p.150.

35 Waters (1997), p.151.

36 [*Waters's Note:*] John Carey's comment about Dickens's imaginative interest in violence is . . . relevant here [*Editor's Note*: Waters refers the reader to an earlier endnote, no. 15 on p.217 of her book, which reads: As John Carey has observed, 'Dickens, who saw himself as the great prophet of cosy, domestic virtue, purveyor of improving literature to the middle classes, never seems to have quite reconciled himself to the fact that violence and destruction were the most powerful stimulants to his imagination'. *The Violent Effigy: A Study of Dickens's Imagination* (London: Faber, 1973), p.16.].

37 Sally Shuttleworth, 'Female Circulation: Medical Discourse and Popular Advertizing in the Mid-Victorian Era' in Mary Jacobus, Evelyn Fox Keller, Sally Shuttleworth, eds, *Body/Politics: Women and the Discourses of Science* (New York: Routledge, 1990), p.62.

38 Waters (1997), pp.151–53, 157–60, 163–65, 169–70, 173–74.

39 William F. Axton, '*Great Expectations* Yet Again', *Dickens Studies Annual*, 2 (1972), p.278.

SELECT BIBLIOGRAPHY

Novels
This list gives the dates of the monthly numbers, or of the monthly or weekly instalments where the novel first appeared in a magazine. The details of the first UK edition follow.

The Posthumous Papers of the Pickwick Club. Monthly numbers, April 1836–November 1837. London: Chapman and Hall, 1837.

Oliver Twist: or, The Parish Boy's Progress. Monthly instalments in *Bentley's Miscellany*, February 1837–March 1839. London: Richard Bentley, 1838.

The Life and Adventures of Nicholas Nickleby. Monthly numbers, April 1838–October 1839. London: Chapman and Hall, 1839.

The Old Curiosity Shop. Weekly instalments in *Master Humphrey's Clock*, April 1840–February 1841. London: Chapman and Hall, 1841.

Barnaby Rudge: A Tale of the Riots of 'Eighty. Weekly instalments in *Master Humphrey's Clock*, February–November 1841. London: Chapman and Hall, 1841.

Life and Adventures of Martin Chuzzlewit. Monthly numbers, January 1843–July 1844. London: Chapman and Hall, 1844.

Dealings with the Firm of Dombey and Son, Wholesale, Retail and for Exportation. Monthly numbers, October 1846–April 1848. London: Bradbury and Evans, 1848.

The Personal History of David Copperfield. Monthly numbers May 1849–November 1850. London: Bradbury and Evans, 1850.

Bleak House. Monthly numbers, March 1852–September 1853. London: Bradbury and Evans, 1853.

Hard Times for These Times. Weekly instalments in *Household Words*, April–August 1854. London: Bradbury and Evans, 1854.

Little Dorrit. Monthly numbers, December 1855–June 1857. London: Bradbury and Evans, 1857.

A Tale of Two Cities. Weekly instalments in *All the Year Round*, April–November 1859. London: Chapman and Hall, 1859.

Great Expectations. Weekly instalments in *All the Year Round*, December 1860–August 1861. 3 vols. London: Chapman and Hall, 1861.

Our Mutual Friend. Monthly numbers, May 1864–November 1865. 2 vols. London: Chapman and Hall, 1865.

The Mystery of Edwin Drood. Monthly numbers April–September 1870 (six numbers of an intended twelve). London: Chapman and Hall, 1870.

Editions of *Great Expectations*
Calder, Angus, ed. *Great Expectations.* Penguin English Library series. Harmondsworth: Penguin, 1965. A widely used paperback edition.

Cardwell, Margaret, ed. *Great Expectations.* The Clarendon Dickens. Oxford:

Clarendon Press, 1993. This is the authoritative text used in this Guide.
Cardwell, Margaret, ed. *Great Expectations*, with introduction by Kate Flint.
Oxford World's Classics series. Oxford: Oxford University Press, 1994; 1998.
This contains the authoritative Clarendon text.

Letters
Walter Dexter, ed. *The Letters of Charles Dickens*. 3 vols. London: Nonesuch
Press, 1938.
The Letters of Charles Dickens. The Pilgrim Edition. Oxford: Clarendon Press
(1965–). Madeline House and Graham Storey, eds, vol. 1: 1820–1839
(1965); vol. 2: 1840–1841 (1969); Madeline House, Graham Storey,
Kathleen Tillotston, eds, vol. 3: 1842–1843 (1974); Kathleen Tillotson, ed.,
vol. 4: 1844–1846 (1977); Graham Storey and K.J. Fielding, eds, vol. 5:
1847–1849 (1981); Graham Storey, Kathleen Tillotson, Nina Burgis, eds,
vol. 6: 1850–1852 (1988); Graham Storey, Kathleen Tillotson, Angus
Easson, eds, vol. 7: 1853–1855 (1993); Graham Storey and Kathleen
Tillotson, eds, vol. 8: 1856–1858 (1995); still in progress.

Speeches
K.J. Fielding, ed. *The Speeches of Charles Dickens*. Oxford: Clarendon Press, 1960.

Working notes
Harry Stone, ed. *Dickens's Working Notes for His Novels*. Chicago: University of
Chicago Press, 1987.

Bibliographies of criticism
General criticism of Dickens
Churchill, R.C. *A Bibliography of Dickensian Criticism: 1836–1975*. London:
Macmillan, 1975.
Cohn, Alan M. and Collins, K.K. *The Cumulated Dickens Checklist: 1970–1979*.
Troy: Whitston, 1982.
Fenstermaker, John J. *Charles Dickens: 1940–1975: An Analytical Subject Index to
Periodical Criticism of the Novels and Christmas Books*. London: George Prior, 1979.
Gold, Joseph. *The Stature of Dickens: A Centennial Bibliography of Dickensian
Criticism: 1836–1975*. London: Macmillan, 1975.

Criticism of *Great Expectations*
Worth, George J. *Great Expectations: An Annotated Bibliography*. Garland
Dickens Bibliographies series. New York: Garland Publishing, 1986.

The MLA (Modern Language Association) Database, which lists books and
journal articles in literature, languages, linguistics, and folklore, is an
invaluable guide to more recent Dickens criticism, though it should not be
regarded as comprehensive. It can be accessed through many university
and college computer systems.

Journals

The Dickensian: A Magazine for Dickens Lovers (1905–)
Dickens Quarterly (1984–)
Dickens Studies: A Journal of Modern Research and Criticism (1965–70)
Dickens Studies Newsletter (1969–84)

Studies of Dickens's working methods, critical reputation, publishing history

Butt, John and Tillotson, Kathleen. *Dickens at Work*. London: Methuen, 1957.
Fielding, K.J. *Charles Dickens*. Bibliographical Series of Supplements to 'British Book News'. London: Longmans, Green for the British Council and the National Book League, 1953.
Ford, George H. *Dickens and His Readers: Aspects of Novel-Criticism Since 1836*. Princeton: Princeton University Press for the University of Cincinnati, 1955.
Patten, Robert L. *Dickens and His Publishers*. Oxford: Clarendon Press, 1978.
Rantavaara, Irma. *Dickens in the Light of English Criticism*. Helsinki: Annales Academiae Scientiarum Fennicae, 1944.

Biographies

Ackroyd, Peter. *Dickens*. London: Sinclair-Stevenson, 1990.
Forster, John. *The Life of Charles Dickens*. 3 vols. London: Chapman and Hall, 1872–74; 2 vols, with introduction by G.K. Chesterton. Everyman's Library no. 78. London: J.M. Dent, 1927; J.W.T. Ley, ed. 1 vol. London: Cecil Palmer, 1928; A.J. Hoppe, ed. 2 vols. London: J.M. Dent, 1966.
Johnson, Edgar. *Charles Dickens: His Tragedy and Triumph*. 2 vols. New York: Simon and Schuster, 1952; London: Gollancz, 1953. Abridged and revised edition: London: Allen Lane, 1977.
Leacock, Stephen. *Charles Dickens: His Life and Work*. London: Peter Davies, 1933.
Lindsay, Jack. *Charles Dickens: A Biographical and Critical Study*. London: Andrew Dakers, 1950.
Pope-Hennessy, Una. *Charles Dickens*. London: Chatto and Windus, 1945.
Priestley, J.B. *Charles Dickens and His World*. London: Thames and Hudson, 1961.
Storey, Gladys. *Dickens and Daughter*. London: Frederick Muller, 1939.
Tomalin, Claire. *The Invisible Woman: The Story of Nelly Ternan and Charles Dickens*. London: Viking, 1990.
Wilson, Angus. *The World of Charles Dickens*. London: Secker and Warburg, 1970; Harmondsworth: Penguin, 1972.

General critical works on Dickens

Carey, John. *The Violent Effigy: A Study of Dickens's Imagination*. London: Faber, 1973.
Chesterton, G.K. *Charles Dickens*. London: Methuen, 1906; 1946. Extracts in

Wall (1970), pp. 244–50; Page (1979), p. 102; Cotsell (1990), pp. 27–28.

Chesterton, G. K. *Appreciations and Criticisms of the Works of Charles Dickens*. London: J. M. Dent, 1911. Extracts in Cotsell (1990), pp. 28–33.

Collins, Philip. *Dickens and Crime*. Cambridge Studies in Criminology, vol. 17. London: Macmillan, 1962.

Connor, Steven. *Charles Dickens*. ReReading Literature series. Oxford: Blackwell, 1985. Extract in Sell (1994), pp. 166–76.

Engel, Monroe. *The Maturity of Dickens*. Cambridge, Massachusetts: Harvard University Press, 1959.

Flint, Kate. *Dickens*. Harvester New Readings series. Brighton: Harvester Press, 1986.

Garis, Robert. *The Dickens Theatre: A Reassessment of the Novels*. Oxford: Clarendon Press, 1965. Extracts in Wall (1970), pp. 492–99; Cotsell (1990), pp. 87–93.

Gissing, George. *Charles Dickens: A Critical Study*. The Victorian Era series. London: Blackie, 1898; The Imperial Edition of the Works of Charles Dickens. Gresham: London, 1902. Extracts in Wall (1970), pp. 222–39; Cotsell (1990), pp. 22–24.

Grant, Allan. *A Preface to Dickens*. Preface Books series. London: Longman, 1984.

Hardy, Barbara. *The Moral Art of Dickens: Essays*. London: Athlone Press, 1970. Extract in Page (1969), pp. 130–40.

House, Humphry. *The Dickens World*. Second edition. Oxford: Oxford University Press, 1940; 1960. Extract in Wall (1970), pp. 323–48.

Jackson, T. A. *Charles Dickens: The Progress of A Radical*. London: Lawrence and Wishart, 1937. New York: Haskell House, 1971.

Leacock, Stephen. *Charles Dickens: His Life and Work*. London: Peter Davies, 1933.

Leavis, F. R. and Q. D. *Dickens the Novelist*. London: Chatto and Windus, 1970.

Lucas, John. *Charles Dickens: The Major Novels*. Penguin Critical Studies series. London: Penguin, 1992.

Miller, J. Hillis. *Charles Dickens: The World of His Novels*. Cambridge, Massachusetts: Harvard University Press, 1958. Extract in Wall (1970), pp. 391–405.

Sadrin, Anny. *Parentage and Inheritance in the Novels of Charles Dickens*. European Studies in English Literature series. Cambridge: Cambridge University Press, 1994.

Stone, Harry. *Dickens and the Invisible World: Fairy Tales, Fantasy and Novel-Making*. London: Macmillan, 1980.

Swinburne, Algernon Charles. *Charles Dickens*. London: Chatto and Windus, 1913.

Tambling, Jeremy. *Dickens, Violence and the Modern State: Dreams of the Scaffold*. London: Macmillan, 1995.

Waters, Catherine. *Dickens and the Politics of the Family*. Cambridge: Cambridge University Press, 1997.

Critical books on *Great Expectations*

Barnes, John. *Critical Commentary on Dickens's 'Great Expectations'*. Macmillan Critical Commentaries series. London: Macmillan, 1966.
Bradbury, Nicola. *Charles Dickens's 'Great Expectations'*. Critical Studies of Key Texts series. New York: St. Martin's Press, 1990.
Newman, Stephen. *'Great Expectations' (Charles Dickens)*. Notes on English Literature series. Oxford: Blackwell, 1975.
Sadrin, Anny. *'Great Expectations'*. Unwin Critical Library series. London: Unwin Hyman, 1988. Extract in Sell (1994), pp. 187–202.
Thomas, R. George. *Charles Dickens: 'Great Expectations'*. Studies in English Literature series no. 19. London: Edward Arnold, 1964.

Other books that discuss Dickens and *Great Expectations*

Page references are given to the most extended discussions of Dickens and *Great Expectations* in the books below, but useful and relevant comments may be found on other pages of these books – use the book's index, where it has one, to check for further references.

Brooks, Peter. *Reading for the Plot: Design and Intention in Narrative*. Cambridge, Massachusetts: Harvard University Press, 1984, pp. 113–42. Extracts in Cotsell (1990), pp. 124–46; Sell (1994), pp. 98–109; Carlisle (1994), pp. 481–501.
Forster, E. M. *Aspects of the Novel*, ed. Oliver Stallybrass. London: Edward Arnold, 1927; Harmondsworth: Penguin, 1976, pp. 33–34, 76–77, 81–82, 169, 172–73. Extract in Wall (1970), p. 277–78.
Friedman, Norman. *Form and Meaning in Fiction*. Athens: University of Georgia Press, 1975, pp. 21–41.
Gilmour, Robin. *The Idea of the Gentleman in the Victorian Novel*. London: George Allen and Unwin, 1981, pp. 105–48. Extracts in Sell (1994), pp. 110–22.
Guerard, Albert J. *The Triumph of the Novel*. New York: Oxford University Press, 1976, pp. 139–42.
House, Humphry. *All in Due Time: The Collected Essays and Broadcast Talks*. London: Rupert Hart-Davis, 1955, pp. 201–20. Extract in Wall (1970), pp. 351–57.
Hughes, Robert. *The Fatal Shore: The Epic of Australia's Founding*. New York: Knopf, 1987, pp. 584–86.
Leavis, F. R. *The Great Tradition: George Eliot; Henry James; Joseph Conrad*. London: Chatto and Windus, 1948; Penguin, 1972, pp. 29–32.
Leavis, Q. D. *Fiction and the Reading Public*. London: Chatto and Windus, 1932; Harmondsworth: Penguin, 1979, pp. 129–31.
Miller, J. Hillis, ed. *Aspects of Narrative: Selected Papers from the* [1969–70] *English Institute*. New York: Columbia University Press, 1971, pp. 47–68, especially pp. 56–68.
Miller, J. Hillis. *Victorian Subjects*. Hemel Hempstead: Harvester Wheatsheaf, 1990, pp. 47–48.

Said, Edward W. *The World, The Text, and the Critic.* Cambridge, Massachusetts: Harvard University Press, 1983; London: Faber and Faber, 1984, pp. 196–200.

Said, Edward W. *Culture and Imperialism.* London: Chatto and Windus, 1993, pp. xv–xviii. Extract in Carlisle (1996), pp. 524–26.

Santayana, George. *Selected Critical Writings of George Santayana,* ed. Norman Henfrey, vol. 1. Cambridge: Cambridge University Press, 1968, pp. 108–22. Essay on 'Dickens' reprinted in Ford and Lane (1961), pp. 135–51; extract from essay in Wall (1970), pp. 258–69.

Sedgwick, Eve Kosofksy. *Between Men: English Literature and Male Homosocial Desire.* New York: Columbia University Press, 1985, pp. 130–32.

Steiner, George. *Language and Silence: Essays 1958–1966.* London: Faber, 1967. Abridged edition, Harmondsworth: Penguin, 1969, pp. 243–44.

Steiner, George. *On Difficulty and Other Essays.* Oxford: Oxford University Press, 1978; paperback edition, 1979, pp. 99–100.

Trilling, Lionel. *The Liberal Imagination: Essays on Literature and Society.* New York: Viking, 1950, p. 211.

Van Ghent, Dorothy. *The English Novel: Form and Function.* New York: Holt, Rinehart and Winston, 1953, pp. 125–38, 370–79. Extract in Dyson (1968), pp. 244–57; Wall (1970), pp. 375–79.

Essay/review collections
On Dickens in general

Collins, Philip, ed. *Dickens: The Critical Heritage.* Critical Heritage series. London: Routledge and Kegan Paul, 1971.

Dyson, A. E., ed. *Dickens: Modern Judgements.* Modern Judgements series. London: Macmillan, 1968.

Ford, George H. and Lane, Lauriat, Jr., eds. *The Dickens Critics.* Ithaca, New York: Cornell University Press, 1961.

Gross, John and Pearson, Gabriel, eds. *Dickens and the Twentieth Century.* London: Routledge and Kegan Paul, 1962.

Johnson, Wendell Stacy. *Charles Dickens: New Perspectives.* Twentieth Century Views series. Englewood Cliffs, New Jersey: Prentice-Hall, 1982.

Partlow, Robert B., Jr. *Dickens the Craftsman: Strategies of Presentation.* Carbondale and Edwardsville: Southern Illinois University Press, 1970.

Price, Martin, ed. *Dickens: A Collection of Critical Essays.* Twentieth Century Views series. Englewood Cliffs, New Jersey: Prentice-Hall, 1967.

Wall, Stephen, ed. *Charles Dickens: A Critical Anthology.* Penguin Critical Anthologies series. Harmondsworth: Penguin, 1970.

On *Great Expectations*

Carlisle, Janice, ed. *Charles Dickens: 'Great Expectations': Complete, Authoritative Text with Biographical and Historical Contexts, Critical History, and Essays from Five Contemporary Critical Perspectives.* Case Studies in Contemporary Criticism series. Boston: Bedford Books of St Martin's Press, 1996.

Cotsell, Michael, ed. *Critical Essays on Charles Dickens's 'Great Expectations'*. Critical Essays on British Literature series. Boston: G. K. Hall, 1990.

Page, Norman, ed. *Charles Dickens: 'Hard Times', 'Great Expectations' and 'Our Mutual Friend': A Casebook*. Casebook series. London: Macmillan, 1979.

Sell, Roger D., ed. *'Great Expectations': Charles Dickens*. New Casebooks series. London: Macmillan, 1994.

Reviews of *Great Expectations*

A., J. *'Great Expectations'. Ladies Companion and Monthly Magazine*, 20 (1861), pp. 218–20.

Anon. 'Charles Dickens'[s] *Great Expectations': The Eclectic Review*, 1 (October 1861), pp. 458–77.

Anon. 'The Collected Works of Charles Dickens'. *British Quarterly Review*, 35 (January 1862), pp. 135–60.

Anon. *'Great Expectations'. The Literary Gazette*, 7:159 (13 July 1861), pp. 32–33.

Anon. *'Great Expectations'. The Saturday Review*, 12 (20 July 1861), pp. 69–70.

[Capes, John Moore and Acton, J.E.E.D.] *'Great Expectations'. The Rambler*, 6 (January 1862), pp. 274–76. Extracts in Collins (1971), pp. 436–38.

[Chorley, H. F.] *'Great Expectations'. Athenaeum*, 159 (2319) (13 July 1861), pp. 43–45. Extracts in Page (1979), pp. 94–96.

[Dallas, E. S.] *'Great Expectations'. The Times* (17 October 1861), p. 6. Extracts in Collins (1971), pp. 430–34; Page (1971), p. 99.

[Forster, John, or Morley, Henry?]. *'Great Expectations'. The Examiner* (20 July 1861), pp. 452–53.

[Oliphant, Margaret]. 'Sensation Novels'. *Blackwood's Edinburgh Magazine*, 91 (May 1862), pp. 564–84. Extracts in Collins (1971), pp. 439–42.

[Townsend, Meredith?]. *'Great Expectations'. The Spectator*, 34 (20 July 1861), pp. 784–86. (Worth (1986), p. 52, incorrectly gives p. 785 as the first page of this review.)

[Trotter, L. J.] 'Mr. Dickens's Last Novel', *Dublin University Magazine*, 68 (December 1861), pp. 685–93. Extracts in Collins (1971), pp. 434–36.

[Whipple, Edwin P.] *'Great Expectations'. Atlantic Monthly*, 40: 8 (September 1861), pp. 380–82. Extracts in Collins (1971), pp. 428–30 and in Page (1979), p. 98.

Forewords and Introductions

Chesterton, G. K. 'Foreword'. Edwin Charles, *Some Dickens Women*. London: T. Werner Laurie, 1926, pp. v–vii.

Lang, Andrew. 'Introduction'. Charles Dickens, *Great Expectations*. Gadshill Edition of The Works of Charles Dickens, vol. 22. London: Chapman and Hall, 1898, pp. v–xi.

Lang, Andrew. 'Charles Dickens'. Charles Dickens, *Reprinted Pieces: The Lamplighter; To Be Read at Dusk, and Sunday under Three Heads, with a General Essay on The Works of Charles Dickens* by Andrew Lang. Gadshill Edition of Dickens, vol. 34. London: Chapman and Hall, 1899, pp. ix–xxxvi.

Shaw, George Bernard. 'Preface'. Charles Dickens, *Great Expectations* (with original ending). New York: Limited Editions Club, 1937, pp. v–xxii.
Shaw, George Bernard. 'Foreword'. Charles Dickens, *Great Expectations*. The Novel Library series. London: Hamish Hamilton, 1947. Reprinted in Wall (1970), pp. 284–97; Cotsell (1990), pp. 33–44.

Essays in Journals and Books
General essays on Dickens

Lang, Andrew. 'Charles Dickens'. *Fortnightly Review*, 64 (December 1898), pp. 944–60. Also in Gadshill Edition of Dickens, vol. 34 (1899), pp. ix–xxxvi.
Lewes, G. H. 'Dickens in Relation to Criticism'. *Fortnightly Review*, 17 (1872), pp. 143–51. Extracts in Alice R. Kaminsky, ed. *Literary Criticism of George Henry Lewes*. Regents Critics series. Lincoln, Nebraska: University of Nebraska Press, 1964, pp. 94–105; Wall (1970), pp. 191–202. Reprinted in Ford and Lane (1961), pp. 54–74.
Orwell, George. 'Charles Dickens'. *Inside the Whale* (London: Gollancz, 1940). Reprinted in Sonia Orwell and Ian Angus, eds, *The Collected Essays, Journalism and Letters of George Orwell: Volume I: An Age Like This: 1920–1940*. Harmondsworth: Penguin in association with Secker and Warburg, 1968, pp. 454–504. Extracts in Ford and Lane (1961), pp. 157–71; Wall (1970), pp. 297–313.
Santayana, George. 'Dickens'. *The Dial*, 71 (1921), pp. 537–49. Reprinted in Santayana (1968); extract in Wall (1970), pp. 258–69.
Swinburne, Algernon Charles. 'Charles Dickens'. *Quarterly Review*, 196 (July 1902), pp. 20–39. Extract in Cotsell (1990), pp. 22–24. Reprinted, incorporating Swinburne's essay on *Oliver Twist*, and two of his marginalia, as Swinburne (1913).
Wilson, Edmund. 'Dickens: The Two Scrooges'. *The Wound and the Bow: Seven Studies in Literature*. London: W. H. Allen, 1941; revised edition, 1942; Methuen, 1961.

Essays and articles on *Great Expectations*

Axton, William F. '*Great Expectations* Yet Again'. *Dickens Studies Annual*, 2 (1972), pp. 278–93.
Brooks, Peter, 'Repetition, Repression, and Return: *Great Expectations* and the Study of Plot', *New Literary History*, 11 (1980), pp. 503–26. Revised version in Brooks (1984), pp. 113–42.
Brown, Carolyn. '*Great Expectations*: Masculinity and Modernity'. *Essays and Studies*, 40 (1987), pp. 60–74.
Byrd, Max. '"Reading" in *Great Expectations*', *PMLA*, 9:2 (1976), pp. 259–65.
Clayton, Jay. 'Is Pip Postmodern? Or, Dickens at the End of the Twentieth Century'. Carlisle (1996), pp. 606–24.
Cohen, William A. 'Manual Conduct in *Great Expectations*'. *ELH* [formerly subtitled *A Journal of English Literary History*], 60 (1993), pp. 217–59. Shortened version in Carlisle (1996), pp. 572–91.

Dessner, Lawrence Jay. '*Great Expectations*: The Tragic Comedy of John Wemmick'. *Ariel: A Review of International English*, 6:2 (April 1975), pp. 65–80.

Dexter, Walter. 'The End of *Great Expectations*'. *The Dickensian*, 34 (Spring 1938), p. 82.

Friedman, Norman. 'Versions of Form in Fiction – *Great Expectations* and *The Great Gatsby*', *Accent*, 14 (Autumn, 1954), pp. 246–63. Revised version in Friedman (1975), pp. 21–41.

Frost, Lucy. 'Taming to Improve: Dickens and the Women in *Great Expectations*'. *Meridian*, 1 (1982), pp. 11–20. Reprinted in Sell (1994), pp. 60–78.

Gregory, Marshall W. 'Values and Meanings in *Great Expectations*: The Two Endings Revisited'. *Essays in Criticism*, 19 (October 1969), pp. 402–9.

Hagan, John H., Jr. 'Structural Patterns in Charles Dickens's *Great Expectations*'. *ELH: A Journal of English Literary History*, 21:1 (March 1954), pp. 54–66.

Hagan, John H., Jr. 'The Poor Labyrinth: The Theme of Social Injustice in Dickens's *Great Expectations*'. *Nineteenth-Century Fiction*, 9 (December 1954), pp. 169–78.

Hardy, Barbara. 'Formal Analysis and Common Sense'. *Essays in Criticism*, 11 (January 1961), p. 112.

Hardy, Barbara. 'Work in Progress IV; Food and Ceremony in *Great Expectations*'. *Essays in Criticism*, 13 (October 1963). Reprinted with small changes in Hardy (1970), pp. 139–55. 1970 version reprinted in Page (1979), pp. 130–40.

House, Humphry. 'G. B. S. on *Great Expectations*'. *The Dickensian*, 44 (Spring and Autumn 1948), pp. 63–70, 183–86. Reprinted in House (1955), pp. 201–20.

Hutter, Albert D. 'Crime and Fantasy in *Great Expectations*'. Frederick Crews, ed. *Psychoanalysis and Literary Process*. Cambridge, Massachusetts: Winthrop, 1970, pp. 26–65.

Kucich, John. 'Action in the Dickens Ending: *Bleak House* and *Great Expectations*'. *Nineteenth-Century Fiction*, 33 (June 1978), pp. 88–109.

Leavis, L. R. 'The Dramatic Narrator in *Great Expectations*'. *English Studies: A Journal of English Language and Literature*, 68:3 (June 1987), pp. 236–48.

Lohman, W. J., Jr. 'The Economic Background of *Great Expectations*'. *Victorians Institute Journal*, 14 (1986), pp. 53–66.

Marcus, Philip L. 'Theme and Suspense in the Plot of *Great Expectations*'. *Dickens Studies Annual*, 2 (1966), pp. 57–73.

Matchett, Willoughby. 'The Strange Case of *Great Expectations*'. *The Dickensian*, 9 (February 1913), pp. 33–36.

Meckier, Jerome. 'Charles Dickens's *Great Expectations*: A Defence of the Second Ending'. *Studies in the Novel*, 25 (1993), pp. 28–58.

Meisel, Martin. 'The Ending of *Great Expectations*'. *Essays in Criticism*, 15 (July 1965), pp. 326–31; reprinted under heading 'The Problem of the Novel's Ending' in Page (1979), pp. 125–29.

Millhauser, Milton. '*Great Expectations*: The Three Endings'. *Dickens Studies Annual*, 2 (1972), pp. 267–77.

Moynahan, Julian. 'The Hero's Guilt: The Case of *Great Expectations*'. *Essays in Criticism*, 10 (January 1960), pp. 60–79. Reprinted in Page (1979), pp. 103–18.

Partlow, Robert B., Jr. 'The Moving I: A Study of the Point of View in *Great Expectations*'. *College English*, 23 (November 1961), pp. 122–31. Extract in Page (1979), pp. 118–24.

Rosenberg, Edgar. 'Last Words on *Great Expectations*: A Textual Brief on the Six Endings'. *Dickens Studies Annual*, 9 (1981), pp. 87–115.

Said, Edward W. 'Molestation and Authority in Narrative Fiction' in Miller (1971), pp. 47–68.

Said, Edward W. 'The Problem of Textuality: Two Exemplary Positions'. *Critical Inquiry*, 4 (Summer 1978), pp. 673–714. Reprinted with small changes in Said (1983), pp. 196–200; Carlisle (1996), pp. 518–24.

Schor, Hilary. '"If He Should Turn to and Beat Her": Violence, Desire, and the Woman's Story in *Great Expectations*'. Carlisle (1994), pp. 541–57.

Stange, G. Robert. 'Expectations Well Lost; Dickens'[s] Fable for His Time'. *College English*, 16 (October 1954), pp. 9–17. Reprinted in Ford and Lane (1961), pp. 294–308; Cotsell (1990), pp. 63–73.

Stone, Harry. 'Fire, Hand, and Gate: Dickens's *Great Expectations*'. *Kenyon Review*, 24 (Autumn 1962), pp. 652–91. Expanded version in Stone (1980), pp. 298–339.

Stone, Harry. 'The Love Pattern in Dickens'[s] Novels' in Partlow (1970), pp. 1–20.

Tambling, Jeremy. 'Prison-Bound: Dickens and Foucault'. *Essays in Criticism*, 36:1 (January 1986), pp. 11–31. Reprinted in Cotsell (1990), pp. 182–98; Sell (1994), pp. 123–42. Revised and expanded version in Tambling (1994), pp. 17–47.

Vasta, Edward. '*Great Expectations* and *The Great Gatsby*'. *The Dickensian*, 60 (1964), pp. 167–72.

Walsh, Susan. 'Bodies of Capital: *Great Expectations* and the Climacteric Economy'. *Victorian Studies: A Journal of the Humanities, Arts and Sciences*, 37:1 (Fall 1993), pp. 73–98.

Wolfe, Peter. 'The Fictional Crux and the Double Structure of *Great Expectations*'. *South Atlantic Quarterly*, 73 (1974), pp. 335–47.

Essays on other topics with significant mentions of *Great Expectations*

Crompton, Donald W. 'The New Criticism: A Caveat'. *Essays in Criticism*, 10:3 (July 1960), pp. 359–64.

Jacobson, Dan. 'Out of Empire'. *New Statesman*, 69:1768 (29 January 1965), pp. 153–54.

Trilling, Lionel. 'Manners, Morals, and the Novel'. *Kenyon Review*, 10 (Winter 1948), pp. 1–27. Reprinted in Trilling (1955), pp. 205–22.

Films of *Great Expectations*

1. *Great Expectations* (1917). Famous Players Film Company (USA). Released by Paramount (USA). With Jack Pickford as Pip.
2. *Great Expectations* (1921 (or 1922?)). Nordisk (Denmark). Director: A.W. Sandberg. Screenplay: Laurids Skands. With Phillips [*sic*] Holmes as Pip, Jane Wyatt as Estella, Henry Hull as Magwitch.
3. *Great Expectations* (1934). Universal Pictures (USA). Director: Stuart Walker. Screenplay: Gladys Unger.
4. *Great Expectations* (1946). Cineguild (UK). Released by J. Arthur Rank. Director; David Lean. Screenplay: Ronald Neame, David Lean, Kay Walsh, Cecil McGivern, Anthony Havelock-Allan. With Anthony Wager as the child Pip, John Mills as the adult Pip, Alec Guinness as Herbert, Jean Simmons as the child Estella, Valerie Hobson as the adult Estella, Finlay Currie as Magwitch, Bernard Miles as Joe Gargery, Martita Hunt as Miss Havisham.
5. *Great Expectations* (1974). Robert Fryer-James Cresson Production (UK). Director: Joseph Hardy. Screenplay: Sherman Yellen. With Michael York as Pip.
6. *Great Expectations* (1998). 20th Century Fox. Director: Alfonso Cuarón. Screenplay: Mitch Glazer. Cast includes Ethan Hawke, Gwyneth Paltrow, Anne Bancroft, Robert de Niro. This is a modernised version.

A commercial video of the 1981 BBC1 TV production of *Great Expectations* is available. Adapted for television by James Andrew Hall. With Gerry Sundquist as Pip, Sarah-Jane Varley as Estella, Stratford Johns as Magwitch and Joan Hickson as Miss Havisham.

Most discussion has focused on the 1946 David Lean version. See, for example:
Baston, Jane. 'Word and Image: The Articulation and Vizualization of Power in *Great Expectations*'. *Literature/Film Quarterly*, 24:3 (1996), pp. 322–31.
Beja, Morris. '*Great Expectations*' in *Film and Literature*. New York: Longman, 1979, pp. 146–55.
DeBona, Guerric. 'Doing Time; Undoing Time: Plot Mutation in David Lean's *Great Expectations*'. *Literature/Film Quarterly*, 20:1 (1992), pp. 77–100.
McFarlane, Brian. 'David Lean's *Great Expectations* – Meeting Two Challenges'. *Literature/Film Quarterly*, 20:1 (1992), pp. 68–76.
Zambrano, Ana L. *Dickens and Film*. New York: Gordon Press, 1977.

ACKNOWLEDGEMENTS

The editor and publishers wish to thank the following for their permission to reprint copyright material: Harvard University Press (for material from *Charles Dickens: The World of His Novels* and *Reading for the Plot: Design and Intention in Narrative*); Athlone Press (for material from *The Moral Art of Dickens*); Oxford University Press (for material from *The Dickens Theatre: A Reassessment of the Novels*); *South Atlantic Quarterly* (for material from 'The Fictional Crux and the Double Structure of *Great Expectations*'); Macmillan (for material from *Dickens and the Invisible World: Fairy Tales, Fantasy and Novel Making* and *Dickens, Violence and the Modern State: Dreams of the Scaffold*); Blackwell (for material from *Charles Dickens*); Chatto and Windus (for material from *Culture and Imperialism*); Cambridge University Press (for material from *Dickens and the Politics of Family*).

Every effort has been made to contact the holders of any copyrights applying to the material quoted in this book. The publishers would be grateful if any such copyright holders whom they have not been able to contact, would write to them.

The editor is most grateful to his wife, Angela Tredell, and to her colleagues in East Sussex Library Services, for their speed and efficiency in obtaining copies of the many books and essays consulted in the preparation of this Guide.

Nicolas Tredell teaches American and English literature, art history, and cultural and film studies for Sussex University. He has contributed widely to journals in the UK and the USA, and his recent books include *Uncancelled Challenge: The Work of Raymond Williams*, *The Critical Decade: Culture in Crisis*, *Conversations with Critics*, *Caute's Confrontations: The Novels of David Caute* and the Icon Critical Guides to *The Great Gatsby*, 'Heart of Darkness' and *The Sound and the Fury* and *As I Lay Dying*, as well as the Icon Readers' Guide to *The Fiction of Martin Amis*.

INDEX

as radical 56, 57, 59
as realist 41–2, 46
representations of women 19, 35, 55,
    71–2
romanticism 31–2, 71, 72
sexual relations 149
snobbishness 55–6, 60, 177(n93)
social attitudes 60, 63
society 30, 32, 59
and Sterne 44
and Ternan 53–4, 62
and Thackeray 47, 48, 49
Dickens Fellowship 51
Dickens world 75, 77, 79, 175(n61)
*The Dickensian: A Magazine for Dickens
    Lovers* 51
Discipline and Punish (Foucault) 21, 136
discovery (anagnorisis) 180(n29)
Dombey and Son 18, 23, 64, 130
domesticity 135, 164
dominance 89–90
Dostoevsky, Fyodor 88
Drummle, Bentley 30, 55, 185(n30)
dualism 62–3
Dublin University Magazine 25, 28, 29–31

eating: *see* food
eccentricity 15, 16, 28, 29, 33, 34, 40
The Eclectic Review 16, 27–8, 61
economics, and class 66
Eliot, George 38, 50
Eliot, T.S. 96, 140
emigration 147
The Empty Chair portrait 36
eroticism 126; *see also* homoeroticism
Estella
    and Biddy 163–5
    characterisation 29, 40, 162, 163–4
    cruelty 33, 55, 85
    Havisham, Miss 16, 43, 85, 129, 162
    inner voice denied 141–2
    as link to plots 128
    Magwitch as father 17, 67, 73, 88, 92
    murderess for mother 73
    and Pip 30–1, 102–3
    Stange 85, 88
    and Ternan 54
    Waters 162, 163–4
Everyman analogy 12, 58, 75, 76, 78, 96
exaggeration 16, 19, 29
The Examiner 16–17

expatriates 114, 146

fairy-tale aspects 114–15, 181(n42)
family life 159–60, 166
farce 29
father–son relationship 85, 116, 118
femininity, stereotypes 33
fiction and reality 37–8
Fielding, Henry 44
Fielding, K.J. 53
fighting 153–4, 185(n30)
Fildes, Sir Luke 36
fire motif 117
first person narrator 7, 42, 71, 104–5, 111
flâneur 81, 83, 179(n15)
Flint, Kate 141–2, 143
folklore 81–2
food
    Magwitch
        in churchyard 100–2
        in London 103–4
    Pip at Satis House 102–3
Ford, George H. 37, 41, 149
forge, double meaning 134–5
Forster, E.M. 113, 181(n33)
Forster, John 7, 13, 16, 36, 37
Fortnightly Review 37, 39
Foucault, Michel 21, 136, 137, 139,
    140–1, 143
France, literary criticism 121
Freud 71
    Beyond the Pleasure Principle 122
    Civilization and its Discontents 105,
        106
    Oedipus complex 130, 183(n16)
    repetition 122–3, 127, 183(n11)
frustrations, societal 106, 107–8

Gadshill Dickens 39, 40–1, 44
Gamp, Mrs. Sarah 17
Gargery, Joe: *see* Joe
Gargery, Mrs. Joe: *see* Mrs. Joe
Garis, Robert
    artifice and illusion 16, 42, 104
    frustrations 106, 107–8
    linguistic performance 20
    Pip 28, 119
    self-discovery 106
    shame 105
    showmanship 113
    snobbishness 105–6